TABLE OF CONTENTS

GETTING STARTED

GETTING STARTED IN STORY MODE

MEET ETHAN WABER

While the Network and Extra Modes allow you to create your own characters, in Story Mode you'll play only as Ethan Waber, a young Guardians recruit. While you can't change Ethan's race or appearance, you can make him your own by changing his class, selecting his weapons, evolving his Partner Machinery and buying him new clothes.

CHANGING CLASSES

Ethan begins Story Mode as a Hunter, but after his Guardians License is updated in Chapter 3, he'll gain the right to switch between the three basic classes. To change your class, visit the Guardians HQ on the fifth floor of Clyez City and speak to one of the women at the counter. She will charge you a small fee, but there is no penalty for changing classes and you may do it as often as you like. Note that when you change classes your weapons and armor will automatically be unequipped and removed from your action palette. Make sure to re-equip your gear before your next mission!

MISSION POINTS AND CLASS ADVANCEMENT

At the end of each timed trial and Free Mission, Ethan will receive a number of Mission Points (MP) as a reward. Just as normal Experience Points cause Ethan to level-up, Mission Points cause Ethan's classes to level-up, leading to an increase in the stat bonuses he receives when he is a member of that class. Each class advances independently, so if you're level 2 and halfway to level 3 when you switch out of the Hunter class, that's exactly where you'll be the next time you play a Hunter.

THE THREE TYPES

HUNTERS: Hunters have more Hit Points and Attack Power than any other class, and they'll need it, since their weapon selection is oriented towards frontline combat. With the ability to use some ranged weapons and Wands, and respectable scores in the TECHNIC Power stat, they are the most versatile of the three classes.

RANGERS: Rangers possess stunning Accuracy Power, which allows them to make the most out of otherwise unreliable weapons like Shotguns and Machine Guns. Rangers are decent in frontline combat, where they can use Long Swords and Spears and enjoy high Evasion and Stamina scores. They can use wands, but have the worst TECHNIC Power of the three classes.

FORCES: Forces focus on TECHNIC use to the exclusion of everything else. They can deal heavy damage with their spells and the ability to equip Rods allows them to have up to four TECHNICs at their fingertips. They have the weakest stats in nearly every category except TECHNIC Power and Mental Strength, and are limited to only seven simple weapons. But their ability to use Bows up to Rank B arguably makes them better at ranged combat than

CHARACTER STATS

Statistic	Description
HP (HIT POINTS)	This is the amount of damage a character can take before becoming incapacitated.
ATP (ATTACK POWER)	Combined with a weapon's Attack score, this stat affects the amount of damage dealt with physical weapons.
ATA (ATTACK ACCURACY)	Combined with a weapon's Accuracy score, this stat affects the odds of connecting with an attack.
TP (TECHNIC POWER)	Combined with a weapon's TECHNIC score, this stat affects the efficacy of TECHNICs cast by a
DFP (DEFENSE POWER)	Combined with the Defense score of a line shield, this stat reduces the damage dealt by enemy physical attacks.
EVP (EVASIVE POWER)	Combined with the Evasion score of a line shield, this stat increases the odds of dodging enemy physical attacks.
MST (MENTAL STRENGTH)	Combined with the Mental score of a line shield, this stat reduces the damage dealt by enemy
STA (STAMINA)	Combined with the Endurance score of a line shield, this stat increases the odds or avoiding negative status conditions.

STORY MODE WEAPONRY RESTRICTIONS

Each class is allowed to use the weapons in its area of specialty (melee, ranged, and Force), but have a limited ability to use the weapons of other classes as well. All weapons have a rank of either C, B, A, or S (the best). You'll encounter only C-Rank weapons during the bulk of Story Mode, but B-, A-, and a precious few S-Rank weapons appear in the final chapters. The chart below shows the maximum ranks of weapons that are usable by each class in Story Mode.

WEAPON	HUNTER	RANGER	FORCE	WEAPON	HUNTER	RANGER	FORCE
1-HAND SWORD	S	B	B	HANDGUN	B	S	B
TWIN BLADES	S	-	-	TWIN HANDGUNS	C	S	-
LONG SWORD	S	B	-	MACHINE GUN	B	S	B
DAGGER	S	B	B	RIFLE	C	S	-
TWIN DAGGERS	S	-	-	BOW	-	S	B
SPEAR	S	B	-	SHOTGUN	C	S	-
CLAW	S	-	-	CROSSBOW	-	S	-
TWIN CLAWS	S	-	-	CANNON	-	S	-
KNUCKLES	S	-	-	WAND	B	B	S
DOUBLE BLADE	S	-	-	ROD	-	-	S

∨∨ | THE FOUR RACES OF PSU

When you begin a game in Network Mode or Extra Mode, your first decision will be a hugely significant one. A character's race determines its strengths and weaknesses, its appearance, and what special abilities it will have access to. Class, on the other hand, is now a completely fluid concept; any race can be any class, and they can switch freely between them.

HUMANS

☐ ☐ ☐ **DEFAULT CLASS:** HUNTER

Humans are the most populous race in the Gurhal System, and make the most well-rounded characters. They have no distinct strengths or weaknesses, and are an excellent choice for players who anticipate class-changing often.

NEWMEN

☐ ☐ ☐ **DEFAULT CLASS:** FORCE

Newmen are natural Forces and boast the highest TECHNIC Power of any race by far. Their natural resistance to enemy TECHNICs, combined with their skill at evading attacks, can help keep them alive despite low HP totals. When it comes to weapon combat, high Accuracy scores make Newmen surprisingly skilled with guns.

BEASTS

☐ ☐ ☐ **DEFAULT CLASS:** HUNTER

With the best scores in the HP and Attack Power categories, and the ability to use Nanoblasts, Beasts arguably make the best Hunters. They can do a respectable job of casting TECHNICs, but their poor accuracy will make it a challenge to succeed as a Ranger.

CASTs

☐ ☐ ☐ **DEFAULT CLASS:** RANGER

The machine-like accuracy of CASTS make them fantastic Rangers, but their high scores in Attack Power, Defense Power and Hit Points make them nearly as good at frontline Hunter combat. CASTS can now use TECHNICs (a major change since Phantasy Star Online) but they aren't very good at it. As a race they have two special abilities: the option to use SUV Weapons and the ability to use high-level traps that can be set by no other race.

PROFICIENCY BY RACE

CATEGORY	HUMAN	BEAST	NEWMAN	CAST
HP (HIT POINTS)	★★	★★★★	★	★★★
ATP (ATTACK POWER)	★★	★★★★	★	★★★
ATA (ATTACK ACCURACY)	★★	★	★★★	★★★★
TP (TECHNIC POWER)	★★★	★★	★★★★	★
DFP (DEFENSE POWER)	★★	★★★	★★	★★★★
EVP (EVASIVE POWER)	★★★	★★	★★★★	★
MST (MENTAL STRENGTH)	★★★	★★	★★★★	★
STA (STAMINA)	★★	★★	★★★	★★★

SPECIAL RACE ABILITIES

Beasts and CASTS have access to special abilities that no other race can use. You won't be able to unlock either ability until you hit level 20, however.

NANOBLASTS: Beasts of level 20 or higher can get a tattoo-like badge inscribed on their arm at Clyez City's Makeover Shop. It costs 10,000 Meseta, but is well worth it—this badge allows Beasts to absorb energy as they are damaged in combat and unleash their true beast nature for a temporary stat boost. When the energy gauge below a Beast's EXP bar is full, press both attack buttons together to transform. While in a Super-Beast state you will only be able to use that Beast's melee attacks. Which stat is boosted depends on which badge you buy; some boost attack scores, while others grant invulnerability or increased agility.

SUV WEAPONS: CASTS of level 20 or higher can equip special Blaster units that are sold at the unit counter of Armor Shops. These units fit into the extra slot of armor and allow their user to absorb damage dealt in combat and use it to unleash a powerful special attack. To use an SUV weapon, wait until the energy gauge below your EXP bar is full, then press both attack buttons together to summon a massive gun from a satellite in space. The exact effect varies based on the unit installed, but you can count on heavily damaging all the enemies in a room.

GENDER DIFFERENCES

Gender makes a fairly significant difference in character creation. Men of all races tend to have more Hit Points and higher Attack Power and Accuracy scores. Women, however, excel at TECHNIC Power, Evasive Power, Mental Strength and Stamina. There is no significant difference between the Defense scores of the two genders.

CLASS RESTRICTIONS IN NETWORK MODE

In Network Mode, the restrictions on weapons are stricter than they are for Ethan in Story Mode, most notably in that TECHNICs are completely forbidden for non-Forces. (Forces, however, now have access to a wider variety of melee weapons.) There are less total weapons available online, and they're capped at Rank B, although this will change in future updates. As in Story Mode, Network Mode players can change their class at any time at the Guardians HQ in Clyez City. By collecting Mission Points they can level-up each class and, at high enough class levels, gain access to Expert Classes that are not available to Ethan. Or so we assume—Expert Classes will not be available until a future update.

MAX CLASS BY RANK

WEAPON	HUNTER	RANGER	FORCE
1-HAND SWORD	B	C	C
TWIN BLADES	B	-	-
LONG SWORD	B	-	-
DAGGER	B	C	C
TWIN DAGGERS	B	-	C
SPEAR	B	C	C
KNUCKLES	B	-	-
HANDGUN	C	B	C
TWIN HANDGUNS	-	B	-
MACHINE GUN	-	B	-
RIFLE	-	B	-
BOW	-	B	B
SHOTGUN	-	B	-
WAND	-	-	B
ROD	-	-	B

WELCOME TO THE GUARDIANS!

Whatever mode you choose, you'll take the role of a new recruit to the Guardians organization. Each Guardian is assigned a room in the barracks of Clyez City, provided with a few basic supplies and granted a Partner Machinery that serves several useful functions. Beyond that, you're on your own; the Guardians are a freelance, for-profit organization, and you'll have to buy new armaments and upgrade your Partner Machinery with the rewards you earn on your missions.

! If you aren't sure how to get started in Network Mode, talk to your Partner Machinery and ask to take the tutorial. In addition to teaching you the basics, your Trainer will give you his or her Partner Card and the Rising Strike Photon Art.

Four different weapons manufacturers produce the tools of the Guardians trade. That includes nearly twenty varieties of weapons, a wide array of line shields, and stat-enhancing units that have all sorts of interesting effects. Spend your Meseta wisely—there's a stunning amount of gear to choose from!

THE FOUR MANUFACTURERS

GRM

Parum's GRM sells weapons with solid attack and accuracy scores, and minimal stat requirements. Their stock of melee weapons grows thin later in Story Mode, but Hunters will enjoy their attack-boosting Line Shield units and a variety of blades made with ice photons. Rangers will love their many specialty ranged weapons, including Machine Guns, Rifles, and Laser Cannons.

YOHMEI CORP

The Yohmei shop on Neudaiz is a dreamland for Forces. Their weapons have the highest PP scores, and they sell the best Wands and Rods. They stock units that boost TECHNIC Power, and in Story Mode they always have the newest TECHNIC discs a chapter early. Hunters and Rangers should check in from time to time too; they can certainly benefit from high-PP weapons themselves. In addition to Wands and Rods, Yohmei Corp specializes in claws for Hunters and Bows for Rangers and Forces. Melee weapon sold here often contain a fire photon.

TENORA WORKS

Moatoob's Tenora Works sells some of the finest line shields in the system and stocks many weapons for Hunters and Rangers, including exclusive Knuckles, Shotguns, and Crossbows. Their weapons have the highest attack scores and good accuracy, but they have the lowest PP capacity. Their favored photon is Electric, and their units primarily boost defensive stats.

KUBARA

Kubara is a catch-all manufacturer for rare and unusual items that are not sold in any store. Some enemies drop Kubara items, and a few Story Mode trials award Kubara items as S-Rank prizes. The Clyez City Mall sells a few Kubara machinery boards, and their Weapon Upgrades shop focuses on Kubara weapons exclusively.

WEAPON UPGRADES

Each manufacturer's store has an upgrade counter where they can upgrade the weapons they manufacture. To attempt an upgrade, unequip the weapon, and find, purchase or synthesize an appropriate Grinder. Bring both items to the counter and they'll give it a shot, but be aware that they may fail and destroy the weapon in the process—and they'll take no responsibility for replacing it! Using a high-quality Grinder will increase your odds of success, as will performing the upgrade on a lucky day. (See the Missions section for more details on lucky days.)

HOW SHOPS WORK IN STORY MODE

HOW SHOPS WORK IN NETWORK MODE

You begin Story Mode with access only to the shops in the Clyez City Mall, but the outlet shops of the major weapons manufacturers will become available one-by-one. At the start of each chapter, those shops will be updated with new stock across all categories, although the outlet shop on the planet where your mission is based will usually have the best new gear. While each outlet shop only sells their own weapons and armor, the Clyez City Mall sells goods from four manufacturers. However, their shop is always a chapter out of date, so you'll need to visit the planets to get access to the newest weapons, armor, and Photon Arts discs.

While Network Mode weapons may share the same name as Story Mode weapons, they have different stats and prices. Shops are not updated as your character advances, and always sell the same stock. The Clyez City Mall sells every weapon from every manufacturer with a rarity level of up to three stars, while manufacturers' outlet shops sell only their own weaponry, and stock items with rarity levels of up to four stars. Currently you cannot buy items with a rarity levels above four stars, but they will become available in future game updates.

WEAPON VALUES

In Network Mode, every weapon is priced according to its rarity value, so the two-star Swords sold by every manufacturer are the exact same price. Buy the one with stats that best fit your play style.

RARITY LEVEL	COST	RESALE VALUE
★	350	52
★★	800	120
★★★	2000	300
★★★★	8600	1290

LINE SHIELDS AND UNITS

The Armor Shops of the Gurhal system sell an all-in-one defensive armor known as a Line Shield. Line Shields boost your Defense and Evasion stats, and also have slots for units, which can boost other stats. Since Units allow you to customize your character's strengths, a line shield with three or four open slots is always worth buying over a Line Shield that is less upgradeable but has slightly better stats. The units that go into Extra slots are particularly useful, as they can regenerate HP, increase PP recovery speed, boost Endurance and give CAST characters access to special SUV Weapons!

As with weapons, each manufacturer makes its own line shields and excels in different areas:

GRM: GRM Line Shields provide average boosts for Defense and Evasion, and always have an available Arm slot. Arm slot units typically boost Attack or Accuracy scores.

YOHMEI CORP: Yohmei's Line Shields favor Defense over Evasion and typically have an open Head slot, into which you can insert a unit that boosts TECHNIC or Mental Strength stats.

TENORA WORKS: Line Shields made by Tenora Works have high Evasion scores that come at the expense of Defense. They specialize in slots for Body units that can further boost your defensive stats.

OTHER SHOPS

Besides combat supplies, each planet also hosts Clothing, Synthesis, and Parts shops.

CLOTHING SHOPS: In Story Mode, Ethan can purchase new clothing in Chapter 6 and beyond. Each planet only sells locally manufactured clothing, so the selection of styles is limited, but the selection of colors is much wider than what you'll find in the Clyez City Mall.

SYNTHESIS SHOPS: Each planet's Synthesis shop sells local materials and machinery boards that can used to make the weapons and Line Shields of the local manufacturer. There is little point visiting them, since the Clyez City Mall has the combined stock of all three planets.

PART SHOPS: CASTs don't wear clothes, so to change their appearance you'll need to buy parts. Of course, Ethan is a human, so these shops are of little use to him. They're there for the sake of CAST characters in Network and Extra Mode.

 There is also a Makeover Shop that can only be found in the Clyez City Mall. It allows any character to change hair, skin, and eye color, and allows Beasts to buy the badges that are the source of their Nanoblast powers.

▽▽ PARTNER MACHINERY

After completing their Guardians training, each character is assigned a helper robot known as a "Partner Machine." Your Partner Machine will hang out in your quarters and provide several useful functions, although not all of these functions will be available at the start of the game in Story Mode.

ITEM STORAGE: Each character's personal inventory has room for sixty items, counting multiple copies of recovery items (up to 10 or 20) and materials (up to 99) as a single item. Despite this impressive capacity, it will fill up quickly, and when it does you can bring the extra items to your Partner Machinery for storage. Even when your inventory has plenty of space, you might as well entrust all of your Materials to your Partner Machinery, since it is the one who will ultimately put them to use.

NEWS REPORTS: In Story Mode, when you select the Talk command in the P Machinery Functions menu, Pete will offer updates on the characters and situations you've encountered during your quest, as well as background information that will be useful in quests to come. In Network Mode, your Partner Machinery will offer you a selection of tutorials.

EVOLUTION: By using the "Give item" command in the P Machinery Functions menu, you can feed items from your inventory to your Partner Machinery (In Story Mode, this option is unlocked in Chapter 4). When your Partner Machinery eats, its stats will rise or fall by a set amount of points. When it gains 100 points in any one stat, it will go up a level in that category and its production level (the total of its levels in all stats) will rise by 1. At certain intervals, your Partner Machinery will evolve into a more advanced machine, and when it hits a production level of 30 in Story Mode or 80 in Network Mode, it will evolve into a doll-like companion that is capable of fighting alongside you in combat! See the fold-out insert in the back of this book for full details on how Partner Machinery evolve.

ITEM SYNTHESIS: Your Partner Machinery can manufacture special weapons, armor and items, provided you have a machinery board (which acts like a recipe) and the necessary material ingredients are in storage. Many rare items can only be made through item synthesis, and even common items are cheaper to synthesize than they are too buy. In Story Mode, this feature is unlocked during Chapter 4.

ITEM SYNTHESIS

Here are the steps necessary to have your Partner Machinery synthesize an item. It can be complicated and time-consuming, but when it pays off the results will more than justify the effort.

1. INSERT A BOARD: Boards are items whose name begin with a "[B]," like "[B] Blaster." Your Partner Machinery can hold up to 32 boards at once. Boards that make consumable items like Trimate can be used many times, but in Story Mode, most weapon and armor Boards can be used only once.

2. CHECK YOUR INGREDIENTS: Select the "Synthesize" command and scroll through your boards to see a list of the materials necessary for synthesis and how many of each are required. If you don't have sufficient ingredients, an X will appear by the name of the Board. If you're only a few materials short, don't despair; you may be able to buy the missing items at a Synthesis Shop.

3. FILL IN THE BLANKS: Some ingredients have a material icon but are listed as "???" This means you may choose any item from that material category to fill in the blank. The item you choose will affect the quality of the weapon and the odds of success. For example, you can infuse an element into the weapon by choosing an elementally-charged photon, or increase the quality of a Line Shield by using better metals. If you use materials that are significantly lower in rarity level

than the item you are trying to create, you will usually create an inferior item instead.

4. CONSIDER THE ODDS: Before you begin, your Partner Machinery will inform you of the odds of success. This is affected by the rarity level of the Board (rarer items are harder to make), the quality of materials (more expensive materials increase the odds) and your Partner Machinery's level (the higher its level in Striking, for example, the better it will be at making melee weapons). If you agree to give it a shot, it will begin synthesis.

5. WAIT AND HOPE: Synthesis can take hours to finish in Network Mode, particularly for rare items, but in Story Mode the process is instantaneous. When the item is done, choose "Take out item" from the P Machinery Functions menu to see what you've created. A failed synthesis will often result in a different item from the one you intended to make—one misplaced screw and that legendary Long Sword could come out as a Koltova Sandwich. At least in Story Mode you can save your game before attempting to synthesize anything.

COMBAT TACTICS

⌄⌄ | EXPLOIT THE ELEMENTS

There are three elemental pairings in Phantasy Star Universe: Fire and Ice, Electric and Ground, and Dark and Light. Monsters of each type are resistant to their own element but weak to its counterpart. So fire attacks will deal additional damage to ice creatures, but less damage to fire creatures.

ELEMENT ICONS		
⬡ FIRE	⬡ ICE	
⬡ ELECTRIC	⬡ GROUND	
⬡ LIGHT	⬡ DARK	

ELEMENTAL PHOTONS

Players can give themselves and their melee weapons elemental properties by using elementally-charged photons. Some weapons and armor have photons built in, but players who use Item Synthesis to create their own weapons and armor can use photon materials to give a specific elemental type to their creations.

The double-edged nature of elements applies to characters as well as monsters; if you're wearing ice armor you'll be resistant to ice attacks, but more vulnerable to fire-based ones. The power level of a photon is reflected by the % after its name; a weapon that is Ice-20% will deal 20% more damage to fire creatures, for example.

! You can assess the elemental type of an enemy by checking the icon that appears to the left of its name when fighting at close range.

ELEMENTAL BULLETS

All ranged weaponry use "bullet" Photon Arts that, when linked to a weapon, grant the weapon that elemental property. In addition to dealing extra damage to creatures of the opposite type, elementally-charged bullets have a chance of causing the status effect associated with each element, such as burning a foe, or freezing it in a block of ice. As bullet Photon Arts increase in level, the power of the photon granted to the weapon and the odds of inflicting the condition increase steadily.

ELEMENT	CONDITION	EFFECT	ELEMENT	CONDITION	EFFECT	ELEMENT	CONDITION	EFFECT
⬡ FIRE	Burn	Loses HP each turn	⬡ ELECTRIC	Shock	Cannot attack	⬡ LIGHT	Confusion	Moves and attacks randomly
⬡ ICE	Freeze	Cannot move or defend	⬡ GROUND	Silence	Cannot use TECHNICs	⬡ DARK	Infection	Loses HP each turn

ELEMENTAL TECHNICs

Forces are tied to the elements even more strongly than Rangers and Hunters. All 24 TECHNICs have some elemental property, and while the power of a TECHNIC may compensate for elemental disadvantages (Fire-type Foie will usually do more damage to a fire-type creature than an Ice-type Barta, for example), it is usually best to use TECHNICs of the type that your foe is vulnerable to.

While Wands and Rods don't have photons, you can give them an elemental charge by filling all of their linked slots with TECHNICs of the same element. A Wand or Rod with two fire TECHNICs will have a 4% fire-element boost, and a Rod with four fire TECHNICs will have a 12% elemental boost! But if even one TECHNIC doesn't match the type, the effect is lost; a Rod with three fire-element TECHNICs and light-element Resta will receive no elemental boost.

GETTING STARTED

STORY MODE

FREE MISSIONS

NETWORK MODE

Your character can switch its class at any time by visiting Guardians HQ in Clyez City and paying a small fee. Certain classes excel in certain areas, and players who are willing to be flexible about their class will be more of an asset to their party. It pays to learn the tactics of each class!

PLAYING A HUNTER

Hunters have access to a wide array of weapons, and their main strategy is using the right weapons against the right foes. Quick weapons like Knuckles and Daggers can keep certain foes "stunned" with their fast attacks, leaving them unable to use TECHNICs or retaliate. Heavier weapons like the long sword deal more damage and can sweep away a group of weaker foes. Different Photon Arts have different properties that may be useful, like knocking foes over or leaping up in the air to hit ranged foes. Fill your action palette with a wide variety of weapons and level-up the Photon Arts of each so you can take advantage of the combos that become available at level 11.

It's the responsibility of Hunters to come to the aid of Rangers and Forces who become surrounded by enemies. This isn't mere altruism; when a monster focuses on another target, you can circle around and hit it in the back, where it will be unable to defend or retaliate.

PLAYING A RANGER

Rangers should keep a lot of guns in their action palette and purchase a wide variety of Photon Arts for each. While Photon Arts may drain the PP of your weapons more quickly, using them constantly will increase their power and accuracy. Since Photon Charges are so rare and expensive, simply switch to another gun when you drain the first. It can be expensive to play a Ranger at low-levels, since they need to recharge all of their weapons between missions. However, Rangers are the easiest class to develop, since they can get a shot in against every foe in battle, earning a share of the Experience Points from each one.

Since Rangers can battle from a distance, they get a unique view of the battle and are in a good position to help out anyone who gets into trouble. When battling beside Hunters, approach your foes and blast them from close range so you can lure them into attacking you. This will expose their backs to the Hunters, and you can continue to battle them safely by backing away as you fire.

PLAYING A FORCE

Forces always make for popular allies, since their spells can heal or boost an entire party. Accumulate rods instead of selling old ones, and fill them with TECHNICs of the same elemental type for a power boost. But devote at least one slot to a gun-and-wand combo, and link recovery TECHNICs like Resta to the wand. Repeated blasts from the handgun will make it easier to wade into battle without getting attacked, so you can provide healing to those in need. This isn't altruism; if you let your Hunters die, you'll be quickly overwhelmed by foes, so a good Force is truly his brother's keeper.

While attack TECHNICs are fun, make sure stat-boosters like Shifta and Zodial are among your early purchases. Call your party together at the beginning of each block and before each boss, and boost as many of their stats as you can. While linking them all to a single staff is convenient, you can also link them alongside the attack TECHNICs of the same element to give those TECHNICs an elemental boost.

⌄⌄ | PHOTON ARTS

Weapons aren't much good (and aren't much fun) until they've been linked with a Photon Art, so buy the Photon Art Discs for your weapons as soon as possible. Photon Art skills give melee weapons more power and flexibility, Photon Art bullets give ranged weapons added power and elemental effects, and Photon Art TECHNICs make Wands and Rods into something other than a paperweight. Remember that after you learn a Photon Art by using a Disc, you must link it your weapon before you can use it.

LEVELING-UP PHOTON ARTS

Whenever you use a Photon Art successfully it will gain a small amount of experience. When it reaches 100%, it will level up, providing a 1-2% increase in attack power and accuracy. After every 10 levels (at levels 11, 21, and so on) it will gain a more significant boost: many melee Photon Arts gain an additional stage to its combo, while bullets and TECHNICs gain an increase in the odds of inflicting a status condition. When they hit these intervals, however, bullets and TECHNICs also increase in PP cost.

In Story Mode, Photon Arts max out at level 30. In Network Mode, the current max is 20. Classes in Network Mode also cap the level of other classes' Photon Arts; a Hunter cannot raise a bullet Photon Art beyond level 10, for example.

Rising Strike Level 10

Rising Strike Level 11

THE PHOTON ART LIMIT

No character can know more than 36 Photon Arts. If you attempt to learn an additional Photon Art, you'll have to forget one you already know (if you relearn it later, it will be back to level 1). 36 sounds like a lot, but if you switch between classes frequently, you'll max it out sooner or later. Anticipate this eventuality by taking it easy early in the game; Rangers should buy no more than one or two Photon Arts for each weapon, and Forces should specialize in certain elements. If a TECHNIC isn't to your liking, stop developing it so it will be less painful when you have to forget it later.

RARE PHOTON ARTS

While stores stock only one Photon Art per melee weapon, there is an additional set of weapon Photon Arts that are currently only available in Story Mode. These are the Photon Arts that your NPC allies use in combat, and only they can give them to you. This will happen roughly 10% of the time when you earn an S-Rank at a trial while they're in your party. Some allies have two Photon Arts to give, so if you're determined to earn them all you'll have to replay Free Missions with each character in your party a great many times. (Note that the TECHNICs given by Maya Shidow are not exclusive and will eventually be sold at shops).

When you earn an S Rank at any trial, there is a small chance (around 1 in 10) that a party member will reward you with an exclusive Photon Art.

CHARACTER	PRIZE 1	PRIZE 2
HYUGA	GRAVITY STRIKE (1-HAND SWORD)	ASSAULT CRUSH (TWIN BLADES)
KAREN	MOUBU SEIRAN-ZAN (TWIN DAGGERS)	--
LEO	SPINNING BREAK (LONG SWORD)	DUS ROBADO (SPEAR)
LUCAIM	BOBBA DONGA (KNUCKLES)	RENZAN SEIDAN-GA (TWIN CLAWS)
MAYA	DIGAS (WAND/ROD)	RENTIS (WAND/ROD)
TONNIO	BUTEN SHOUREN-ZAN (DAGGER)	SENTEN KANZAN-GA (CLAW)
LOU	SPIRAL DANCE (DOUBLE BLADE)	--

MISSIONS

∨∨∨ FINDING A MISSION

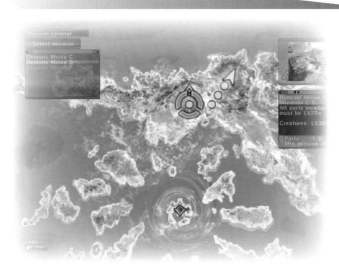

Your adventure begins at Clyez City, from which you can fly to any of the planets in the Gurhal system. There you'll find the entry points of various Guardians missions; most start at the town's Flyer Base, but some begin at other points such as train platforms. In Story Mode you'll find both story-driven missions that disappear after being completed and Free Missions that can be attempted at any time. In Network Mode there are currently only Free Missions.

One change in Network Mode is that missions end not where they began, but at areas known as Field Lobbies. From a Field Lobby you can return to the city or attempt new missions that are exclusive to that area. To begin the Sleeping Warriors mission, for example, you must complete the Mad Creatures mission that will take you from Holtes City to a Field Lobby known as the Raffon Meadow Field Base.

⌄⌄ FORMING A PARTY

While you're free to take on solo missions in Network Mode, the missions are easier and more fun with a party. To invite a character to join you, approach him or her and, when the yellow targeting crosshairs appears, select "Invite to Party" from the Community Menu.

USING PARTNER CARDS

You can also form a party with Partner Cards. To give another player your card, target them and select "Send Card" from the Community Menu. Once you have their Partner Card, you can invite them to join your party by choosing "Form Party" from the Community Menu and selecting their Partner Card. This will only work if they are currently online, in the same world, and not currently in another party. (The icon by their name will reveal their current availability.) The mission will begin as soon as the leader accepts it, but all party characters must make their own way to the mission site. In Story Mode, using Partner Cards is often the only way to recruit NPCs for Free Missions.

LUCKY DAYS IN NETWORK MODE

You may notice that some characters have twinkling stars by their name. Every day, characters of a certain race and sex will be luckier than others, and will enjoy increased odds of finding rare items. Since the leader's luck applies to the whole party, you should always put the luckiest character (the one with the most and largest stars) in the leader role.

NPC ALLIES

Just as Ethan uses computer-controlled allies in Story Mode, Network Mode players can fill out their party with up to two NPC (Non-Playable Character) allies. Only the party leader can invite NPCs; if leadership changes, the NPCs added by the leader will automatically be removed from the party.

    The first NPC ally available to each player is his or her Guardians Trainer. To get your trainer's Partner Card, talk to your Partner Machine and agree to take the tutorial. Trainers will always be three levels higher than your character, but tend not to be very aggressive in combat. Your other potential NPC ally is the Partner Machine itself; it will evolve into a combat ally when it hits level 80, and provide you with a Partner Card.

Each character is assigned a trainer based on race.

PC RACE	NPC TRAINER
HUMAN	HYUGA
NEWMAN	MAYA
BEAST	LEO
CAST	LOU

⌄⌄ STORY MODE TRIALS

Most Story Mode missions include three "trials," which are timed portions of the game in which you must complete a specific objective, like clearing an area of foes or defeating a boss. At the end of each challenge you'll be graded on your performance and awarded a ranking. The entirety of each Free Mission is a trial as well.

    Trials are a very important part of the Story Mode. Scoring well will earn you significant amounts of Meseta, and trials are the only way to earn the Mission Points that increase the level of your current class. If you can earn an S-Rank you'll also receive a high-value prize (such as a new weapon) and possibly an exclusive Photon Art from one of your comrades.

RANKING CRITERIA

At the end of each trial your performance will be judged in up to three areas. Time is always a factor, and the amount of enemies slain is a factor in most non-boss trials. Depending on the situation, you may also be judged on the number of times you allow a party member to become incapacitated, the number of SEED you clear, or the number of traps you disarm. Each field is tallied at the end, and awarded a certain number of points. The maximum amount of points you can earn is 1,000, and you'll need to earn that exact number to earn an S-Rank. If you're one second late or miss a single enemy along the way, you can kiss that S-Rank prize goodbye!

SCORE	RANK
1000	S
700-999	A
400-699	B
0-399	C

Gravity Strike received from Hyuga Ryght.

TRIAL STRATEGIES

Every second counts in trials, so you'll need to be at your absolute best to earn an S-Rank. You'll find specific strategies for every trial in the walkthrough that follows, but here are a few general tips.

PREPARATION IS KEY: Trials typically begin at the start of a new block, immediately after a Save Marker. Always save your game so you'll be able to log out and replay the trial if you aren't happy with your score. If the trial occurs in the middle of a mission, it will usually be at a mission waypoint, so you'll be allowed to return to town for a PP recharge or new supplies.

BE THOROUGH: Earning an S-Rank means killing every single enemy that appears on the map. So instead of finding the quickest route to the end of the trial, you'll have to visit every dead end simply to clear out the foes that appear there. You may not have time to pick up items, but many foes are spawned only when you destroy item boxes. Whenever you enter an empty room, shoot the treasure boxes to flush them out!

USE TECHNICS: When trial enemies attack in large packs, the quickest way to dispose of them is with area-effect TECHNICs like Rabarta, Gifoie and Regrants. Link up a staff or wand with a variety of TECHNICs that have an elemental advantage against the local foes, and don't be shy about using it whenever you have the chance to kill two foes in one shot.

MAKE A TRIAL WAND: As soon as you can afford them, buy the Shifta and Zodial TECHNICs, and link both to a wand (which any class can use in Story Mode). Cast both TECHNICs on yourself before each trial begins, and when the clock starts ticking you'll enjoy a significant boost in attack power and accuracy for the first few minutes. This is especially important on boss trials, where the boost can easily shave 30 seconds off your time.

NETWORK MODE TRIALS

All Network Mode Missions are trials. There are no prizes to win, but Mission Points and Meseta are more valuable and harder to come by in Network Mode, so S-Ranking is no less important.

TRIAL STRATEGIES

There's no timer in Network Mode Trials, because time doesn't matter; the only factors that count are the number of enemies your party slays and the number of times a character is incapacitated.

BE AWARE OF MAP VARIATIONS: As with Story Mode trials, you'll need to kill every enemy that appears in the mission to earn an S-Rank. But that task is a bit trickier in Network Mode, where each mission has three geographic variations (of which one will be chosen randomly). Each variation has different amounts of enemies, and each has its own unique little nooks where they can hide. Parties that seek an S-Rank should fan out to find them all.

WATCH OUT FOR NPCS: You'll lose points every time any character in your party dies during the mission. While human companions can be counted on to heal themselves when their health becomes dire, many NPC's—especially Trainers—cannot. While it can be helpful to fill out a small party with NPC's, they can be a liability to your ranking if you aren't vigilant about healing them.

EXTRA MODE

After completing Chapter 4 of Story Mode, you'll unlock Extra Mode. Extra Mode allows you to make a character of any race and use it offline to play the Free Missions you've unlocked in Story Mode. As you play Story Mode, you will also unlock NPC allies that can accompany your Extra Mode character. There is no content exclusive to Extra Mode (except for a single Free Mission that is unlocked when you beat Story Mode), but the Makeover Shop will open so that Beasts can use Nanoblasts, and CAST characters will be able to win SUV Weapon Units as S-Rank prizes from Free Missions. Extra Mode is entirely self-contained; it is not possible to transfer characters or items to Story Mode or Network Mode characters.

NETWORK MODE UPDATES

While this book covers the state of Phantasy Star Universe's Network Mode at launch, Sega plans to update the game regularly. In addition to opening the gates to Moatoob and offering many new Network Missions, future updates will include:

EXPERT CLASSES: Those who reach certain levels at normal classes will be able to switch to expert classes that enhance the power of one class, combine the strengths of two classes, or add new abilities!

STORY MISSIONS: In addition to Network Missions, updates will include Story Missions that continue the story that began in Story Mode.

NEW WEAPONS: Network Mode players will finally be able to use the Double Blades, Claws, Twin Claws, Crossbows and Cannons that were available in Story Mode. In addition, there will be all-new weapons including Axes, Cards, and Grenade Launchers.

S-RANK MISSIONS: A new version of each Network Mission will be selectable for higher-level characters.

HIGHER LEVEL CAPS: The level cap on characters will rise from 50 to 60, and the level cap on Photon Arts will rise from 20 to 30.

NEW GEAR: You'll be able to find and buy higher-level weapons and armor, as well as new clothes, parts, and room decorations.

CHAPTER 1

OF LIGHT AND DARKNESS

[GUARDIANS COLONY]
CLYEZ CITY

PARTNERS

NONE

CHAPTER OBJECTIVES

- [ ] Take Lumia to the Linear Line

- [ ] Chase the pickpocket

- [ ] **1** Seek Leo for help

- [ ] **2** Raid the emergency supplies

- [ ] **3** Join the Vol Brothers

- [ ] **4** TRIAL: Race to the Linear Line Platform

- [ ] **5** Save the woman in the rubble

- [ ] **6** TRIAL: Defeat the SEED-Vance

TAKE LUMIA TO THE LINEAR LINE

Your adventure begins on the ground floor of the Clyez City Mall. Both escalators are blocked, so you'll need to take the elevator between them to reach the 4th floor. Run to the end of the floor and hang a right to reach the Linear Line Station.

CHASE THE PICKPOCKET

When you arrive at your stop, a thief will swipe Lumia's Meseta Card. Chase him through the station, towards the green-lit, unlocked door. Matters will spiral quickly from bad to worse.

He was headed towards the viewing plaza.

GETTING STARTED
STORY MODE
FREE MISSIONS
NETWORK MODE

[GUARDIANS COLONY]
LINEAR LINE A & B

PARTNERS
NONE

OBJECTIVES 1 TO 2

1 SEEK LEO FOR HELP

But I don't think I can get myself out of here!

The aftershocks of the SEED attack have collapsed the tunnel, trapping Lumia behind a wall of debris. Follow the green-lit doors past the bodies of fallen civilians—there's nothing you can do for them. Leo has suffered a wound himself, but will help by giving you his gear: a standard-issue Saber, Handgun, Carline Line Shield, and 5 doses of Monomate. Ethan will equip all of the gear and assign the weapons and Monomate to his action palette automatically.

2 RAID THE EMERGENCY SUPPLIES

Proceed north through Block B-2, where you'll encounter the first pack of Pannon monsters. These creatures aren't very aggressive, so take the opportunity to practice your Saber skills as Leo instructs. In the next room, the Pannon will be joined by a deadlier Delsaban, but you'll have time to soften it up with a few Handgun blasts before it can reach you.

When the room is clear of enemies, examine the loop in the northeast corner of the map; despite the random contents of most chests, you'll always find a Sword in this place. Equip this massive two-handed blade to your action palette so you can switch to it whenever you like. The Sword does more damage than your trusty Saber and has a much wider range—but since you haven't yet learned the Sword Photon Art, this weapon will be less useful than the Saber.

MONSTERS

PANNON

LVL	1	TYPE: DARK
HP	49	ATT 34
EXP	4	DEF 11

DELSABAN

LVL	1	TYPE: DARK
HP	70	ATT 45
EXP	8	DEF 14

PARTNERS

NAME	LVL (Ethan's +...)	RACE	CLASS
1. Do Vol	+0	Beast	Hunter
2. No Vol	+1	Human	Ranger

③ JOIN THE VOL BROTHERS

You'll run into No Vol and Do Vol at point C, and the pair are willing to put aside the 'tude and team up for safety's sake. Both Twin Handgun-packing No Vol and Knuckle-wearing Do Vol pack a punch, but they're pretty shy in combat, so you'll have to take the lead.

④ TRIAL   RACE TO THE LINEAR LINE PLATFORM

When you approach the locked door in the northwest part of Block C-1, you'll receive a message from Leo and the game's first trial will begin. Trials last until you complete an objective, and then your performance is ranked on a number of factors. Accordingly, you will be rewarded with Meseta, Mission Points, and—if you earn an S-Rank—an item. This first trial doesn't award Mission Points and the prize is only a dose of Trimate, so there isn't too much at stake.

! Before you attempt the challenge, save at the Save Marker and heal up by standing on the glowing green spot.

ITEM HUNTING IN THE LINEAR LINE...

Gamotite? Par Wood? Photons? What is this stuff? Most of the items you'll find in chests and on the bodies of fallen foes are ingredients with no clear use. These won't come into play until much later in the game, but if you collect them now you'll be glad you did later. You'll also find many recovery items, mostly Monomate, but with a precious few Photon Charges mixed in. Photon Charges sell for 1500 Meseta (when they're sold at all) so if you're lucky enough to find some, hoard them for future use instead of wasting them here.

MONSTERS

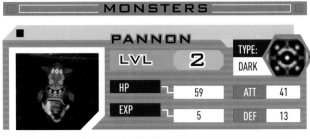

PANNON

LVL	2
TYPE:	DARK
HP	59
ATT	41
EXP	5
DEF	13

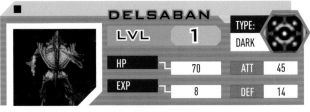

DELSABAN

LVL	1
TYPE:	DARK
HP	70
ATT	45
EXP	8
DEF	14

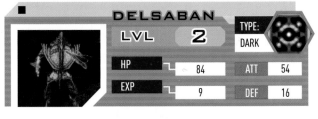

DELSABAN

LVL	2
TYPE:	DARK
HP	84
ATT	54
EXP	9
DEF	16

MONSTERS

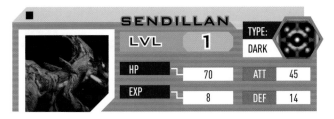

SENDILLAN
LVL 1
TYPE: DARK

| HP | 70 | ATT | 45 |
| EXP | 8 | DEF | 14 |

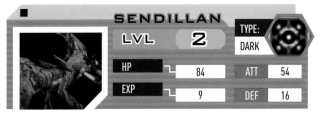

SENDILLAN
LVL 2
TYPE: DARK

| HP | 84 | ATT | 54 |
| EXP | 9 | DEF | 16 |

There are several new twists to trip you up during the trial. In the first room you'll be ambushed by a pack of Sendillan enemies, aggressive beasts who can send you flying with a head butt. These creatures can only damage you from the front, so attack their sides to be safe.

There are also locked doors that can only be opened with a key that appears when you exterminate a certain group of foes. The key will show up as a red dot on your auto-map, so use that to find it if you don't see it appear.

If you're gunning for an S-Rank, you'll need to reach the tracks of the Linear Line Platform within 9 minutes; run for the key to the west before Leo even stops talking. Fight with your Saber and Photon Arts and count on your frequent level-ups to provide the healing you need. Don't try to save time by skipping dead ends such as the one to the right as you enter Block C-2; there are Pannon in there and you need to kill every last one of the 67 enemies that appear in these two blocks to earn an S Rank. Save time by skipping the treasure chests in the loops of both Block C-2 and C-3. You can't skip the chests in the seemingly empty room at the west end of Block C-2, however, as that room's monster pack will only appear when the first chest is destroyed. When you reach the Linear Line Platform, run all the way to the left to find the stairs that are the official end point of the trial.

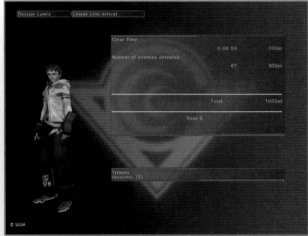

TRIAL RANKING

CONDITIONS

1 CLEAR TIME 9:00 VALUE 700pts
PENALTY -1 point per second late

2 ENEMIES 67 VALUE 300pts
PENALTY -5 points per enemy missed

RANKING INFORMATION

SCORE	RANK	MESETA	MP	PRIZE
1000	S	300	-	Trimate
700 - 999	A	200	-	-
400 - 699	B	100	-	-
0 - 399	C	-	-	-

(4)

(5) SAVE THE WOMAN IN THE RUBBLE

After settling your affairs with the Vol Brothers, you'll find a survivor trapped beneath some rubble. Leo will explain how to use the goggles in your action palette to identify weak points in the rubble. Slap on the goggles and focus your crosshairs on what looks like a glowing green orb. When the crosshairs flash red, swap the goggles for a weapon and hack the weak point three times to free the survivor. Repeat the process again to clear the barrier to the south. As you proceed, use your goggles on other piles of rubble, and you may find one that conceals a dose of Trimate.

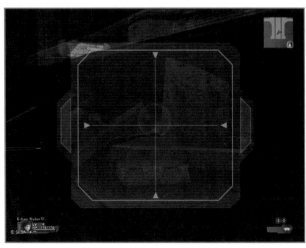

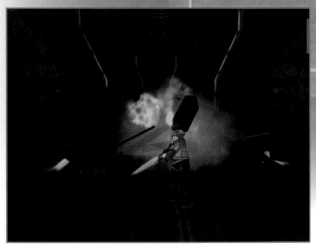

⑥ TRIAL   DEFEAT THE SEED-VANCE

At the end of the line you'll find a powerful alien standing between you and your sister. Forget conservative Handgun-strafing tactics; this boss battle is also a trial and you'll need to fight hard to earn a Rising Crush (the Photon Art for twin blade weapons) as your S-Rank Prize. Charge at the SEED-Vance with your Saber and use your Rising Strike at close range. The damage will knock it over, allowing you to get a few normal swings in. When it rises again, repeat the process until it dies. You may take a few flesh wounds, but you'll earn an S-Rank with time to spare.

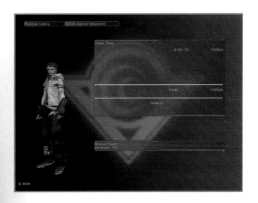

BOSS ONE
SEED-VANCE

⬡⬡⬡⬡⬡⬡⬡ BOSS

SEED-VANCE ●

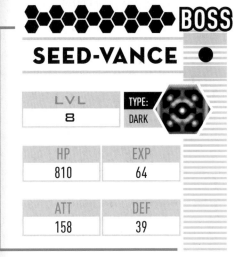

LVL	TYPE:
8	DARK

HP	EXP
810	64

ATT	DEF
158	39

TRIAL RANKING

CONDITIONS

1 CLEAR TIME **0:50** VALUE **1000pts**
PENALTY **-5 points per second late**

RANKING INFORMATION

SCORE	RANK	MESETA	MP	PRIZE
1000	S	300	-	Rising Crush
700 - 999	A	200	-	-
400 - 699	B	100	-	-
0 - 399	C	-	-	-

TYPICAL LIVES

MISSION: MEADOW PURIFY

CHAPTER OBJECTIVES

- [ ] Meet Pete
- [ ] Receive your assignment at Guardians HQ
- [ ] Visit the Holtes City Guardians Branch
- [ ] Meet the team at the West District Open Café
- 1 [ ] Touch base with Norphe
- 2 [ ] Fell trees for extra items
- 3 [ ] The fork in the road: left
- 4 [ ] The fork in the road: right
- 5 [ ] The art of SEED removal
- 6 [ ] TRIAL: Clear the SEED infestation!
- 7 [ ] Chase down Kalam
- 8 [ ] TRIAL: Slay the mad Gol Dolva

[GUARDIANS COLONY]
CLYEZ CITY

PARTNERS

NONE

MEET PETE

Chapter 2 begins in your quarters in Clyez City, where you'll be awakened by Pete, your new Partner Machine. Pete doesn't yet have all of the functions Network Mode players may be familiar with, so for now you'll have to settle for using it as storage. Your inventory has space for only 60 different items (although you can have multiple copies of each), so clear out the #5 tab of your inventory by giving Pete all of your Wenceline, Par Wood, and such.

RECEIVE YOUR ASSIGNMENT AT GUARDIANS HQ

The mall elevators are out, so you'll have to take the escalators to the fifth-floor Guardians HQ. You can hit the shops on the way, purchasing the Tornado Break Photon Art for your Sword or a new weapon-and-photon-art duo. Nothing available at this point is any higher-level than the gear you already own, but a Twin Saber or a Twin Handgun with an elemental Photon Art will add some variety and versatility to your next mission.

[GUARDIANS COLONY]
SHOP REPORT

Ethan is too busy to shop for clothes or get a makeover, so the only shops worth visiting at this point are on the second floor. The armor shop doesn't sell anything better than what you already have, so spend your cash at the weapon shop or save it for a later chapter. Note that the shops in Holtes City carry the same stock at the same prices, so it doesn't matter whether you do your shopping now or after you return from your trip to Parum.

ITEM SHOP

ITEMS	COST
MONOMATE	30
SOL ATOMIZER	100
MOON ATOMIZER	500
GRINDER C+1	300
GRINDER C+2	800
GRINDER C+3	1500
DAMAGE TRAP	50
BURN TRAP	100
FREEZE TRAP	120

ROOM DECORATIONS

DECORATIONS	COST
SUNFLOWER	1000
GREEN LIGHT	1000
PINK LIGHT	1000
REFRESHING GREEN	1000
GOLD TROPHY	5000
SILVER TROPHY	3000
COSMO FOUNTAIN	3000
MOATOOB SOTETS	5000
STRANGE FLOWER	5000
PURPLE FLOWER	5000
LAUTUS FLOWER	8000
MUSHROOMS	8000
BUGEATER CACTUS	12000
MOATOOB KAZLA	12000
RAHULI RAHULE	25000
SCROLL	25000
REFRESHING JELLY	25000
PAPER LANTERN	25000
TOURO	30000
KOBLE TROPHY	1000
ROUND LANTERN	30000
BLUE LIGHT	1000
PHOTON STAR	45000
GUMBALL MACHINE	45000
HOURGLASS	45000
OKIKU DOLL	45000
G FLYER (BLUE)	80000
G FLYER (ORANGE)	80000

WEAPON SHOP   *GRM*

MELEE WEAPONS	COST	PP	ATT	ACC	ELEMENTS	ATP
SWORD	250	115	80	80	-	25 (LONG SWORD)
TWIN SABER	300	120	33	80	-	25 (TWIN BLADES)
TWIN DAGGER	280	130	21	80	-	25 (TWIN DAGGERS)
SABER	220	85	61	83	-	25 (1-HAND SWORD)
DAGGER	200	90	40	84	ICE-20%	25 (DAGGER)

RANGED WEAPONS	COST	PP	ATT	ACC	ELEMENTS	ATA
TWIN HANDGUN	290	125	35	34	-	8 (TWIN HANDGUNS)
HANDGUN	180	95	31	34	-	8 (HANDGUN)

DISCS	COST	ATTACHES TO
TORNADO BREAK	500	LONG SWORD
RISING CRUSH	500	TWIN BLADES
RENKAI BUYOU-ZAN	480	TWIN DAGGERS
RISING STRIKE	350	1-HAND BLADE
SHUNBU SHOUREN-ZAN	450	DAGGER
TWIN BURN	400	TWIN HANDGUN
TWIN FREEZE	400	TWIN HANDGUN
TWIN PLASMA	400	TWIN HANDGUN
BURNING HIT	400	HANDGUN
FROZEN HIT	400	HANDGUN
PLASMA HIT	400	HANDGUN

ARMOR SHOP

ARMOR	COST	DEF	EVA	SLOTS	ELEMENTS	DFP
CARLINE	300	15	30	0	-	3
LIGHTLINE	300	14	32	1	-	3

UNITS	COST	ATT	ACC
CAR / POWER	200	6	0
CAR / HIT	200	0	6

[PARUM] HOLTES CITY

PARTNERS

NONE

VISIT THE HOLTES CITY GUARDIANS BRANCH

After receiving your assignment and learning all you can from the folks at Guardians HQ, take a PPT Shuttle on the 4th floor to the planet Parum. You'll land in the Central Square of Holtes City, where you'll need to turn to your right and step onto a moving walkway that leads to the East District. Check in at the local Guardians Branch, where you'll be sent to meet your team at a West District café.

MEET THE TEAM AT THE WEST DISTRICT OPEN CAFE

You'll meet your partner Hyuga and your trainer Karen at the café at the opposite end of the area. After completing a brief tutorial about recruiting and dismissing party characters, the group will separate. Find Karen nearby and ask her to join you, then return to the East District to track down Hyuga; he should be waiting near the moving walkway. When your party is complete, head up the stairs to the East District Flyer Base and accept the Meadow Purify Mission.

22

MISSION: MEADOW PURIFY

1st training mission. Suppress the altered livestock and other creatures. Purify the SEED infection in Raffon Meadow. Meet with the client on-site.

Required	1 Karen
	2 Hyuga
Party	3/3

[PARUM]
RAFFON MEADOW A

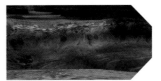

PARTNERS

NAME	LVL (Ethan's +...)	RACE	CLASS
1. Hyuga Ryght	+0	Human	Hunter
2. Karen Erra	+3	Newman	Hunter

OBJECTIVES ① TO ④

1   TOUCH BASE WITH NORPHE

You'll meet your client in the monster-free Block A-1, where she'll send you deeper into Raffon Meadow in search of a boy named Kalam. The enemies here are much tougher than the ones you faced in the Linear Line, but the same tactics should prove effective. Polty behave similar to the Pannon, and the new Koltova and Vahra have roughly the same attack patterns as the Sendillan and Delsaban foes you know so well.

MONSTER TACTIC:
THE KING OF THE VAHRA

There are actually two variations of the Vahra enemy found in the meadow. Your garden-variety Vahra can only swipe with its claws, but rarer "king" Vahra have the ability to boost the Attack and Defense of their comrades and can cast Resta to heal the whole pack. They also deal and require more damage, but provide about 40% more EXP to compensate for the trouble.

The data box that appears when you fight an enhanced Vahra usually has a little yellow crown icon in it, but you can tell from farther away by examining their left arms. Unlike normal, symmetrical Vahra, the left arms of the kings have a thick tan and green bone shield. They may be tougher prey, but take the kings out first, before they can boost and heal their subjects.

MONSTERS

POLTY

LVL	5	TYPE: ELEC
HP	122	ATT 79
EXP	7	DEF 24

POLTY

LVL	6	TYPE: ELEC
HP	136	ATT 88
EXP	8	DEF 26

KOLTOVA

LVL	5	TYPE: FIRE
HP	122	ATT 79
EXP	12	DEF 24

VAHRA

LVL	5	TYPE: ELEC
HP	122	ATT	79
EXP	12	DEF	24

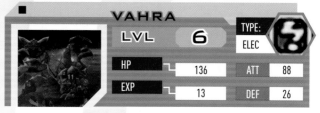

VAHRA

LVL	6	TYPE: ELEC
HP	136	ATT	88
EXP	13	DEF	26

SHAGREECE

LVL	5	TYPE: FIRE
HP	85	ATT	103
EXP	18	DEF	24

② TOPPLE TREES FOR EXTRA ITEMS

After you clear the first batch of enemies out of Block A-2's second area, slip on your goggles and take a look at the tree. Not every tree has a weak point that you can isolate, but the ones that do often offer rewards that are far better than the typical random items in the area. There are six destructible trees in all; look for the icons on the area maps.

ITEM HUNTING IN RAFFON MEADOW...

The barrels and hay bales in Raffon Meadow usually conceal minor items like Monomate, Dimate, Par Wood, and Photons. The trees hold much more exciting supplies, including Star Atomizers, Moon Atomizers, and even Scape Dolls, all of which you'll want to save until later in the game. But the best of all is a random enemy drop: Polty—especially the level 6 Polty that appear in the Block A-4 Cave and in Block C-1—sometimes drop Brand weapons. The Brand is the two-star version of the Saber and it packs double the power as well as an ice-element Photon Art that deals additional damage to the Fire-type Koltova and Shagreece enemies.

③ THE FORK IN THE ROAD: LEFT

When you clear the area to the north of the Block A-4 cave, you'll encounter a fork in the road. The area to the left is optional, but if you can fight your way through a pair of Wyvern-like Shagreece enemies, you'll unlock a Heal Spot and a few well-hidden hay bales. To beat the fast-moving Shagreece, switch to a ranged weapon and blast them from a distance—if you can get one shot in, the creature's flinch will allow you to score several more. You can't auto-target the Shagreece when they're flying high, but you can target them manually if you switch to the first-person view. Be careful, however, as this leaves you rooted in place and vulnerable to their mid-air flame jets.

④ THE FORK IN THE ROAD: RIGHT

Take a look at the arms of the Vahra that attack as you approach the Block A-4 Exit. While only one has the crown, each of these Vahra deals far more damage than usual; you'll be dead within seconds if you let them surround you. Circle around the pack so you can unload Photon Arts into their backs and then get out of the way before they can retaliate. Keep an eye on your lifebar and a Monomate at the ready; just a few enhanced-Vahra hits can send you to the brink of death.

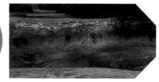
PARTNERS

NAME	LVL (Ethan's +...)	RACE	CLASS
1. Hyuga Ryght	+0	Human	Hunter
2. Karen Erra	+3	Newman	Hunter

⑤ THE ART OF SEED REMOVAL

You'll encounter the first SEED-Zoma a short distance into Block B-1. This strange being is immune to damage, but Karen will teach you how to eradicate it with a Photon Eraser. (The one she gives you goes straight to your item menu, so you'll need to manually assign it to your action palette.) Use your goggles to isolate the invisible SEED-Blewmes and lock onto them to dispel their shroud of invisibility. Then switch to your Photon Eraser and blast the blewme until it turns gray. When all four blewmes are cleansed the zoma will become vulnerable, and you can destroy it with any weapon. You don't need to smash the gray blewmes, but if you do you may find common random items like Photons and Par Wood. The Zoma themselves often hold the higher-tier items (like Star Atomizers and Scape Dolls) that can be found in destructible trees.

MONSTERS

SEED-VANCE

LVL	**5**	TYPE: DARK
HP	610	ATT	119
EXP	51	DEF	29

POLTY

LVL	**6**	TYPE: ELEC / FIRE
HP	136	ATT	88
EXP	8	DEF	26

VAHRA

LVL	**5**	TYPE: ELEC / FIRE
HP	122	ATT	79
EXP	12	DEF	24

KOLTOVA

LVL	**6**	TYPE: FIRE
HP	136	ATT	88
EXP	13	DEF	26

VAHRA

LVL	**6**	TYPE: ELEC / FIRE
HP	136	ATT	88
EXP	13	DEF	26

MONSTERS   CONTINUED

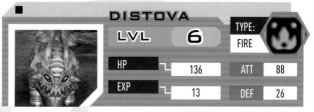

6 TRIAL   CLEAR THE SEED INFESTATION!

When you cross the next gate a trial will begin, so you may want to backtrack and save your game first. In this trial you have 12 minutes to clear four SEED-Zoma and kill 43 monsters. The first two Zoma cleansings are similar to the one you trained on, but by the third you'll be fighting off monsters as you search for blewmes tucked in corners or behind tall grass. Keep an eye out for the lava pools that usually (but not always) reveal the locations of blewmes, and make sure to search the hill behind the fourth Zoma; you'll find two of its blewmes up there, guarded by a SEED-Vance and other monsters!

To save time, entrust the cleansing to Karen and Hyuga whenever possible. If they're nearby, just walk past a red blewme and they should draw their Photon Erasers. As soon as ones begins to fire you can move on to find the next blewme, confident that they won't move on until they've finished the job. Save time by ignoring the dead blewmes and most of the chests you pass, but do take a few seconds to smash the yellow containers that appear both between the first and second Zoma, and following the fourth one—these boxes hold rare items.

> Many of the Polty and Vahra enemies you'll encounter in Block B are fire-element variants that have new attacks like Foie fireballs!

TRIAL RANKING

CONDITIONS

1 CLEAR TIME 12:00 VALUE 300pts

PENALTY -1 point per second late

2 ENEMIES 43 VALUE 300pts

PENALTY -5 points per enemy missed

3 SEEDS PURIFIED 4 VALUE 400pts

PENALTY -200 points per SEED-Zoma missed

SCORE	RANK	MESETA	MP	PRIZE
1000	S	1500	-	Pike
700 - 999	A	500	-	-
400 - 699	B	200	-	-
0 - 399	C	-	-	-

7 CHASE DOWN KALAM

You'll spot Kalam here, but you'll have to chase him through all of Block C. He triggers blue laser gates that won't fall until all the enemies are slain, forcing you to clear an area of enemies before you can proceed. When pursuing him, use your map to figure out which route you haven't yet taken; it's easy to get lost since you won't always see which gate has disappeared.

8 **TRIAL** SLAY THE MAD GOL DOLVA

After you save at the Save Marker, you can return to Holtes City by going back through the Block C door. You'll resume exactly where you left off, so take the opportunity to return to town if you're low on healing items—you may need a few for this boss fight.

The safest place to fight the Gol Dolva is from behind. From there you only need to worry about the shockwave attack, and you can dodge it by running when the Gol Dolva rears up on its hind legs. The key to scoring an S-Rank is getting as much participation out of Hyuga and Karen as possible; if they don't chase the Gol Dolva with you, lead it back to them. Not only will their attacks help whittle away its HP, but the Gol Dolva won't run as much if it has adjacent targets to attack. If you got an S-Rank in the last trial, use your Pike prize for this fight—even without a Photon Art this is the weapon that will deal the most damage.

GETTING STARTED

STORY MODE

FREE MISSIONS

NETWORK MODE

BOSS TWO
GOL DOLVA

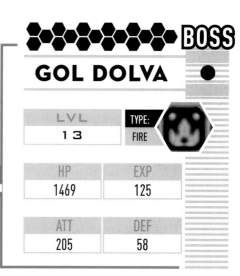

◆◆◆◆◆◆◆◆◆◆ **BOSS**

GOL DOLVA

LVL	TYPE:
13	FIRE

HP	EXP
1469	125

ATT	DEF
205	58

TRIAL RANKING

⑧

CONDITIONS

1 CLEAR TIME 1:00 VALUE 1000pts
PENALTY -5 points per second late

RANKING INFORMATION

SCORE	RANK	MESETA	MP	PRIZE
1000	S	1500	-	Agtaride
700 - 999	A	500	-	-
400 - 699	B	200	-	-
0 - 399	C	-	-	-

RELICS

[GUARDIANS COLONY]
CLYEZ CITY

PARTNERS

NONE

UPDATE YOUR GUARDIANS LICENSE

You'll awaken to a hologram of Hyuga telling you to meet him on the fourth floor of the mall, and a message from Guardians HQ telling you to stop in on the fifth. Since Hyuga is late, head straight to the fifth floor, skipping the shops on the way (you'll find much better shopping opportunities at Holtes City).

Speak to Mina behind the counter of Guardians HQ, and she'll update your Guardians License with the ability to do Free Missions and change your type. If you want to change your type now, from Hunter to Force or Ranger, speak to the woman on the other side of the counter. We would advise against switching to Force this early in the game, however.

MEET UP WITH HYUGA AND KAREN

After updating your license, you'll find Hyuga near the elevator by the Parum PPT gate. He'll give you his partner card and explain how the partner card system works. You'll find Karen waiting when you arrive at Holtes City, and she'll give you her card as well. You can now use partner cards to invite Hyuga and Karen to your party without having to find them in town.

[PARUM]
HOLTES CITY

PARTNERS

NONE

[GUARDIANS COLONY]
SHOP REPORT

[NOTE: PURPLE TEXT DENOTES THAT THIS IS NEW TO THE SHOP.]

WEAPON SHOP   GRM

MELEE WEAPONS	COST	PP	ATT	ACC	ELEMENTS	ATP
SWORD	250	115	80	80	-	25 (LONG SWORD)
PIKE	1800	152	156	80	-	45 (SPEAR)
TWIN SABER	300	120	33	80	-	25 (TWIN BLADES)
TWIN DAGGER	280	130	21	80	-	25 (TWIN DAGGERS)
SABER	220	85	61	83	-	25 (1-HAND SWORD)
BRAND	1600	110	126	83	ICE-16%	45 (1-HAND SWORD)
DAGGER	200	90	40	84	ICE-20%	25 (DAGGER)

RANGED WEAPONS	COST	PP	ATT	ACC	ELEMENTS	ATA
TWIN HANDGUN	290	125	35	34	-	8 (TWIN HANDGUNS)
HANDGUN	180	95	31	34	-	8 (HANDGUN)
POWERGUN	1350	123	65	34	-	13 (HANDGUN)

FORCE WEAPONS	COST	PP	TECH	ELEMENTS	TP
STAFF	1500	156	126	-	28 (ROD)

DISCS	COST	ATTACHES TO
TORNADO BREAK	500	LONG SWORD
DUS DAGGAS	2500	SPEAR
RISING CRUSH	500	TWIN BLADES
RENKAI BUYOU-ZAN	480	TWIN DAGGERS
RISING STRIKE	350	1-HAND BLADE
SHUNBU SHOUREN-ZAN	450	DAGGER
TWIN BURN	400	TWIN HANDGUN
TWIN FREEZE	400	TWIN HANDGUN
TWIN PLASMA	400	TWIN HANDGUN
BURNING HIT	400	HANDGUN
FROZEN HIT	400	HANDGUN
PLASMA HIT	400	HANDGUN
FOIE	1000	WAND/STAFF
BARTA	1000	WAND/STAFF
ZONDE	1000	WAND/STAFF
RESTA	1000	WAND/STAFF

The shops in Clyez City still sell the same low-level stuff they did in Chapter 2, but the Holtes City G.R.M. shop has been updated with several tempting items. The Perpaline armor is a must-buy, as it will boost your defensive stats and give you some protection against fire-element attacks (it will also reduce your resistance to ice-element attacks, but you aren't likely to encounter those soon). For a mere extra 200 Meseta you can buy a unit for your armor that will boost either your Attack or Accuracy scores.

You can exploit the power of elemental photons on offense as well. Since fire-type critters will abound in this Chapter, pick up a Brand if you don't have one already. If you've gone the Ranger route, buy a Powergun and the Frozen Hit Photon Art to give yourself the same capability.

Finally, you'll notice that a Staff and four Technics have appeared in the shop. In Story Mode even Hunters can use wands, so if you have 3700 Meseta to burn you can buy a Wand and a pair of Technics to attach to it (Resta and Foie are your best choice for the missions ahead). Don't have that kind of cash on hand? Buy what you can now and come back after completing the Free Mission a few times to buy the rest.

ARMOR SHOP

ARMOR	COST	DEF	EVA	SLOTS	ELEMENTS	DFP
CARLINE	300	15	30	0	-	3
PERPALINE	2500	33	58	1	FIRE-8%	5
LIGHTLINE	300	14	32	0	-	3
BRANDLINE	2500	30	56	1	-	5

UNITS	COST	ATT	ACC
CAR / POWER	200	6	0
CAR / HIT	200	0	6

ITEM SHOP

ITEMS	COST
MONOMATE	30
SOL ATOMIZER	100
MOON ATOMIZER	500
GRINDER C+1	300
GRINDER C+2	800
GRINDER C+3	1500
DAMAGE TRAP	50
BURN TRAP	100
FREEZE TRAP	120

GETTING STARTED

STORY MODE

FREE MISSIONS

NETWORK MODE

Your official mission isn't ready yet, so get the party together and sign up for the Flyer Base's "Creature Discomfort" Free Mission. This quick and lucrative mission consists of only a single Raffon Meadow block with 25 foes. You'll earn cash from fallen foes and your trial ranking, but the biggest rewards are the healing items you can find in yellow containers and destructible trees. Moon Atomizers, Scape Dolls and the like can be resold for big money; you can potentially earn several thousand Meseta each time you play the Creature Discomfort mission. And since it's a Free Mission, you can replay it as many times as you want!

MISSION: CREATURE DISCOMFORT

Native creatures that lived in Raffon Meadow because of the SEED influence became savage and as a result, they are causing damage in the local area.

		Required	-
LOC	Raffon Meadow	Party	1-4

① TRIAL — DEFEAT ENEMIES EN ROUTE

The Creature Discomfort trial begins as soon as you land, but you have little hope of earning an S-Rank at this point. You can come back for that when you're stronger, but for now aim for an A. Don't rush so much that you pass up any of the yellow containers that hold the great loot.

At the start of the mission, run to your right to reach a peninsula in the lake guarded by two Shagreece. Blow them out of the sky, then help yourself to the contents of two yellow containers (you can break the tree, too). Then head in the other direction, where you'll battle low-level Distova and Vahra on the way to the exit. At the end you'll face 12 Vahra in alternating waves of normal and enhanced versions, but they're no tougher than the ones you fought in Chapter 2. Before you go for the exit, search out the hidden path concealed by the tall grass and hit three more yellow containers.

TRIAL RANKING

CONDITIONS

1 CLEAR TIME 2:00 VALUE 700pts
PENALTY -1 point per second late

2 ENEMIES 25 VALUE 300pts
PENALTY -5 points per enemy missed

RANKING INFORMATION

SCORE	RANK	MESETA	MP	PRIZE
1000	S	300	20	PPT Shuttle
700 - 999	A	150	10	-
400 - 699	B	50	5	-
0 - 399	C	-	-	-

2 MEET YOUR CLIENT AT THE GUARDIANS BRANCH

When you've repeated the Free Mission enough times to afford the weapon of your dreams, visit the Holtes City Guardians Branch to begin your real mission. After you meet Dr. Dorson, you'll be able to select "Relics Inquiry" at the Flyer Base. Hyuga and Karen should already be in your party, so you're ready to go!

MISSION: RELICS INQUIRY

Per the request of the client, Dr. Dorson, head to the Relics site in Raffon Meadow. Investigate it and protect the doctor.

Required
1 Karen
2 Hyuga

 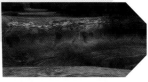

LOC	Raffon Meadow Shore	Party	3-3

[PARUM]

RAFFON MEADOW SHORE D&E

PARTNERS

NAME	LVL (Ethan's +...)	RACE	CLASS
1. Hyuga Ryght	+0	Human	Hunter
2. Karen Erra	+3	Newman	Hunter
3. Dr. Dorson	-3	Human	Civilian

OBJECTIVES 3 TO 5

MONSTERS

DISTOVA LVL 10 TYPE: FIRE

HP	188	ATT	122
EXP	19	DEF	36

KOLTOVA LVL 11 TYPE: FIRE

HP	200	ATT	130
EXP	21	DEF	40

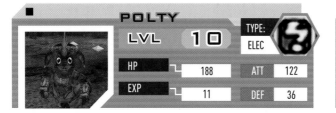

POLTY

LVL	10	TYPE: ELEC

HP	188	ATT	122
EXP	11	DEF	36

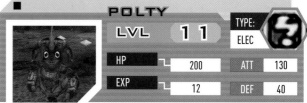

POLTY

LVL	11	TYPE: ELEC

HP	200	ATT	130
EXP	12	DEF	40

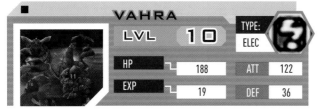

VAHRA

LVL	10	TYPE: ELEC

HP	188	ATT	122
EXP	19	DEF	36

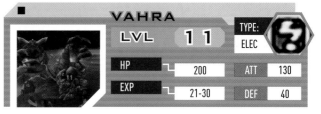

VAHRA

LVL	11	TYPE: ELEC

HP	200	ATT	130
EXP	21-30	DEF	40

3 TRIAL   CLEAR LAKESHORE AREA

You must race through a new area of Raffon Meadow to reach the Relic site; this is an arduous task. The X factor here is Dr. Dorson, who will cost you 100 points if he gets knocked out. The doctor is pretty smart about staying off the front lines, but keep an eye on his lifebar and heal him with a Resta Technic or a Star Atomizer if it ever turns yellow.

To kill all 69 monsters you'll need to explore every dead end. Start by heading to the northwest, where you'll find a few foes and a hidden path through the trees. Make sure to smash the three yellow containers at the end of the path, not just for the treasure, but also to lure out three Vahra. Continue west and smash the gray chests you find there to spawn another batch of foes.

As you progress through the later parts of the trial, use your auto-map to make sure you don't get lost. Many of this area's keys are on small islands you can only reach with teleporters (they activate automatically when an area is clear of foes), and these keys may be far from the doors they unlock. Make sure to hit all the possible dead ends before you pass through the last door of Block D-2, where the trial ends.

TRIAL RANKING

CONDITIONS

1 CLEAR TIME 11:00 VALUE 600pts
PENALTY -1 point per second late

2 ENEMIES 69 VALUE 300pts
PENALTY -5 points per enemy missed

3 DR. DORSON FAINTS 0 VALUE 100pts
PENALTY -100 points per Dr. Dorson incapacitation

RANKING INFORMATION

SCORE	RANK	MESETA	MP	PRIZE
1000	S	2000	60	Agtaride
700 - 999	A	1000	30	-
400 - 699	B	-	10	-
0 - 399	C	-	5	-

④ TRIAL — SURVIVE THE DE RAGAN

After the first trial, you'll end up in an abandoned base. You'll find a Save Marker and Heal Spot in the northeast, not far from the door to Block E-1. The E Block is short and straightforward, but ends with a rare mid-mission boss trial!

The De Ragan boss in Block E-2 compensates for its low defense score with scaly armor that protects it from all but a small fraction of your attack power. The armor is weakest in its head and neck area, so that's the place to strike. Your best weapon by far is the Brand; Rising Strike will allow you to hit it high in vulnerable spots and the Brand's ice-element photon will deal additional damage. If you've switched to the Ranger type, use an ice-element Photon Art and make sure your crosshairs are centered on De Ragan's head or neck when you fire. If you bought the Perpaline armor you can afford to be somewhat aggressive here, as its fire photon will protect you from much of the De Ragan's damage.

BOSS THREE
DE RAGAN

◆◆◆◆◆◆◆◆◆ BOSS

DE RAGAN ●

LVL	TYPE:
18	FIRE

HP	EXP
3900	440

ATT	DEF
214	19

GETTING STARTED · STORY MODE · FREE MISSIONS · NETWORK MODE

TRIAL RANKING

RANKING INFORMATION

CONDITIONS

1 CLEAR TIME 1:00 VALUE 900pts
PENALTY -1 point per second late

2 DR. DORSON FAINTS 0 VALUE 100pts
PENALTY -100 points per Dr. Dorson incapacitation

SCORE	RANK	MESETA	MP	PRIZE
1000	S	2000	60	Gigush
700 - 999	A	1000	30	-
400 - 699	B	-	10	-
0 - 399	C	-	5	-

5 STOCK UP AT BRUCE'S SHOP

Former Guardians Bruce will meet you at the entrance to the Relic, where he's selling a few basic weapons and recovery items. Ranged attacks are going to be important in the Relic, so pick up a Powergun if you don't have any good long-range weapons.

WEAPON SHOP Bruce's

MELEE WEAPONS	COST	PP	ATT	ACC	ELEMENTS	ATP
PIKE	1800	152	156	80	-	45 (SPEAR)
BRAND	1600	110	126	83	ICE-16%	45 (1-HAND SWORD)

RANGED WEAPONS	COST	PP	ATT	ACC	ELEMENTS	ATA
POWERGUN	1350	123	65	34	-	13 (HANDGUN)

FORCE WEAPONS	COST	PP	TECH	ELEMENTS	TP
STAFF	1500	156	126	-	28 (ROD)

ITEM SHOP

ITEMS	COST
MONOMATE	30
SOL ATOMIZER	100

[PARUM] THE RAFFON RELIC

PARTNERS

NAME	LVL (Ethan's +...)	RACE	CLASS
1. Hyuga Ryght	+0	Human	Hunter
2. Karen Erra	+3	Newman	Hunter
3. Dr. Dorson	-3	Human	Civilian

OBJECTIVES 6 TO 12

MONSTERS

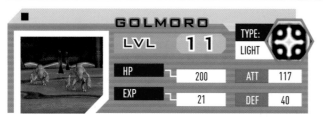

GOLMORO — LVL 11 — TYPE: LIGHT

HP	200	ATT	117
EXP	21	DEF	40

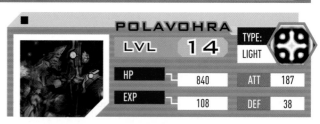

POLAVOHRA — LVL 14 — TYPE: LIGHT

HP	840	ATT	187
EXP	108	DEF	38

ITEM HUNTING IN THE RAFFON RELIC...

MONSTERS CONTINUED

BADIRA

LVL	11	TYPE: FIRE
HP	140	ATT	98
EXP	12	DEF	32

Chests appear only rarely in the Raffon Relic and are usually empty. The few items you do find will be mostly familiar, but there are a few new items, including [B] Dimate, the first Board item. Boards function as recipes in item synthesis, an ability of Pete's that will be unlocked in Chapter 4.

6   STRIKE GOLMORO FROM A DISTANCE

The monsters in the Raffon Relic give Force and Ranger tactics a chance to shine. While Badira are straightforward creatures that can be easily swept aside by Hunter ice-element weapons like the Gigush and Brand, quick-hopping, hard-slashing Golmoro will give melee fighters fits. To safely approach a Golmoro you'll need to walk in an arc to dodge its claws, and even then you'll only get in a hit or two before it hops away. It is far easier to kill them with guns and Force Technics like Foie.

7   BRING DOWN THE MIGHTY POLAVOHRA

The Polavohra that attacks at Point B is like a giant, slow-moving Koltova. But unlike the Koltova, Polavohra can use a shockwave attack that knocks away anyone nearby. Melee fighters will need to fight conservatively to dodge Polavohra attacks, but Technic and Handgun-users will have little trouble blasting these slow-moving behemoths from a distance.

GETTING STARTED

STORY MODE

FREE MISSIONS

NETWORK MODE

8 NEVER TRUST RELIC TREASURE BOXES

Whenever you see isolated treasure boxes, use a Handgun to destroy them from a distance. The center chest here contains a pack of Badira, while the chests at either end hold lone Golmoro. Keep blasting the monsters from your current position so you can kill them before they can close the distance. This will reveal the key. More trick boxes are ahead, so stay wary!

9 THE STATERIA DISCOVERY

The event at Point D will end with a monster ambush, and you'll need to act quickly to save Dr. Dorson. This is an ideal time to use the Tornado Break Photon Art for a two-handed Sword; it will sweep the enemies away and give you a chance to cut open an escape route for the doctor. Let Karen and Hyuga provide a distraction as you finish off the pack from a distance.

10 THE OPTIONAL C BLOCK

From the Save Marker in Block B-2 you can head either southwest to Block C-1, or southeast to the boss. Block C-1 is a loop that leads past several monster-filled areas to a room with five chests (but with the same low odds that they hold anything good). If you've had your fill of Badira and Golmoro monsters, skip Block C entirely and head straight to the boss area.

11 TRIAL DEFEAT SVALTUS

Svaltus is skilled at Swordplay, so this is yet another time when Technics and guns are your best option. As an added bonus, the doctor tends to stick close to you, and pursuing ranged attacks will make it easier to keep him out of trouble. (It will also make it easier to treat his wounds). When Svaltus is distracted by Hyuga and Karen you can fire Foie Technics and Power Gun rounds freely, but when he has a bead on you you'll need to wait for him to swing his Sword, and retaliate after you sidestep the long-range energy blast. If you insist on fighting at melee range, try to stay behind Svaltus and watch its arms closely; he always lifts them to attack, giving you time to flee its shockwaves. A melee win is doable, but a stream of Foie fireballs is by far the easiest way to earn an S-Rank and the ultra-rare Svaltus Edge material prize (retail value: 150,000 Meseta).

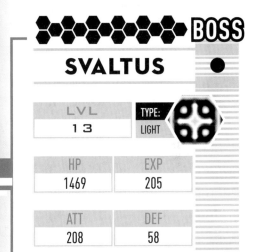

BOSS FOUR
SVALTUS

BOSS

SVALTUS ●

LVL	TYPE:
1 3	LIGHT

HP	EXP
1469	205

ATT	DEF
208	58

TRIAL RANKING

RANKING INFORMATION

⑪

CONDITIONS

1. CLEAR TIME **1:00** VALUE **900pts**
   PENALTY **-1 point per second late**

2. DR. DORSON FAINTS **0** VALUE
   PENALTY **-100 points per Dr. Dorson**
   incapacitation

SCORE	RANK	MESETA	MP	PRIZE
1000	S	2000	60	Svaltus Edge
700 - 999	A	1000	30	-
400 - 699	B	-	10	-
0 - 399	C	-	5	-

 ⑫ **LEAD DR. DORSON TO SAFETY**

After the boss battle, Hyuga and Karen will stay to hold back the Stateria while you escort Dr. Dorson to safety. The first room you cross contains another Svaltus and a horde of foes, but the door at the other side is open and you can flee without engaging them. Dr. Dorson isn't quite as fleet of foot, however, so turn around and cover his escape with a ranged weapon. The door will take you back to Block A-1, where you will face no further opposition.

GETTING STARTED

STORY MODE

FREE MISSIONS

NETWORK MODE

CHAPTER 4

ROGUES

[GUARDIANS COLONY]
CLYEZ CITY

PARTNERS

NONE

CHAPTER OBJECTIVES

☐ Go shopping with Lumia

☐ Party up with Lucaim Nav

① ☐ TRIAL: Destroy the Dilla Griena

② ☐ TRIAL: Destroy the Gohma Dilla

③ ☐ Clear a path to Car 5

④ ☐ TRIAL: Regain control of the train

⑤ ☐ Run to Karen's side

⑥ ☐ TRIAL: Defeat the Vol Brothers

MISSION: THE MILATE 04

GO SHOPPING WITH LUMIA

You promised Lumia you'd take her shopping, so meet her at the Central Table and let her drag you around the mall for a few minutes. Your outing will end at the Synthesis shop, where Lumia will buy you a Synthesis kit. Bring the kit to your room, and Pete will upgrade itself to include Synthesis functions. You can now insert boards into Pete. (If you have the necessary materials in storage, have Pete synthesize the board item.) You can also feed Pete extra items to level it up, increasing its Synthesis abilities and ultimately evolving it into a combat ally! Synthesize a dose of Trimate with the Board that came with the kit, then check out the Synthesis shop to see what else you can cook up.

! Three new Free Missions have opened up, including one right here on the Guardians Colony. Give them a shot if you need cash or want to level up before your next mission.

[GUARDIANS COLONY]
SHOP REPORT

The shops in Clyez City now sell the new items that were added to the G.R.M. store in Chapter 3, but if you want anything new you'll have to make it yourself. If you've been collecting ingredients, you probably have what you need to whip up a Gigush, Twin Brand or the not-yet-for-sale Blaster. The missing Neu Wood and Mot Wood required to make a Ryo-Stizashi or Gudda Brana can be purchased at the next counter, but you'll need three and five pieces of each material respectively, and that can get expensive. The Zon-photon you need for the Stellaline armor upgrade is not yet available.

Today's mission will entail guarding the cargo of this train, the Milate 04.

SYNTHESIS SHOP

BOARDS	COST
[B] GIGUSH	500
[B] TWIN BRAND	500
[B] RYO-STIZASHI	1000
[B] GUDDA BRANA	1500
[B] BLASTER	1000
[B] PERPALINE	300
[B] STELLALINE	800
[B] MONOMATE	5
[B] DIMATE	10
[B] GRINDER C	100

CONVERTERS	COST
[B] ORE C. 1 > 2	50
[B] ORE C. 2 > 3	200
[B] METAL CONV. C > B	200
[B] METAL CONV. B > A	1500
[B] WOOD CONV. C > B	200
[B] WOOD CONV. B > A	1500

MATERIALS	COST
PHOTON	300
EL-PHOTON	800
IM-PHOTON	800
CARLIAN	200
MEGANITE	200
HARNIUM	200
GAMOTITE	200
SOURAL	200
ACENALINE	100
WENCELINE	300
HOT BERRY	50
COLD BERRY	50
SWEET BERRY	50
BITTER BERRY	50
STAMINA BERRY	50
TRANS ACID	100
GRINDER BASE C	100
PAR WOOD	200
MOT WOOD	200
NEU WOOD	200

PARTY UP WITH LUCAIM NAV

On your way out of your room, Karen will call and ask you to meet her and Hyuga at the Guardians Branch in Holtes City. When you do, you'll meet Lucaim Nav, the academy headmaster and the leader on this mission. He'll give you his partner card so you can bring him on the Milate 04 mission, but he doesn't seem to mind if you drag him on Free Missions as well. Note that this mission leaves out of the train system across from the G.R.M. shop, and not from the usual Flyer Base.

I'm looking forward to seeing what you've got!

GETTING STARTED

STORY MODE

FREE MISSIONS

NETWORK MODE

MISSION: MILATE 04

Guard the A-Photon reactors found in the Raffon Relics while they're being transported aboard the Milate 04.

Required	1 Karen	2 Hyuga	3 Nav

NOTE: Cannot return to city during mission.

LOC	On board the Milate 04	Party	4/4

SHOP REPORT

The G.R.M. shop has a few new toys, including the Knife, Twin Knife, and Twin Powergun. You can also buy a Gigush or Twin Brand, although it would be cheaper to synthesize them. Technic-users will find plenty of treats on G.R.M. shelves, primarily the second tier of elemental Technics. If you have more Technics than you can fit on a Wand, you can always buy a second one, but the simplest solution is to replace Foie with Rabarta. Ice-element Rabarta will destroy the fire-element foes you'll face in the next two missions and all but guarantee you an S-Rank in two lucrative trials.

WEAPON SHOP — GRM

[NOTE: PURPLE TEXT DENOTES THAT THIS IS NEW TO THE SHOP.]

MELEE WEAPONS	COST	PP	ATT	ACC	ELEMENTS	ATP
SWORD	250	115	80	80	-	25 (LONG SWORD)
GIGUSH	3000	149	166	80	ICE-16%	45 (LONG SWORD)
PIKE	1800	152	156	80	-	45 (SPEAR)
TWIN SABER	300	120	33	80	-	25 (TWIN BLADE)
TWIN BRAND	2900	156	69	80	-	45 (TWIN BLADE)
TWIN DAGGER	280	130	21	80	-	25 (TWIN DAGGER)
TWIN KNIFE	2700	169	45	80	ICE-20%	45 (TWIN DAGGER)
SABER	220	85	61	83	-	25 (1-HAND SWORD)
BRAND	1600	110	126	83	ICE-16%	45 (1-HAND SWORD)
DAGGER	200	90	40	84	ICE-20%	25 (DAGGER)
KNIFE	2000	117	83	84	-	45 (KNIFE)

RANGED WEAPONS	COST	PP	ATT	ACC	ELEMENTS	ATA
TWIN HANDGUN	290	125	35	34	-	8 (TWIN HANDGUN)
TWIN POWERGUN	2400	162	72	34	-	13 (TWIN HANDGUN)
HANDGUN	180	95	31	34	-	8 (HANDGUN)
POWERGUN	1350	123	65	34	-	13 (HANDGUN)

FORCE WEAPONS	COST	PP	TECH	ELEMENTS	TP
STAFF	1500	156	126	-	28 (ROD)

DISCS	COST	ATTACHES TO
TORNADO BREAK	500	LONG SWORD
DUS DAGGAS	2500	SPEAR
RISING CRUSH	500	TWIN BLADES
RENKAI BUYOU-ZAN	480	TWIN DAGGERS
RISING STRIKE	350	1-HAND BLADE
SHUNBU SHOUREN-ZAN	450	DAGGER
TWIN BURN	400	TWIN HANDGUN
TWIN FREEZE	400	TWIN HANDGUN
TWIN PLASMA	400	TWIN HANDGUN
BURNING HIT	400	HANDGUN
FROZEN HIT	400	HANDGUN
PLASMA HIT	400	HANDGUN
FOIE	1000	WAND/STAFF
RAFOIE	3500	WAND/STAFF
JELLEN	3500	WAND/STAFF
BARTA	1000	WAND/STAFF
RABARTA	3500	WAND/STAFF
ZALURE	1500	WAND/STAFF
ZONDE	1000	WAND/STAFF
RAZONDE	3500	WAND/STAFF
ZOLDEEL	1500	WAND/STAFF
RESTA	1000	WAND/STAFF
REVERSER	3000	WAND/STAFF

[PARUM]
THE MILATE 04 : PART 1
PARTNERS

NONE

OBJECTIVES 1 TO 2

1 TRIAL — DESTROY THE DILLA GRIENA

When Lucaim Nav discovers a hacking attempt during your two-man patrol, you'll be sent to hunt down the trio of Dilla Griena that have infiltrated the nearest car. Dilla Griena follow the same basic pattern as SEED-Vance, so you can battle them with the usual Rising Strike or Rising Crush moves. But for the easiest (and quickest) victory, blast them with Technics. Rabarta is the best choice for these fire-element foes, but even Foie fireballs will deal enough damage to earn you an S-Rank. Technic-users will particularly enjoy the prize, too: a three-star Machine Gun they can pair with their Wand!

TRIAL RANKING

RANKING INFORMATION

CONDITIONS

1 CLEAR TIME 1:10 VALUE 1000pts
PENALTY -5 points per second late

SCORE	RANK	MESETA	MP	PRIZE
1000	S	2500	70	Greasegun
700 - 999	A	1200	40	-
400 - 699	B	100	20	-
0 - 399	C	-	10	-

MONSTERS

DILLA GRIENA — LVL 15 — TYPE: FIRE
HP 504 | ATT 245
EXP 133 | DEF 50

GOHMA DILLA — LVL 15 — TYPE: FIRE
HP 252 | ATT 163
EXP 46 | DEF 50

Save your game and heal up after rejoining Hyuga and Karen, because a longer, tougher trial awaits when you pass through that next door. This time you'll need to slay nearly a dozen Gohma Dilla, and once again a Wand with ice-element spells is your best hope of victory. You may not have enough PP to destroy all the Gohma Dilla with Technics, so use it with reserve; hit each enemy once and then finish it with a melee weapon, unloading multiple ice blasts only when you can hit two or more Gohma Dilla with each shot.

In melee combat, Gohma Dilla emit circles of blue light that give a few seconds of warning to anyone attacking them before a force wave sends them flying. Both dodging and taking the hit are time-consuming, so you should try to head the attacks off entirely by using quick weapons like Twin Daggers and Twin Sabers. As soon as there's a lull at the end of your combo, use a Photon Art to knock the foe back, and then repeat. This will prevent the Gohma Dilla from being able to attack for as long as it lives; but turn and run as soon as the yellow Exp marker pops up, because Gohma Dilla always self-destruct when they die.

There is one nasty twist in this trial. When you enter the second part of Car 3, a pair of stationary guns in the back of the car will pepper you with laser fire. Try to keep the battle as close to the door as you can so you're out of cannon range, then dash past the cannons without destroying them (they don't count as part of the trial).

Karen Erra
Disperse and move in to attack!

TRIAL RANKING

CONDITIONS

1 CLEAR TIME 4:00 VALUE 1000pts
PENALTY -5 points per second late

RANKING INFORMATION ②

SCORE	RANK	MESETA	MP	PRIZE
1000	S	2500	70	Hourglass
700 - 999	A	1200	40	-
400 - 699	B	700	20	-
0 - 399	C	-	10	-

[PARUM]
THE MILATE 04 : PART 2

PARTNERS

NAME	LVL (Ethan's +...)	RACE	CLASS
1. Hyuga Ryght	+0	Human	Hunter
2. Lucaim Nav	+5	CAST	Hunter

OBJECTIVES 3 TO 6

MONSTERS

DILLA GRIENA
LVL **16** TYPE: FIRE

HP	504	ATT	245
EXP	133	DEF	50

GOHMA DILLA
LVL **16** TYPE: FIRE

HP	266	ATT	172
EXP	54	DEF	52

DILLA GRIENA
LVL **17** TYPE: FIRE

HP	632	ATT	258
EXP	180	DEF	52

GOHMA DILLA
LVL **17** TYPE: FIRE

HP	278	ATT	180
EXP	63	DEF	54

---

3 CLEAR A PATH TO CAR 5

In a brief lull between trials, Hyuga and Lucaim Nav will join you on a mission to clear a path from Car 1 to Car 4. Lucaim Nav is a powerhouse of a fighter, and is hearty enough that you can literally use him as a Shield if you battle with ranged weaponry. Expect a lot of return fire, however, as you'll face both Rogue (Jasse) and cannon-equipped Gohma Dilla foes. Both of these enemies fire at distant targets when they aren't engaged at melee range. Run past them to get Hyuga and Lucaim into the fray, then blast them while they're distracted.

You'll probably take some hits here, so you won't want to miss the healing spot in Car 3. To reveal it, activate the switches on either side as you enter the car; they'll lift the gates at the other end. Another healing spot awaits in Car 4, where you'll find a Save Marker, Bruce's shop, and the entrance to another trial.

ROGUE (JASSE)
LVL **15** TYPE: --

HP	454	ATT	261
EXP	31	DEF	50

ROGUE (JASSE)
LVL **16** TYPE: --

HP	479	ATT	275
EXP	36	DEF	52

WEAPON SHOP — Bruce's

MELEE WEAPONS	COST	PP	ATT	ACC	ELEMENTS	ATP
GIGUSH	3000	149	166	80	ICE-16%	45 (LONG SWORD)
TWIN BRAND	2900	156	69	80	-	45 (1-HAND SWORD)
TWIN KNIFE	2700	169	45	80	ICE-20%	45 (TWIN DAGGERS)
KNIFE	2000	117	83	84	-	45 (DAGGER)

RANGED WEAPONS	COST	PP	ATT	ACC	ELEMENTS	ATA
TWIN POWERGUN	2400	162	72	34	-	13 (TWIN HANDGUNS)

ITEM SHOP

ITEMS	COST
MONOMATE	30
SOL ATOMIZER	100

④ TRIAL — REGAIN CONTROL OF THE TRAIN

If you rush through this trial, killing just enough foes to open the doors to proceed, you'll be several foes short when you reach the final car. The trickery begins in Car 5, where slaying two batches of enemies will open the door before the car is truly clear. After the doors open, go back towards the entrance to reveal a well-hidden Dilla Griena that didn't appear the first time around. Killing it will earn you the key to the locked treasure room in this car (the entrance is through the doors to the south), and while time is tight, it's a detour worth taking: The chests contain rare random items that may include a Breaker Long Sword or one of several Recipe Boards.

The lights are out in Car 6, making it tough to track down the slippery Rogue (Jasse) foes. Run to the opposite end of the car, turn to the right and hack through some boxes to reveal a red light switch on the floor. Tripping it will make it easier to clear the car and reveal the second key. Turn around and head north to enter the treasure room, where you'll find three Rogues among the loot. If you can spare a few seconds to continue to the second part of the treasure room (through the east door to Car 5), you'll find a few more rare item chests.

There are two paths through the final room of Car 7. You'll meet a pair of Rogues at either entrance, and a pair of Rogues with a Della Griena in between. After slaying the Della Griena, make sure to run down the entrance path you didn't take in order to trigger the final batch of enemies. Slaying them will end the trial, so if you have time to spare, hit the chests in the middle of the room first (they disappear when the trial ends).

MONSTERS CONTINUED

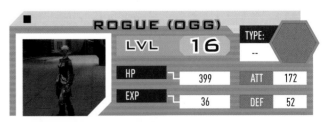

ROGUE (OGG)

LVL **15** — TYPE: --

HP	378	ATT	163
EXP	31	DEF	50

ROGUE (OGG)

LVL **16** — TYPE: --

HP	399	ATT	172
EXP	36	DEF	52

TRIAL RANKING

CONDITIONS

1 CLEAR TIME **10:00** VALUE **1000pts**
PENALTY -5 points per second late

2 ENEMIES **32** VALUE **300pts**
PENALTY -5 points per enemy missed

RANKING INFORMATION

SCORE	RANK	MESETA	MP	PRIZE
1000	S	2500	70	Scape Doll
700 - 999	A	1200	40	-
400 - 699	B	700	20	-
0 - 399	C	-	10	-

---

⑤

RUN TO KAREN'S SIDE

Hyuga needs to stay with Lucaim Nav, so it's up to you to reach Karen at the far end of the train and save her from the Vol Brothers. The good treasure is mostly gone, but you should still hit the key-locked rooms on your way. Car 5 has fallen into darkness, and you'll find the light switch in the treasure room accessible through Car 6. The brothers are waiting in Car 4, just past the Save Marker and Bruce's shop.

---

⑥ **TRIAL**   ## REGAIN CONTROL OF THE TRAIN

Before you begin this battle, assign Resta and your deadliest Technic to the same Staff. The best way to survive this battle (and earn an S-Rank in the process) is to charge at Hiru Vol and discharge all of your Technic PP into him as quickly as possible. Hiru alone has the power to heal the brothers, and if you don't use a Technic or an extremely powerful weapon to damage him, he'll quickly recover from the damage you deal. Once he falls, you shouldn't have much trouble mopping up his brothers with conventional melee weapons (focus on No Vol first, so he can't blast you while you strike his brother). If you're gunning for an S-Rank, drink an Agtaride to hasten their demise.

BOSS FIVE
VOL BROTHERS

 **BOSS**

HIRU VOL • DO VOL • NO VOL

LVL	TYPE:
19/18/16	FIRE

HP	EXP
912 / 730 / 730	275 / 240 / 240

ATT	DEF
394 / 161 / 189	78 / 58 / 58

TRIAL RANKING

CONDITIONS

1 CLEAR TIME **1:20** VALUE **1000pts**
PENALTY -5 points per second late

RANKING INFORMATION

SCORE	RANK	MESETA	MP	PRIZE
1000	S	2500	70	Neta Note
700 - 999	A	1200	40	-
400 - 699	B	700	20	-
0 - 399	C	-	10	-

GETTING STARTED

STORY MODE

FREE MISSIONS

NETWORK MODE

THE DIVINE MAIDEN

CHAPTER OBJECTIVES

[GUARDIANS COLONY] CLYEZ CITY

PARTNERS

NONE

MEET THE GANG AT GUARDIANS HQ

Everyone is waiting for you at Guardians HQ, so skip the shops and head straight to the fifth floor. Check in with Mina, and she'll take you to Lucaim Nav's meeting room. This mission is on the planet Neudaiz, so check in with Mina again after the briefing to get your license updated with new travel permissions. You'll find Karen waiting outside, and you can follow her straight to the Neudaiz PPT Gate. You might as well—the Clyez City Mall has new stock in the Synthesis and Armor shops, but you should wait until you see the selection at Neudaiz's Ohtoku City before you make any decisions about what to buy.

[NEUDAIZ] OHTOKU CITY

PARTNERS

NONE

JOIN FORCES WITH MAYA SHIDOW

Your mission will begin as soon as your shuttle touches down on Neudaiz. After intervening to save the Maiden, let Guardians Maya Shidow escort you to the local Guardians Branch. There you'll receive word that the Maiden is in trouble again, and this chapter's true mission will go up on the Flyer Base Board. Exchange cards with Maya Shidow, then invite her to your party. (If Lucaim is in your party, you'll have to disband and form a new party without him.) The Flyer Base is right nextdoor, but don't leave Ohtoku City before you check out the Yohmei Shop.

MISSION: RESCUE THE MAIDEN

The Maiden's shuttle has crashed in Muzraki C.D. This location is overflowing with SEED-altered life forms. Rescue the Maiden at once.

Required
1 Karen
2 Hyuga
3 Maya

Party 4/4

LOC	Mizuraki C.D.

[OHTOKU CITY]
SHOP REPORT

Nearly all of the gear you've seen so far has been manufactured by G.R.M., but you won't find any of that here. Yohmei makes their own weapons and armor; and while they usually can't compete with G.R.M. in terms of attack power and accuracy, they have more PP and are capable of augmenting Mental Powers. Yohmei is the manufacturer of choice for the Force type, and has plenty to offer Rangers as well. But virtually nothing here is of interest to Hunters, who should do most of their shopping with G.R.M (which also has new stock). If you are a Hunter, seriously consider returning to Guardians HQ for a class change; this mission will be much easier for Forces and Rangers.

Whatever you choose, make sure your arsenal includes ranged weapons and Wands with ice and fire Photon Arts and Technics. The Compadri Bow is a great choice for both Forces and Rangers, but Hunters can't use them; they should buy a Blaster Rifle and its appropriate Photon Art at the G.R.M. shop instead. Forces who already know Foie and Rabarta should skip the Disc shop—a Rayharod is a much better investment than the pricy new Technics. You can attach up to four Technics to a Rod, and they have higher Tech scores and a much higher PP capacity. Sta-senba armor and a Tech-enhancing Sta / Force unit is also a good buy. If you're having trouble affording all this stuff, you can always come back for more after completing each section of the mission.

[NOTE: PURPLE TEXT DENOTES THAT THIS IS NEW TO THE SHOP.]

ITEM SHOP

ITEMS	COST
MONOMATE	30
DIMATE	150
SOL ATOMIZER	100
MOON ATOMIZER	500
PHOTON CHARGE	1500
GRINDER C+1	300
GRINDER C+2	800
GRINDER C+3	1500
DAMAGE TRAP	50
BURN TRAP	100
FREEZE TRAP	120

WEAPON SHOP — Yohmei

MELEE WEAPONS	COST	PP	ATT	ACC	ELEMENTS	ATP
BREAKAUD	3750	189	225	76	FIRE-18%	97 (LONG SWORD)
LACANATA	3500	193	212	76	-	97 (SPEAR)
BASTARA	3200	140	171	78	-	97 (1-HANDED BLADE)
STINA-ZASHI	3000	148	112	79	-	97 (DAGGER)

RANGED WEAPONS	COST	PP	ATT	ACC	ELEMENTS	ATA
COMPADRI	3550	341	307	25	-	26 (BOW)
ORTOTORE	2900	156	88	28	-	26 (HANDGUN)

FORCE WEAPONS	COST	PP	TECH	ELEMENTS	TP
RAYHAROD	4000	363	198	-	62 (ROD)
BATNARA	3400	198	171	-	62 (WAND)

SHOPS CONTINUED ▶

WEAPON SHOP
CONTINUED *Yohmei*

DISCS	COST	ATTACHES TO
TORNADO BREAK	500	LONG SWORD
DUS DAGGAS	2500	SPEAR
RISING CRUSH	500	TWIN BLADES
RENKAI BUYOU-ZAN	480	TWIN DAGGERS
RISING STRIKE	350	1-HAND BLADE
SHUNBU SHOUREN-ZAN	450	DAGGER
ENSEI-SOU	3000	BOW
REISEI-SOU	3000	BOW
RAISEI-SOU	3000	BOW
JISEI-SOU	3000	BOW
TWIN BURN	400	TWIN HANDGUN
TWIN FREEZE	400	TWIN HANDGUN
TWIN PLASMA	400	TWIN HANDGUN
TWIN GRAV	3000	TWIN HANDGUN
BURNING HIT	400	HANDGUN
FROZEN HIT	400	HANDGUN
PLASMA HIT	400	HANDGUN
GRAV HIT	3000	HANDGUN
FOIE	1000	WAND/STAFF
RAFOIE	3500	WAND/STAFF
DAMFOIE	4500	WAND/STAFF
SHIFTA	2500	WAND/STAFF
JELLEN	3500	WAND/STAFF
BARTA	1000	WAND/STAFF
RABARTA	3500	WAND/STAFF
DAMBARTA	4500	WAND/STAFF
DEBAND	2500	WAND/STAFF
ZALURE	1500	WAND/STAFF
ZONDE	1000	WAND/STAFF
RAZONDE	3500	WAND/STAFF
NOSZONDE	4500	WAND/STAFF
ZODIAL	4000	WAND/STAFF
ZOLDEEL	1500	WAND/STAFF
DIGA	450	WAND/STAFF
RADIGA	3500	WAND/STAFF
DAMDIGA	4500	WAND/STAFF
NOSDIGA	4500	WAND/STAFF
RESTA	1000	WAND/STAFF
REVERSER	3000	WAND/STAFF
RETIER	4000	WAND/STAFF

SYNTHESIS SHOP

BOARDS	COST
[B] GIGUSH	500
[B] TWIN BRAND	500
[B] RYO-STIZASHI	1000
[B] GUDDA BRANA	1500
[B] HARISEN BATTLE FAN	3000
[B] FLUORESCENT BULB	3000
[B] VAHRA CLAW	3000
[B] DUO HARISEN FANS	3000
[B] TWIN FLUOR. BULBS	3000
[B] AUTOGUN	1200
[B] BLASTER	1000
[B] COMPADRI	1000
[B] BATNARA	1000
[B] SLYROD	3000
[B] PERPALINE	300
[B] STELLALINE	800
[B] STA-SENBA	800
[B] MONOMATE	5
[B] DIMATE	10
[B] GRINDER C	100

CONVERTERS	COST
[B] ORE C. 1 > 2	50
[B] ORE C. 2 > 3	200
[B] ORC C. 3 > 4	400
[B] METAL CONV. C > B	200
[B] METAL CONV. B > A	1500
[B] WOOD CONV. C > B	200
[B] WOOD CONV. B > A	1500

ARMOR SHOP

ARMOR	COST	DEF	EVA	SLOTS	ELEMENTS	DFP
STA-SENBA	5000	50	87	1	LIGHT-8%	7
REIHA-SENBA	5500	48	85	1	-	7

UNITS	COST	TECH	MENT
STA / FORCE	3200	6	0
STA / MIND	2000	0	6

[HOLTES CITY]
SHOP REPORT

G.R.M. has some serious competition from Yohmei, but they're still in the game. Hunters and Rangers can purchase improved Stellaline line shields and Perpa units here, as well as a few choice weapons. The Shot and Fury series of Photon Arts for Rifles and Machine Guns are also finally available, even in the rare ground element (but stick with ice or fire for now). G.R.M. does have the updated recovery item stock you saw at the Yohmei Shop. However, the Holtes City Synthesis Shop hasn't had the same Board stock update that Ohtoku and Clyez City have. No matter; with no new ingredients for sale, you probably can't synthesize any of that stuff anyway.

WEAPON SHOP — GRM

[NOTE: PURPLE TEXT DENOTES THAT THIS IS NEW TO THE SHOP.]

MELEE WEAPONS	COST	PP	ATT	ACC	ELEMENTS	ATP
GIGUSH	3000	149	166	80	ICE-16%	45 (LONG SWORD)
BREAKER	3800	172	250	80	GROUND-16%	97 (LONG SWORD)
PIKE	1800	152	156	80	-	45 (SPEAR)
TWIN BRAND	2900	156	69	80	-	45 (TWIN BLADE)
TWIN BUSTER	3300	180	104	80	-	97 (TWIN BLADE)
TWIN KNIFE	2700	169	45	80	ICE-20%	45 (TWIN DAGGER)
BRAND	1600	110	126	83	ICE-16%	45 (1-HAND BLADE)
KNIFE	2000	117	83	84	-	45 (DAGGER)

RANGED WEAPONS	COST	PP	ATT	ACC	ELEMENTS	ATA
BLASTER	3000	266	36	-	-	26 (RIFLE)
TWIN POWERGUN	2400	162	72	34	-	13 (TWIN HANDGUN)
POWERGUN	1350	123	65	34	-	13 (HANDGUN)
GREASEGUN	2800	147	22	16	-	26 (MACHINEGUN)

FORCE WEAPONS	COST	PP	TECH	ELEMENTS	TP
STAFF	1500	156	126	-	28 (WAND)

[NOTE: 1-STAR EQUIPMENT IS NOT SHOWN, BUT IS STILL FOR SALE.]

DISCS	COST	ATTACHES TO
TORNADO BREAK	500	LONG SWORD
DUS DAGGAS	2500	SPEAR
RISING CRUSH	500	TWIN BLADES
RENKAI BUYOU-ZAN	480	TWIN DAGGERS
RISING STRIKE	350	1-HAND BLADE
SHUNBU SHOUREN-ZAN	450	DAGGER
BURNING SHOT	3000	RIFLE
FROZEN SHOT	3000	RIFLE
PLASMA SHOT	3000	RIFLE
GRAV SHOT	3000	RIFLE
TWIN BURN	400	TWIN HANDGUN
TWIN FREEZE	400	TWIN HANDGUN
TWIN PLASMA	400	TWIN HANDGUN
BURNING HIT	400	HANDGUN
FROZEN HIT	400	HANDGUN
PLASMA HIT	400	HANDGUN
BURNING FURY	3000	MACHINEGUN
FROZEN FURY	3000	MACHINEGUN
PLASMA FURY	3000	MACHINEGUN
GRAV FURY	3000	MACHINEGUN
FOIE	1000	WAND/STAFF
RAFOIE	3500	WAND/STAFF
JELLEN	3500	WAND/STAFF
BARTA	1000	WAND/STAFF
RABARTA	3500	WAND/STAFF
ZALURE	1500	WAND/STAFF
ZONDE	1000	WAND/STAFF
RAZONDE	3500	WAND/STAFF
ZOLDEEL	1500	WAND/STAFF
RESTA	1000	WAND/STAFF
REVERSER	3000	WAND/STAFF

ARMOR SHOP — GRM

ARMOR	COST	DEF	EVA	SLOTS	ELEMENTS	DFP
CARLINE	300	15	30	0	-	3
PERPALINE	2500	33	58	1	FIRE-8%	5
STELLALINE	5500	52	85	1	ELECTRIC-10%	7
LIGHTLINE	300	14	32	0	-	3
BRANDLINE	2500	30	56	1	-	5
BUSTERLINE	5000	50	84	1	-	7

UNITS	COST	TECH	MENT
CAR / POWER	200	6	0
CAR / HIT	200	0	6
PERPA / POWER	2500	14	0
PERPA/ HIT	2000	0	10

PARTNERS

NAME	LVL (Ethan's +...)	RACE	CLASS
1. Hyuga Ryght	+0	Human	Hunter
2. Karen Erra	+3	Newman	Hunter
3. Maya Shidow	-2	Newman	Force

OBJECTIVES ① TO ②

① MEET THE BEASTS OF NEUDAIZ

Maya may be the lowest-level member of your party, but she's hardly a liability. She's quick with the Resta Technics when someone gets wounded, and will even cure status conditions like the poison inflicted by the Ageeta. Watch her life-bar and run towards her when you see it drop into the yellow so you can get your share of the Resta.

The Ageeta and the Ollaka are similar to foes you've fought before, but the Goshin are new and quite powerful. They burrow underground and emerge at your feet, afflicting anyone nearby with a condition that lowers attack strength for a minute or so. Once they're above ground they'll swing in circles to knock away melee attacks and breathe fireballs at distant targets. Technics and ranged attacks are by far your best hope of victory, especially the Rabarta Technic. Keep an eye on your auto-map so you can monitor them when they're underground and avoid their jack-in-the-box surprise attacks.

MONSTERS

AGEETA

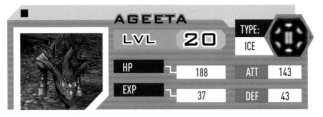

LVL	20	TYPE: ICE

HP	188	ATT	143
EXP	37	DEF	43

OLLAKA

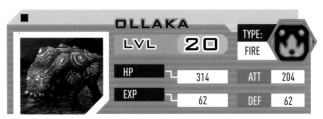

LVL	20	TYPE: FIRE

HP	314	ATT	204
EXP	62	DEF	62

GOSHIN

LVL	20	TYPE: FIRE

HP	314	ATT	224
EXP	62	DEF	62

TENGOHG

LVL	20	TYPE: FIRE

HP	628	ATT	306
EXP	260	DEF	74

② SLAY THE TENGOHG

You'll face a lone Tengohg at the end of Block A-3. These winged demons are vicious at close-range, where they can ensnare you in both whirlwind attacks and a ground-smashing shockwave. Bows and Rifles are the best weapons to use against them, but you can catch them with ice-element Technics when they're near the ground. This Tengohg isn't so tough, but you'll be battling them in pairs and trios soon.

[NEUDAIZ]
MIZURAKI C.D. - BLOCK B

PARTNERS

NAME	LVL (Ethan's +...)	RACE	CLASS
1. Hyuga Ryght	+0	Human	Hunter
2. Karen Erra	+3	Newman	Hunter
3. Maya Shidow	-2	Newman	Force

OBJECTIVES   ③

③ TRIAL   PURIFY THE ICE CONTAMINATION

Block B has fallen into the clutches of an icy SEED infestation, and you'll need to wipe out four Zoma, slay 58 monsters and traverse three blocks of forest within 15 minutes to score an S-Rank on this brutally challenging trial.

    The trial begins with an untimed tutorial in which Maya will teach you how to reveal photon spots with your goggles, and then how to destroy ice blewmes by standing on the spots and firing your new Photon Reflector. The trial will begin as soon as you slay the Zoma, so run for the green-lit door even as Maya is concluding the lesson.

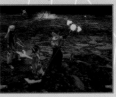

ITEM HUNTING IN MIZURAKI...

The random treasure boxes and destructible rock clusters in the Mizuraki C.D. contain the same sorts of items you found in Parum, but with a higher concentration of elemental photons (particularly Im-Photons and El-Photons) and with Neu Wood and Neu Ash replacing the Par equivalents. If you use your goggles you'll find a few destructible trees that hold rare recovery items, but they're much less common than they were in Raffon Meadow.

The best items are dropped by enemies, and only very rarely. Lucky players may win a Sta / Mind unit from a Gohmon, but the truly charmed will score a Tengohg Bow (you can guess who drops that). The Tengohg Bow is so powerful that probably only Rangers will have a high enough Accuracy score to use it without first leveling up a few times.

RANKING INFORMATION

③

CONDITIONS

1 CLEAR TIME **15:00** VALUE **300pts**
PENALTY -1 point per second late

2 ENEMIES **58** VALUE **300pts**
PENALTY -5 points per enemy missed

3 SEEDS PURIFIED **4** VALUE **400pts**
PENALTY -200 points per SEED-Zoma missed

SCORE	RANK	MESETA	MP	PRIZE
1000	S	7500	80	Autogun
700 - 999	A	3000	50	-
400 - 699	B	1500	30	-
0 - 399	C	-	20	-

It will take several minutes before you reach the first Zoma, as you'll encounter heavy opposition from ice versions of Goshin and Tengohg, as well as Gohmon foes. Every monster in Block B is ice-type, so swap your ranged-weapon Photon Arts for flame versions and make sure you have Foie spells at the ready. Bow and Rifle shots are the best options for slaying Gohmon at long range, as the casting time required by Technics can leave you unable to dodge their freezing Barta attacks. To save time, use ranged attacks to reduce the Gohmon packs to a manageable two or three, then move in and strike at their sides with melee weapons. Ranged attacks are also the safest way to deal with Tengohg, but if you're aiming for an S-Rank you'll find it much faster to defeat them with repeated uses of the Rising Strike Photon Art. Save your Foie PP for the burrowing Goshin.

MONSTERS

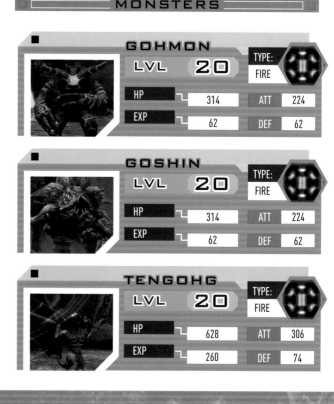

GOHMON

LVL	**20**	TYPE: FIRE

HP	314	ATT	224
EXP	62	DEF	62

GOSHIN

LVL	**20**	TYPE: FIRE

HP	314	ATT	224
EXP	62	DEF	62

TENGOHG

LVL	**20**	TYPE: FIRE

HP	628	ATT	306
EXP	260	DEF	74

You can't count on your friends to handle the blewmes the way they did in Raffon Meadow, but if you reveal the photon spots before engaging enemies, you may return to find that they've fried a blewme or two. Remember that you also need to kill every enemy, so after clearing the fourth Zoma don't run northeast to the exit, but instead run through a thin passage to the southwest where you'll find a Warp Spot. That Warp Spot will take you to an island where you'll encounter the final batch of foes.

[NEUDAIZ]
MIZURAHI C.D. - BLOCK C

PARTNERS

NAME	LVL (Ethan's +...)	RACE	CLASS
1. Hyuga Ryght	+0	Human	Hunter
2. Karen Erra	+3	Newman	Hunter
3. Maya Shidow	-2	Newman	Force

OBJECTIVES ④ TO ⑥

④ HUNT THE TREASURE IN BLOCK C

It is quite easy to dash through the two maps of Block C, since you can skip nearly half of each map if you run straight to the exit. However, thorough explorers will find several treats off the beaten path. In Block C-1, head northwest after opening the laser gates and you'll find a pair of Warp Spots. Use the one on the left, and it will take you to an island with several destructible rocks and a key. Warp back, and unlock the gate to the south. Inside you'll find containers with rare items, one of which always holds a charmingly unconventional Saber known as the Harisen Battle Fan.

MONSTERS

OLLAKA
LVL **21**   TYPE: FIRE
HP 328   ATT 213
EXP 62   DEF 64

TENGOHG
LVL **21**   TYPE: FIRE
HP 656   ATT 320
EXP 264   DEF 77

GOHMON
LVL **21**   TYPE: FIRE
HP 292   ATT 205
EXP 75   DEF 64

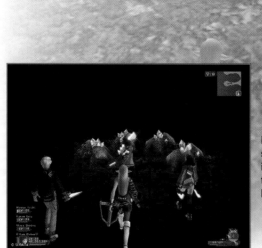

From the center of Block C-2, you can go north to the exit or west to a series of caves. The caves are full of destructible rocks (with minor random items), but smashing them will make enemies appear on the path back to the central area. This is a good opportunity to get in a few extra battles before the boss if you're close to leveling up.

⑤ CLEAR THE TENGOHG NEST

After completing Block C-2, you'll find the Maiden in peril at the Tengohg Nest. There are four Tengohg attacking her, led by a king Tengohg with enhanced stats. In this vast area, it's tempting to blast them all from a distance with a ranged weapon, but you'll want to save the PP of your Rifle or Bow for the boss to come. Instead use up your Technic PP, since magic isn't much use against the Onmagoug.

⑥ TRIAL   SLAY THE ONMAGOUG

The Onmagoug rarely descends to the ground willingly, so you'll need to bring it down by force. Equip your Bow or Rifle (Handguns will work in a pinch, but Machine Guns won't), and switch to the first-person view when you're within range of your target. Aim at the Onmagoug's wings and fire rapidly to ensure you get in a few hits. After the wings take 150-200 points of damage, the Onmagoug will come crashing down.

The fallen Onmagoug has impressive resistance to Technics (even to ice-based Technics) so switch to your best melee weapon and use whatever Photon Art has the longest and most powerful combo to hit it while it's down. (Rising Strike is always a reliable choice, especially when the Onmagoug stands up, since you'll still be able to hit it in the face.) Eventually the wings will heal and the Onmagoug will take to the sky again, but a character whose level is in the 20's should be able to defeat the Onmagoug in just two cycles of shooting its wings and attacking it on the ground. If your aim is good, this should take well under two minutes.

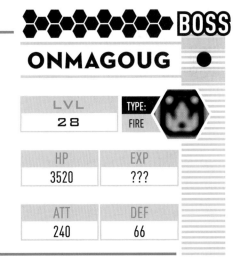

BOSS

ONMAGOUG ●

BOSS SIX
ONMAGOUG

LVL	TYPE:
28	FIRE

HP	EXP
3520	???

ATT	DEF
240	66

TRIAL RANKING

CONDITIONS

1 CLEAR TIME 2:00 VALUE 1000pts
PENALTY -5 points per second late

RANKING INFORMATION

SCORE	RANK	MESETA	EXP	PRIZE
1000	S	7500	80	Rising Fury
700 - 999	A	3000	50	-
400 - 699	B	1500	30	-
0 - 399	C	-	20	-

CHAPTER 6

CAPTIVES OF MOATOOB

MISSION: KIDNAPPER INQUIRY

CHAPTER OBJECTIVES

- [ ] Meet your replacement instructors
- [ ] Shop for some new digs
- [ ] Explore gritty Dagora City
- 1 [ ] Eradicate the Vanda tribes
- 2 [ ] TRIAL: Clear the canyon area
- 3 [ ] Slay the mine guardians
- 4 [ ] TRIAL: Clear the Rogues' trap field
- 5 [ ] Defeat the Vol Brothers: Round 2
- 6 [ ] Squash the BUG swarms
- 7 [ ] Follow Liina to the Landeel dock
- 8 [ ] TRIAL: Destroy the Grinna Bete S trio

[GUARDIANS COLONY] CLYEZ CITY

PARTNERS

NONE

MEET YOUR REPLACEMENT INSTRUCTORS

When you get the call from Hyuga, head out and meet him near the Central Table's fountain. You'll soon be joined by your new instructors: good old Leo and an impish Small Beast by the name of Tonnio. They won't give you their partner cards yet, so if you'd like to attempt the newly unlocked Mizuraki Devastation and Cargo Train Rescue Free Missions before blasting off for Moatoob, you'll need to settle for a team of Hyuga, Maya, and Lucaim.

SHOP FOR SOME NEW DIGS

If you're tired of staring at Ethan's exposed bellybutton, you've finally earned the ability to do something about it. There are currently three clothing manufacturers in the Gurahl System: Mutan in Neudaiz, ASFA in Moatoob, and Cubic Star in Parum. All of their clothing lines are available in Clyez City, but the mall clothing shop typically only stocks two colors per item. Stop in there to see what styles are available, then visit the manufacturer's store on its home planet if you aren't satisfied with the color choices.

CLOTHES SHOPS

MUTAN — Neudaiz

Seyagya

CLOTHES	COST
SEYAGYA VEST	14000
SEYAGYA PANTS	8000
SEYAGYA SHOES	7500

Kusatarika

CLOTHES	COST
KUSATARIKA VEST	14000
KUSATARIKA PANTS	8500
KUSATARIKA SHOES	7000

ASFA — Moatoob

Gojgoj

CLOTHES	COST
GOJGOJ VEST	10000
GOJGOJ SHORTS	6500
GOJGOJ BOOTS	5000

CUBIC STAR — Parum

Innocent

CLOTHES	COST
INNOCENT JACKET	85000
INNOCENT SLACKS	58000
INNOCENT SHOES	25000

Speeders

CLOTHES	COST
SPEEDERS JERSEY	15000
SPEEDERS SHORTS	9500
SPEEDERS SHOES	7000

[MOATOOB]
DAGORA CITY

PARTNERS

NONE

EXPLORE GRITTY DAGORA CITY

Speak to Mina at Clyez City Guardians HQ to update your travel permissions, then hop a shuttle to Dagora. You'll meet the gang and receive your mission briefing at the local Guardians Branch, but you may want to do a bit more exploring before departing for Galenigare Canyon. The Tenora Works shop has a few interesting items for Hunters and Rangers, and the locals have plenty to say—everyone except for the local barkeep, who clams up after dropping a hint about your farther.

MISSION: KIDNAPPER INQUIRY

A-Photon scholars are being kidnapped one after another. Investigate the abandoned mine, believed to be a hideout for the kidnappers.

Required | 1 Leo | 2 | 3 Tonnio
| 2 Hyuga |

| LOC | Galenigare Canyon | Party | 4/4 |

[DAGORA CITY]
SHOP REPORT

Tenora Works creates a wide array of weapons that are powerful but somewhat lacking in accuracy. Hunters will find the most items to enjoy, including a new Mukpat spear and the Gudda Brana, a Knuckle weapon that is much more enticing now that you can buy the Bogga Zubba Photon Art. Players who are transitioning from Force to Hunter should pick up a W'ganba Wand that will allow them to optimize their usage of Technics. Rangers can buy the Shigga Wadda Shotgun here, as well as a variety of elemental Photon Arts for it.

　　　The other manufacturers have also updated their stock, but with only a few items apiece. Highlights include the Gi- series of Technics that are now available in Neudaiz and a variety of interesting recipes that are easiest to find in Clyez City.

SHOPS BEGIN ·································▶

ARMOR SHOP

Tenora Works

ARMOR	COST	DEF	EVA	SLOTS	ELEMENTS	DFP
RABOL STELLA	5000	53	83	1	DARK-10%	7
RABOL MIDRA	5500	52	82	1	-	7

UNITS	COST	DEF	EVA
STELLA / GUARD	2800	18	0
STELLA / LEGS	2800	0	18

[NOTE: PURPLE TEXT DENOTES THAT THIS IS NEW TO THE SHOP.]

WEAPON SHOP

Tenora Works

MELEE WEAPONS	COST	PP	ATT	ACC	ELEMENTS	ATP
SODA BREKKA	3600	172	275	72	-	97 (LONG SWORD)
GUDDA BRANA	5500	165	150	77	-	97 (KNUCKLES)
MUKPAT	3500	175	259	72	-	97 (SPEAR)
ALSEVA BATA	3800	180	115	72	-	97 (TWIN BLADES)
ALDAGA STEG	3750	195	75	72	ELEC-23%	97 (TWIN DAGGERS)
SEVA SATA	3200	127	209	75	-	97 (1-HAND BLADE)
DAGA STEG	3000	135	137	76	ELEC-23%	97 (DAGGER)

RANGED WEAPONS	COST	PP	ATT	ACC	ELEMENTS	ATA
SHIGGA WADDA	5700	307	55	19	-	26 (SHOTGUN)
ARB OGA	5400	187	120	24	-	26 (TWIN HANDGUN)
B'DUKI OGA	3800	142	108	24	-	10 (HANDGUN)

FORCE WEAPONS	COST	PP	TECH	ELEMENTS	TP
W'GANBA	3000	180	209	-	62 (WAND)

WEAPON SHOP

Yohmei

MELEE WEAPONS	COST	PP	ATT	ACC	ELEMENTS	ATP
BREKAUD	3750	189	225	76	FIRE-18%	97 (LONG SWORD)
LACANATA	3500	193	212	76	-	97 (SPEAR)
RYO-BASTA	3500	198	94	76	-	97 (TWIN BLADES)
RYO-STIZASHI	3450	214	61	76	-	97 (TWIN DAGGERS)
BASTARA	3200	140	171	78	-	97 (1-HAND BLADE)
STINA-ZASHI	3000	148	112	79	-	97 (DAGGER)

RANGED WEAPONS	COST	PP	ATT	ACC	ELEMENTS	ATA
COMPADRI	3550	341	307	25	-	26 (BOW)
RYO-ORTOTORE	5500	206	98	28	-	26 (TWIN HANDGUN)
ORTOTORE	2900	156	88	28	-	26 (HANDGUN)

FORCE WEAPONS	COST	PP	TECH	ELEMENTS	TP
RAYHAROD	4000	363	198	-	62 (ROD)
BATNARA	3400	198	171	-	62 (WAND)

WEAPON SHOP *GRM*

MELEE WEAPONS	COST	PP	ATT	ACC	ELEMENTS	ATP
GIGUSH	3000	149	166	80	ICE-16%	45 (LONG SWORD)
BREAKER	3800	172	250	80	GROUND-16%	97 (LONG SWORD)
PIKE	1800	152	156	80	-	45 (SPEAR)
TWIN BRAND	2900	156	69	80	-	45 (TWIN BLADES)
TWIN BUSTER	3300	180	104	80	-	97 (TWIN BLADES)
TWIN KNIFE	2700	169	45	80	ICE-20%	45 (TWIN DAGGERS)
BRAND	1600	110	126	83	ICE-16%	45 (1-HAND SWORD)
KNIFE	2000	117	83	84	-	45 (DAGGER)

RANGED WEAPONS	COST	PP	ATT	ACC	ELEMENTS	ATA
BLASTER	3000	285	266	36	-	26 (RIFLE)
TWIN POWERGUN	2400	162	72	34	-	13 (TWIN HANDGUNS)
POWERGUN	1350	123	65	34	-	13 (HANDGUN)
AUTOGUN	3900	142	98	34	-	26 (HANDGUN)
GREASEGUN	2800	147	22	16	-	26 (MACHINEGUN)

FORCE WEAPONS	COST	PP	TECH	ELEMENTS	TP
STAFF	1500	-	126	-	28 (ROD)

DISC SHOPS

[NOTE: G.C. = GUARDIANS COLONY // PAR = PARUM // NEU = NEUDAIZ // MOT = MOATOOB]

DISCS	COST	ATTACHES TO	G.C.	PAR	NEU	MOT
TORNADO BREAK	500	LONG SWORD	X	X	X	X
BOGGA ZUBBA	6000	KNUCKLES	-	-	-	X
DUS DAGGAS	2500	SPEAR	X	X	X	X
RISING CRUSH	500	TWIN BLADES	X	X	X	X
RENKAI BUYOU-ZAN	480	TWIN DAGGERS	X	X	X	X
RISING STRIKE	350	1-HAND BLADE	X	X	X	X
SHUNBU SHOUREN-ZAN	450	DAGGER	X	X	X	X
BURNING SHOT	3000	RIFLE	X	X	X	X
FROZEN SHOT	3000	RIFLE	X	X	X	X
PLASMA SHOT	3000	RIFLE	X	X	X	X
GRAV SHOT	3000	RIFLE	X	X	X	X
BARADA BANGA	4000	SHOTGUN	-	-	-	X
BARADA RIGA	4000	SHOTGUN	-	-	-	X
BARADA INGA	4000	SHOTGUN	-	-	-	X
BARADA DIGA	4000	SHOTGUN	-	-	-	X
ENSEI-SOU	3000	BOW	X	X	X	X
REISEI-SOU	3000	BOW	X	X	X	X
RAISEI-SOU	3000	BOW	X	X	X	X
JISEI-SOU	3000	BOW	X	X	X	X
TWIN BURN	400	TWIN HANDGUN	X	X	X	X
TWIN FREEZE	400	TWIN HANDGUN	X	X	X	X
TWIN PLASMA	400	TWIN HANDGUN	X	X	X	X
TWIN GRAV	3000	TWIN HANDGUN	X	X	X	X
BURNING HIT	400	HANDGUN	X	X	X	X
FROZEN HIT	400	HANDGUN	X	X	X	X
PLASMA HIT	400	HANDGUN	X	X	X	X
GRAV HIT	3000	HANDGUN	X	X	X	X
BURNING FURY	3000	MACHINEGUN	X	X	X	X
FROZEN FURY	3000	MACHINEGUN	X	X	X	X

DISCS	COST	ATTACHES TO	G.C.	PAR	NEU	MOT
PLASMA FURY	3000	MACHINEGUN	X	X	X	X
GRAV FURY	3000	MACHINEGUN	X	X	X	X
FOIE	1000	WAND / STAFF	X	X	X	X
RAFOIE	3500	WAND / STAFF	X	X	X	X
DAMFOIE	4500	WAND / STAFF	X	X	-	X
GIFOIE	8000	WAND / STAFF	-	-	-	X
SHIFTA	2500	WAND / STAFF	X	X	X	X
JELLEN	3500	WAND / STAFF	X	X	X	X
BARTA	1000	WAND / STAFF	X	X	X	X
RABARTA	3500	WAND / STAFF	X	X	X	X
DAMBARTA	4500	WAND / STAFF	X	X	X	X
GIBARTA	8000	WAND / STAFF	-	-	-	X
DEBAND	2500	WAND / STAFF	X	X	X	X
ZALURE	1500	WAND / STAFF	X	X	X	X
ZONDE	1000	WAND / STAFF	X	X	X	X
RAZONDE	3500	WAND / STAFF	X	X	X	X
GIZONDE	8000	WAND / STAFF	-	-	-	X
NOSZANDE	4500	WAND / STAFF	X	X	X	X
ZODIAL	4000	WAND / STAFF	X	X	X	X
ZOLDEEL	1500	WAND / STAFF	X	X	X	X
DIGA	450	WAND / STAFF	X	X	X	X
RADIGA	3500	WAND / STAFF	X	X	X	X
DAMDIGA	4500	WAND / STAFF	X	X	X	X
GIDIGA	8000	WAND / STAFF	-	-	-	X
NOSDIGA	4500	WAND / STAFF	X	X	X	X
RESTA	1000	WAND / STAFF	X	X	X	X
GIRESTA	9800	WAND / STAFF	-	-	-	X
REVERSER	3000	WAND / STAFF	X	X	X	X
RETIER	4000	WAND / STAFF	X	X	X	X

SHOPS CONTINUED

[NOTE: G.C. = GUARDIANS COLONY // PAR = PARUM // NEU = NEUDAIZ // MOT = MOATOOB]

BOARDS	COST	G.C.	PAR	NEU	MOT
[B] GIGUSH	500	X	X	-	-
[B] TWIN BRAND	500	X	-	-	-
[B] RYO-STIZASHI	1000	X	X	X	-
[B] MISAKI	3500	X	-	X	-
[B] GUDDA BRANA	1500	X	-	-	X
[B] HARISEN BATTLE FAN	3000	X	-	-	-
[B] FLUORESCENT BULB	3000	X	-	-	-
[B] VAHRA CLAW	3000	X	-	-	-
[B] DUO HARISEN FANS	3000	X	-	-	-
[B] TWIN FLUOR. BULBS	3000	X	-	-	-
[B] AUTOGUN	1200	X	X	-	-
[B] REPEATER	2500	X	X	-	-
[B] BLASTER	1000	X	X	-	-
[B] COMPADRI	1000	X	-	X	-
[B] SHIGGA BIGUL	2500	X	-	-	X
[B] BATNARA	1000	X	-	X	-
[B] SLYROD	3000	X	-	X	-
[B] PERPALINE	300	X	X	-	-
[B] STELLALINE	800	X	X	-	-
[B] MEGALINE	2500	X	X	-	-
[B] STA-SENBA	800	X	-	X	-
[B] ME-SENBA	2500	X	-	X	-
[B] RABOL STELLA	800	X	-	-	X
[B] RABOL MEGA	2500	X	-	-	X
[B] MONOMATE	5	X	X	X	X
[B] DIMATE	10	X	X	X	X
[B] TRIMATE	50	X	X	X	X
[B] GRINDER C	100	X	X	-	X

CONVERTERS	COST	G.C.	PAR	NEU	MOT
[B] ORE C. 1 > 2	50	X	X	X	X
[B] ORE C. 2 > 3	200	X	X	X	X
[B] ORE C. 3 > 4	400	X	X	X	X
[B] METAL CONV. C > B	100	X	X	X	X
[B] METAL CONV. B > A	1500	X	X	X	X
[B] WOOD CONV. C > B	200	X	X	X	X
[B] WOOD CONV. B >A	1500	X	X	X	X

MATERIALS	COST	G.C.	PAR	NEU	MOT
PHOTON	300	X	X	X	X
EL-PHOTON	800	X	X	X	X
IM-PHOTON	800	X	X	X	X
BAN-PHOTON	500	X	X	X	X
RAY-PHOTON	500	X	X	X	X
ZAN-PHOTON	500	X	X	X	X
DI-PHOTON	500	X	X	X	X
CARLIAN	200	X	X	X	X
MEGANITE	200	X	X	X	X
HARNIUM	200	X	X	X	X
GAMOTITE	200	X	X	X	X
SOURAL	200	X	X	X	X
ACENALINE	100	X	X	X	X
WENCELINE	300	X	X	X	X
NANOSILICA	200	X	X	X	X
HOT BERRY	50	X	X	X	X
COLD BERRY	50	X	X	X	X
SWEET BERRY	50	X	X	X	X
BITTER BERRY	50	X	X	X	X
STAMINA BERRY	50	X	X	X	X
TRANS ACID	100	X	X	X	X
GRINDER BASE C	100	X	X	X	X
PAR WOOD	200	X	X	-	-
NEU WOOD	200	X	-	X	-
MOT WOOD	200	X	-	-	X

[MOATOOB]
GALENIGARE CANYON - BLOCK A

PARTNERS

NAME	LVL (Ethan's +...)	RACE	CLASS
1. Hyuga Ryght	+0	Human	Hunter
2. Leogini S. Berafort	+2	Beast	Hunter
3. Tonnio Rhima	+1	Beast	Hunter

OBJECTIVES **1** TO **2**

1 ERADICATE THE VANDA TRIBES

Elementally-charged ranged weapons are particularly effective in Block A-1, where you can often maneuver to put a chasm between yourself and your foes. You can then pick off the poor creatures with a Bow or Rifle while they attempt to charge at you.

Much like the monsters of Neudaiz, the beasts of Moatoob are primarily fire- and ice-type creatures. Barta and Rabarta are the Technics of choice against the populous Vanda tribes, whose shoulder-to-shoulder battle formations allow you to hit three at once with a well-placed ice blast. Foie and other fire-type Technics are a better choice against ice-type Lapucha and Jishagara foes.

MONSTERS

VANDA

LVL	25	TYPE: FIRE
HP	380	ATT 247
EXP	68 / 97	DEF 76

It seems a shame to rely solely on ranged attacks when you have a trio of powerful Hunters behind you. They won't be able to contribute unless you charge into the fray, so consider leading them into melee range when battling the Lapucha and Jishagara. But beware of large Vanda packs led by a Vanda king (who is easily distinguished by his sword and helmet). With the king's spells boosting the strength of the tribe, those who do battle at melee range may be overwhelmed quickly.

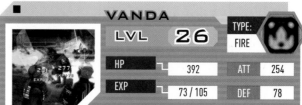

VANDA

LVL	26	TYPE: FIRE
HP	392	ATT 254
EXP	73 / 105	DEF 78

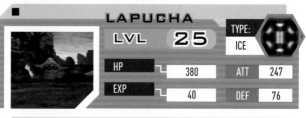

LAPUCHA

LVL	25	TYPE: ICE
HP	380	ATT 247
EXP	40	DEF 76

LAPUCHA

LVL	26	TYPE: ICE
HP	392	ATT 254
EXP	43	DEF 78

TRIAL RANKING

CONDITIONS

1. CLEAR TIME 15:00 VALUE 700pts
   PENALTY -1 point per second late

2. ENEMIES 84 VALUE 300pts
   PENALTY -5 points per enemy missed

RANKING INFORMATION

SCORE	RANK	MESETA	MP	PRIZE
1000	S	9000	90	Kubara Wood
700 - 999	A	3500	60	-
400 - 699	B	1200	40	-
0 - 399	C	-	20	-

There's no time for sniping in Blocks B-1 and B-2, where hordes of Vanda join massive Kog Nadd beasts in a lengthy time trial. Use your Technics to wipe out the Vanda hordes, but lead your team into melee combat against the Technic-resistant Kog Nadd. Bring them down with multi-hit Photon Arts or swings from Long Swords, which can hit them in three different places at once.

Each of the two blocks in the trial appear to be a loop, but walls of rock prevent you from being able to complete the circles. Run straight for the rock walls (to the east of the entrance in both maps) to kill all the enemies in that direction, then loop back and take the correct path to reach the other side of the rock wall before moving on to the exit.

Block B-2 has two unpopulated treasure rooms that you can safely skip if you're tight on time. The first is to the east of the entrance, and the second is just past the exit. If you do have time for the second treasure room, you'll find the key in the second of the three parallel tunnels in the northeast corner of the map (break a box to reveal it). The northernmost tunnel contains one of two keys that open the exit, and the other will appear only when you clear the area of enemies.

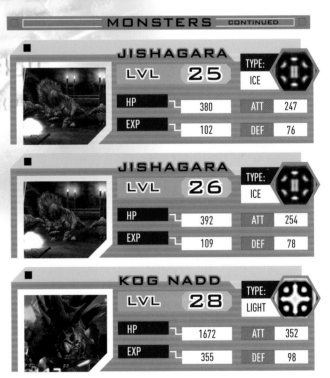

MONSTERS CONTINUED

JISHAGARA
LVL **25**
TYPE: ICE

| HP | 380 | ATT | 247 |
| EXP | 102 | DEF | 76 |

JISHAGARA
LVL **26**
TYPE: ICE

| HP | 392 | ATT | 254 |
| EXP | 109 | DEF | 78 |

KOG NADD
LVL **28**
TYPE: LIGHT

| HP | 1672 | ATT | 352 |
| EXP | 355 | DEF | 98 |

[MOATOOB]
GALENIGARE MINES - BLOCK A-B

PARTNERS

NAME	LVL (Ethan's +...)	RACE	CLASS
1. Hyuga Ryght	+0	Human	Hunter
2. Leogini S. Berafort	+2	Beast	Hunter
3. Tonnio Rhima	+1	Beast	Hunter

OBJECTIVES **3** TO **6**

GETTING STARTED
STORY MODE
FREE MISSIONS
NETWORK MODE

3 SLAY THE MINE GUARDIANS

Block A-1 of the mine is home to higher-level versions of the Vanda, Jishagara and Lapucha that roamed outside. With plenty of room to maneuver and no ticking clock, you can afford to take it slow and conserve the PP of your best weapons for the time trial ahead. The final hallway requires two keys to enter, and you'll find one on either side of the chasm. You won't even need to fight to get the key on the east side of the gulch—it's in plain sight.

143
EXP+105

MONSTERS

VANDA
LVL	**26**	TYPE: FIRE
HP	392	ATT 254
EXP	73 / 105	DEF 78

ROGUE (JASSE)
LVL	**26**	TYPE: --
HP	588	ATT 254
EXP	73	DEF 78

LAPUCHA
LVL	**26**	TYPE: ICE
HP	392	ATT 254
EXP	43	DEF 78

ROGUE (OGG)
LVL	**26**	TYPE: --
HP	588	ATT 254
EXP	73	DEF 78

JISHAGARA
LVL	**26**	TYPE: ICE
HP	392	ATT 254
EXP	109	DEF 78

GOHMA METHNA
LVL	**26**	TYPE: FIRE
HP	392	ATT 254
EXP	109	DEF 78

YG-01Z BUG
LVL	**26**	TYPE: ELEC
HP	392	ATT 254
EXP	94	DEF 78

In Blocks B-1 and B-2 you'll have to battle Rogues and their flame-throwing Gohma Methna creations, all while dodging traps and turrets. The traps have mostly been placed in the connecting hallways and bridges, and in front of many of the treasure chests. To spot them, flip on your goggles and hone in on each trap to reveal it. You can then detonate the trap safely with a ranged weapon. It is possible to run past or away from traps in the interval between when they appear and explode, but expect your friends to take a hit when you try this. In addition, you'll need to reveal and destroy at least eight traps to get an S-Rank on this trial.

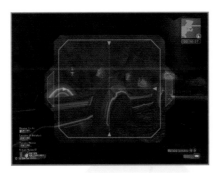

Turrets are typically found in empty rooms and hallways, so you should be able to approach and destroy them with a ranged weapon before they can lock in on you. The mounted guns explode after three hits, regardless of the power of the attack, so quick-firing machineguns are the weapon of choice for turret eradication.

You'll find treasure rooms east of the entrance in Block B-1 and at the far west end of the map, and another pair east of the entrance in Block B-2 and at that map's northwest corner. It isn't necessary to gather the treasures, but you'll need to destroy the treasure boxes to make a wave of enemies appear in each room. (Usually there are traps to disarm near the boxes.) In Block B-1, destroying the enemy waves will open treasure rooms or reveal keys to other treasure rooms, but neither of those secondary areas hold enemies and both can be ignored. In Block B-2, however, you need to pick up the key dropped by the Gohma Methna to access the northwest treasure room that is populated with monsters.

TRIAL RANKING

④

CONDITIONS

1 CLEAR TIME 13:00 VALUE 300pts
PENALTY -1 point per second late

2 ENEMIES 70 VALUE 300pts
PENALTY -5 points per enemy missed

3 TRAPS 8 VALUE 400pts
PENALTY -50 points per trap missed

RANKING INFORMATION

SCORE	RANK	MESETA	MP	PRIZE
1000	S	9000	90	Palasra
700 - 999	A	3500	60	-
400 - 699	B	1200	40	-
0 - 399	C	-	20	-

Barta and Rabarta Technics remain the easiest way to destroy groups of foes, but they aren't much use against the evasive Rogue (Jasse). Instead of chasing down the Jasse, use a heat-seeking Technic like Damdiga to catch them for you.

5   DEFEAT THE VOL BROTHERS: ROUND 2

You won't find a Save Marker or Heal Spot here, so cast your Resta Technics just after the trial ends. Once again you'll be facing the Vol Brothers solo, but this match-up will be a bit easier than the last one, as Hiru's healing abilities can no longer compete with your damage-dealing power. As usual, you should target Hiru first, either with powerful spells or fast melee combos. Then maneuver around Do Vol's knuckle attacks as you strike at No Vol with quick melee combos.

BOSS SEVEN
VOL BROTHERS

BOSS

HIRU VOL · DO VOL · NO VOL

LVL	TYPE:
26/26/26	FIRE

HP	EXP
1176 / 980 / 980	365 / 365 / 365

ATT	DEF
508 / 254 / 216	101 / 78 / 78

6   SLAY THE BUG SWARMS

After the battle, a swarm of YG-01Z BUGs will attack your party. These creatures are skilled at evasion, but you don't need to take special measures to hit them in mid-air. Even ground-skimming Technics like Damdiga can score hits, and Rabarta will kill them in droves. Grab their items as they drop them (they often drop rare Inverter Circuits), since you'll be expelled from the area when the battle ends.

PARTNERS

NAME	LVL (Ethan's +...)	RACE	CLASS
1. Tonnio Rhima	+1	Beast	Hunter
2. Liina Sukaya	+1	Beast	Hunter

OBJECTIVES ⑦ TO ⑧

---

⑦ FOLLOW LIINA TO THE LANDEEL DOCK

Liina claims the Rogues have nothing to hide, and offers to escort you and Tonnio to the Landeel flagship. After saving and recharging your weapons, you can reach the Landeel quite easily by heading directly to the north through Block C-1. None of the doors are locked, so you don't even need to stop and fight off the swarms of BUGs in the way.

If you aren't done treasure hunting, or hope to go up a level before the boss fight, hang a right at the entrance to the Landeel Dock and enter Block D-1. As Liina will warn you, Block D-1 is a dead end, but there are plenty of enemies to slay and several treasure chests to break open (including a few that hold Photon Charges). When you return to Block C-1 the enemies will respawn, and you can continue to go back and forth between Block C and D to gather all the loot and experience points you desire.

MONSTERS

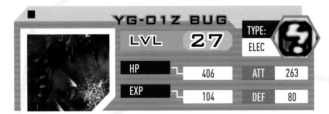

YG-01Z BUG

LVL	27	TYPE: ELEC
HP	406	ATT 263
EXP	104	DEF 80

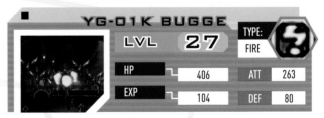

YG-01K BUGGE

LVL	27	TYPE: FIRE
HP	406	ATT 263
EXP	104	DEF 80

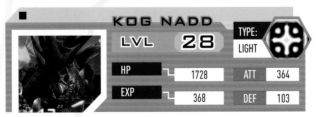

KOG NADD

LVL	28	TYPE: LIGHT
HP	1728	ATT 364
EXP	368	DEF 103

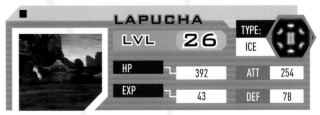

LAPUCHA

LVL	26	TYPE: ICE
HP	392	ATT 254
EXP	43	DEF 78

⑧ ▶ TRIAL — DESTROY THE GRINNA BETE S TRIO

The key to the Landeel Dock battle is to focus your attacks on only one of the three Grinna Bete S at a time. Your lone companion for the first minute of battle is Tylor, so follow his lead and double-team his target. Exploit your foes' weakness to Ground-type attacks by using the Diga Technic or the Ground-infused Breaker Long Sword, and be on the look out for opportunities to hit multiple targets with Technics that affect a large area—just don't forget which enemy to follow when they separate. Hyuga and Leo will join the battle at the one-minute mark, and together you can swarm the remaining targets.

BOSS EIGHT
GRINNA BETE S

Two minutes seems generous for those seeking an S-Rank, but you don't have quite as much time as it seems. You need to slay at least two of the Grinna Bete S within the first 70 or so seconds, or they will begin to use a special attack and spin wildly around the room. The Grinna Bete are invulnerable to attack while spinning, so all you'll be able to do is run for your life while precious time ticks away.

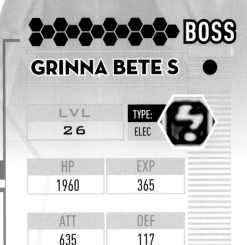

⬡⬡⬡⬡⬡⬡⬡⬡ BOSS

GRINNA BETE S ●

LVL	TYPE:
26	ELEC

HP	EXP
1960	365

ATT	DEF
635	117

TRIAL RANKING

RANKING INFORMATION

CONDITIONS

1 CLEAR TIME 2:00 VALUE 1000pts
PENALTY -5 points per second late

SCORE	RANK	MESETA	MP	PRIZE
1000	S	7500	80	Stella / Power S
700 - 999	A	3000	50	-
400 - 699	B	1500	30	-
0 - 399	C	-	20	-

CHAPTER 7

PHOTON SEALING

[NEUDAIZ] OHTOHU CITY

PARTNERS

NONE

CHAPTER OBJECTIVES

- [ ] Help Hyuga and Maya save Karen
- 1 [ ] TRIAL: Cross the swamp on a floader
- 2 [ ] Get reacquainted with Neudaiz fauna
- 3 [ ] TRIAL: Bring down the Onmagoug
- 4 [ ] Face tougher foes in Block D
- 5 [ ] Clear the temple defenses
- 6 [ ] Pick up a Real Hand Gun
- 7 [ ] Raid Dohgi's office
- 8 [ ] TRIAL: Dismantle Dohgi's war machine

MISSION: KAREN'S RESCUE

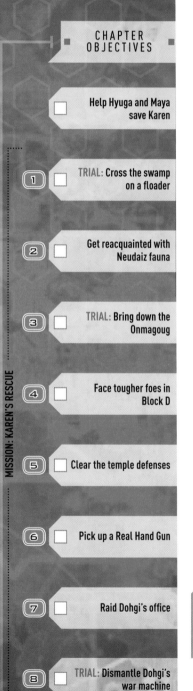

HELP HYUGA AND MAYA SAVE KAREN

You're officially a Guardian, but there's no time to celebrate—Karen is in trouble! Shove Leo, Tonnio, and Lumia aside as you rush to the PPT Spaceport and hop a shuttle to Neudaiz. There you'll meet Hyuga, Maya, and a surprise third party member. She won't give you a Partner Card, so form a party with just Hyuga and Maya and head to the Flyer Base when you're ready to begin. But don't miss your chance to visit the Yohmei shop first; there's new stock everywhere, but the best of it is right here on Neudaiz.

MISSION: KAREN'S RESCUE

Karen has been kidnapped. Her father is the perpetrator. Infiltrate the research facility where he is hiding and rescue Karen.

Required	1 Maya	2 Hyuga

LOC	Shikon Islands	Party	3/3

[DAGORA CITY]
SHOP REPORT

The engineers at G.R.M. and Tenora Works have been busy, but they can't compete with the master weaponsmiths at Yohmei. They have new four-star versions of every weapon they stock, including two new options for Hunters: the Claw and Double Claw. Buying either with its respective Photon Art will set you back around 25,000 Meseta, but the single Misaki Claw is a nice choice for Saber-weary Hunters who like to keep a gun in their left hand.

The new Septara wand and SlyRod rod provide a significant upgrade for Forces. You'll be commanding a Force-heavy party in this mission, and would be better off switching to Hunter type and focusing on melee weapons. But if your Tech stat is high enough to equip it, any class will welcome the significant PP boost the Septara provides over the Tenora Works W'ganda. The Yohmei Disc shop now offers the Megid series of Megid dark-element Wand/Rod Technics to play with, but fire and electric Technics will be more useful in the mission ahead.

GRM has the four-star Shooter Rifle and Repeater Machine Gun in stock, while Tenora Works offers the Gudda Waya Knuckles, the excellent Shigga Bigul Shotgun, and the newly-developed Cubol Upinde Crossbow (with corresponding Photon Arts).

Every manufacturer is offering new armor with roughly equal stats, so you should make your armor choice based on the Unit you intend to install. Budget-conscious consumers should hit the Synthesis shops, where you can now buy the metal materials you may have had trouble finding previously. Most of the new Boards require very rare ingredients, but if you've won the Kubara Wood as an S-Rank prize and earned a White Glove as a rare item drop from a Rogue, you may be able to whip up a Real Hand Gun or Real Twin Hand Gun. Both are fine weapons, but one of each will be available later in the chapter.

ARMOR SHOP
GRM

[NOTE: PURPLE TEXT DENOTES THAT THIS IS NEW TO THE SHOP.]

ARMOR	COST	DEF	EVA	SLOTS	ELEMENTS	DFP
PERPALINE	2500	33	58	1	FIRE-8%	5
STELLALINE	5500	52	85	1	ELECTRIC-10%	7
MEGALINE	18000	70	113	2	-	10
BRANDLINE	2500	30	56	1	-	5
BUSTERLINE	5000	50	84	1	-	7
ZEETLINE	19000	65	110	2	-	10

[NOTE: 1-STAR ITEMS ARE NOT SHOWN, BUT ARE STILL FOR SALE]

ARMOR SHOP
Yohmei

ARMOR	COST	DEF	EVA	SLOTS	ELEMENTS	DFP
STA-SENBA	5000	50	87	1	LIGHT-8%	7
ME-SENBA	18000	67	116	2	-	10
REIHA-SENBA	5500	48	85	1	-	7

UNITS	COST	TECH	MENT
STA / FORCE	3200	20	0
STA / MIND	2000	0	10
ME / QUICK	8000	-14	0

ARMOR SHOP
Tenora Works

ARMOR	COST	DEF	EVA	SLOTS	ELEMENTS	DFP
RABOL STELLA	5000	53	83	1	DARK-10%	7
RABOL MEGA	18000	73	110	2	-	10
RABOL MIDRA	5500	52	82	1	-	7

WEAPON SHOP
Tenora Works

MELEE WEAPONS	COST	PP	ATT	ACC	ELEMENTS	ATP
SODA BREKKA	3600	172	275	72	-	97 (LONG SWORD)
GUDDA BRANA	5500	165	150	77	-	97 (KNUCKLES)
GUDDA WAYA	9500	187	201	98	-	150 (KNUCKLES)
MUKPAT	3500	175	259	72	-	97 (SPEAR)
ALSEVA BATA	3800	180	115	72	-	97 (TWIN BLADES)
ALDAGA STEG	3750	195	75	72	ELEC-23%	97 (TWIN DAGGERS)
SEVA SATA	3200	127	209	75	-	97 (1-HAND BLADE)
DAGA STEG	3000	135	137	76	ELEC-23%	97 (DAGGER)

RANGED WEAPONS	COST	PP	ATT	ACC	ELEMENTS	ATA
SHIGGA WADDA	5700	307	55	19	-	26 (SHOTGUN)
SHIGGA BIGUL	10000	348	74	41	-	39 (SHOTGUN)
ARB OGA	5400	187	120	24	-	26 (TWIN HANDGUN)
B'DUKI OGA	3800	142	108	24	-	10 (HANDGUN)
CUBO UPINDE	8800	163	168	43	-	39 (CROSSBOW)

FORCE WEAPONS	COST	PP	TECH		ELEMENTS	TP
W'GANBA	3000	180	209		-	62 (WAND)

WEAPON SHOP   *Yohmei*

MELEE WEAPONS	COST	PP	ATT	ACC	ELEMENTS	ATP
BREKAUD	3750	189	225	76	FIRE-18%	97 (LONG SWORD)
CLAYMAUD	11000	215	302	96	-	150 (LONG SWORD)
LACANATA	3500	193	212	76	-	97 (SPEAR)
PARZANATA	10000	218	284	96	-	150 (SPEAR)
RYO-BASTA	3500	198	94	76	-	97 (TWIN BLADES)
RYO-PALASRA	10000	224	126	96	-	150 (TWIN BLADES)
RYO-STIZASHI	3450	214	61	76	-	97 (TWIN DAGGERS)
RYO-SAGAZASHI	9500	243	82	96	FIRE-25%	150 (TWIN DAGGERS)
RYO-MISAKI	11500	233	156	96	-	150 (TWIN CLAWS)
BASTARA	3200	140	171	78	-	97 (1-HAND BLADE)
PALASRA	9000	158	229	97	-	150 (1-HAND BLADE)
STINA-ZASHI	3000	148	112	79	-	97 (DAGGER)
SAKANO-ZASHI	8800	168	151	98	-	150 (DAGGER)
MISAKI	9000	162	266	96	-	150 (CLAW)

RANGED WEAPONS	COST	PP	ATT	ACC	ELEMENTS	ATA
COMPADRI	3550	341	307	25	-	26 (BOW)
RIKALBARI	9000	387	413	46	-	39 (BOW)
RYO-ORTOTORE	5500	206	98	28	-	26 (TWIN HANDGUN)
RYO-LOUKTORE	9800	233	132	48	-	39 (TWIN HANDGUN)
ORTOTORE	2900	156	88	28	-	26 (HANDGUN)
LOUKTORE	8500	177	119	48	-	39 (HANDGUN)

FORCE WEAPONS	COST	PP	TECH	ELEMENTS	TP
RAYHAROD	4000	363	198	-	62 (ROD)
SLYROD	11000	411	266	-	92 (ROD)
BATNARA	3400	198	171	-	62 (WAND)
SEPTARA	9500	224	229	-	92 (WAND)

ITEM SHOP   *EVERYWHERE*

ITEMS	COST
MONOMATE	30
DIMATE	150
SOL ATOMIZER	100
MOON ATOMIZER	500
GRINDER C+1	300
GRINDER C+2	800
GRINDER C+3	1500
GRINDER B+1	3000
GRINDER B+2	6000
GRINDER B+3	10000
DAMAGE TRAP	50
BURN TRAP	100
FREEZE TRAP	120

SHOPS CONTINUED ⋯⋯⋯⋯⋯⋯⋯▶

GETTING STARTED

STORY MODE

FREE MISSIONS

NETWORK MODE

WEAPON SHOP *GRM*

MELEE WEAPONS	COST	PP	ATT	ACC	ELEMENTS	ATP
BREAKER	3800	172	250	80	GROUND-16%	97 (LONG SWORD)
TWIN BUSTER	3300	180	104	80	-	97 (TWIN BLADES)

RANGED WEAPONS	COST	PP	ATT	ACC	ELEMENTS	ATA
BLASTER	3000	285	266	36	-	26 (RIFLE)
SHOOTER	9000	323	357	58	-	39 (RIFLE)
AUTOGUN	3900	142	98	34	-	26 (HANDGUN)
GREASEGUN	2800	147	22	16	-	26 (MACHINEGUN)
REPEATER	9500	166	30	28	-	39 (MACHINEGUN)

[NOTE: 1-2 STAR ITEMS ARE NOT SHOWN, BUT ARE STILL FOR SALE]

DISC SHOPS

[NOTE: G.C. = GUARDIANS COLONY // PAR = PARUM // NEU = NEUDAIZ // MOT = MOATOOB]

DISCS	COST	ATTACHES TO	G.C.	PAR	NEU	MOT
TORNADO BREAK	500	LONG SWORD	X	X	X	X
BOGGA ZUBBA	6000	KNUCKLES	X	X	X	X
DUS DAGGAS	2500	SPEAR	X	X	X	X
RISING CRUSH	500	TWIN BLADES	X	X	X	-
RENKAI BUYOU-ZAN	480	TWIN DAGGERS	X	X	X	X
BUKUU RENSEN-GA	14000	TWIN CLAWS	-	-	X	-
RISING STRIKE	350	1-HAND BLADE	X	X	X	X
SHUNBU SHOUREN-ZAN	450	DAGGER	X	X	X	X
SHOUSEN TOTSUZAN-GA	14000	CLAW	-	X	-	-
BURNING SHOT	3000	RIFLE	X	X	X	X
FROZEN SHOT	3000	RIFLE	X	X	X	X
PLASMA SHOT	3000	RIFLE	X	X	X	X
GRAV SHOT	3000	RIFLE	X	X	X	X
BANGA	4000	SHOTGUN	X	X	X	X
RIGA	4000	SHOTGUN	X	X	X	X
INGA	4000	SHOTGUN	X	X	X	X
DIGA	4000	SHOTGUN	X	X	X	X
ENSEI-SOU	3000	BOW	X	X	X	X
REISEI-SOU	3000	BOW	X	X	X	X
RAISEI-SOU	3000	BOW	X	X	X	X
JISEI-SOU	3000	BOW	X	X	X	X
TWIN BURN	400	TWIN HANDGUN	X	X	X	X
TWIN FREEZE	400	TWIN HANDGUN	X	X	X	X
TWIN PLASMA	400	TWIN HANDGUN	X	X	X	X
TWIN GRAV	3000	TWIN HANDGUN	X	X	X	X
BURNING HIT	400	HANDGUN	X	X	X	X
FROZEN HIT	400	HANDGUN	X	X	X	X
PLASMA HIT	400	HANDGUN	X	X	X	X
GRAV HIT	3000	HANDGUN	X	X	X	X
YAK BANGA	7000	CROSSBOW	-	-	-	X
YAK RIGA	7000	CROSSBOW	-	-	-	X
YAK INGA	7000	CROSSBOW	-	-	-	X
YAK DIGA	7000	CROSSBOW	-	-	-	X
BURNING FURY	3000	MACHINEGUN	X	X	X	X
FROZEN FURY	3000	MACHINEGUN	X	X	X	X

DISCS	COST	ATTACHES TO	G.C.	PAR	NEU	MOT
PLASMA FURY	3000	MACHINEGUN	X	X	X	X
GRAV FURY	3000	MACHINEGUN	X	X	X	X
FOIE	1000	WAND / STAFF	X	X	X	X
RAFOIE	3500	WAND / STAFF	X	X	X	X
DAMFOIE	4500	WAND / STAFF	X	X	X	X
GIFOIE	8000	WAND / STAFF	X	X	X	X
SHIFTA	2500	WAND / STAFF	X	X	X	X
JELLEN	3500	WAND / STAFF	X	X	X	X
BARTA	1000	WAND / STAFF	X	X	X	X
RABARTA	3500	WAND / STAFF	X	X	X	X
DAMBARTA	4500	WAND / STAFF	X	X	X	X
GIBARTA	8000	WAND / STAFF	X	X	X	X
DEBAND	2500	WAND / STAFF	X	X	X	X
ZALURE	1500	WAND / STAFF	X	X	X	X
ZONDE	1000	WAND / STAFF	X	X	X	X
RAZONDE	3500	WAND / STAFF	X	X	X	X
GIZONDE	8000	WAND / STAFF	X	X	X	X
NOSZANDE	4500	WAND / STAFF	X	X	X	X
ZODIAL	4000	WAND / STAFF	X	X	X	X
ZOLDEEL	1500	WAND / STAFF	X	X	X	X
DIGA	450	WAND / STAFF	X	X	X	X
RADIGA	3500	WAND / STAFF	X	X	X	X
DAMDIGA	4500	WAND / STAFF	X	X	X	X
GIDIGA	8000	WAND / STAFF	X	X	X	X
NOSDIGA	4500	WAND / STAFF	X	X	X	X
RESTA	1000	WAND / STAFF	X	X	X	X
GIRESTA	9800	WAND / STAFF	X	X	X	X
REVERSER	3000	WAND / STAFF	X	X	X	X
REGRANT	14000	WAND / STAFF	-	X	-	-
RETIER	4000	WAND / STAFF	X	X	X	X
MEGID	450	WAND / STAFF	-	X	-	-
RAMEGID	3500	WAND / STAFF	-	X	-	-
DAMMEGID	4500	WAND / STAFF	-	X	-	-
NOSMEGID	8000	WAND / STAFF	-	X	-	-

SYNTHESIS SHOPS

[NOTE: G.C. = GUARDIANS COLONY // PAR = PARUM // NEU = NEUDAIZ // MOT = MOATOOB]

BOARDS	COST	G.C.	PAR	NEU	MOT
[B] DOUBLE SABER	10000	X	X	-	-
[B] RYO-STIZASHI	1000	X	X	X	-
[B] MISAKI	3500	X	-	X	-
[B] GUDDA BRANA	1500	X	-	-	X
[B] JITSEEN	5000	X	X	-	-
[B] HARISEN BATTLE FAN	3000	X	-	-	-
[B] FLUORESCENT BULB	3000	X	-	-	-
[B] VAHRA CLAW	3000	X	-	-	-
[B] DUO HARISEN FANS	3000	X	-	-	-
[B] TWIN FLUOR. BULBS	3000	X	-	-	-
[B] AUTOGUN	1200	X	X	-	-
[B] REPEATER	2500	X	X	-	-
[B] BLASTER	1000	X	X	-	-
[B] LASER CANNON	5000	X	X	-	-
[B] COMPADRI	1000	X	-	X	-
[B] BAYBARI	8000	X	-	X	-
[B] SHIGGA BIGUL	2500	X	-	-	X
[B] REAL HAND GUN	8000	X	-	-	-
[B] BEAMGUN	5000	X	X	-	-
[B] REAL TWIN H.GUN	10000	X	-	-	-
[B] BATNARA	1000	X	-	X	-
[B] SLYROD	3000	X	-	X	-
[B] STELLALINE	800	X	X	-	-
[B] MEGALINE	2500	X	X	-	-
[B] STA-SENBA	800	X	-	X	-
[B] ME-SENBA	2500	X	-	X	-
[B] RABOL STELLA	800	X	-	-	X
[B] RABOL MEGA	2500	X	-	-	X
[B] DIMATE	10	X	X	X	X
[B] TRIMATE	50	X	X	X	X
[B] GRINDER C	100	X	X	X	X
[B] GRINDER B	800	X	X	X	X

CONVERTERS	COST	G.C.	PAR	NEU	MOT
[B] ORE C. 3 > 4	400	X	X	X	X
[B] ORE C. 4>5	800	X	X	-	-
[B] METAL CONV. C > B	200	X	X	X	X
[B] METAL CONV. B > A	1500	X	X	X	X
[B] WOOD CONV. C > B	200	X	X	X	X
[B] WOOD CONV. B >A	1500	X	X	X	X

MATERIALS	COST	G.C.	PAR	NEU	MOT
PHOTON	300	X	X	X	X
EL-PHOTON	800	X	X	X	X
IM-PHOTON	800	X	X	X	X
BAN-PHOTON	500	X	X	X	X
RAY-PHOTON	500	X	X	X	X
ZAN-PHOTON	500	X	X	X	X
DI-PHOTON	500	X	X	X	X
CARLIAN	200	X	X	X	X
PEPARIAN	1000	X	-	-	-
MEGANITE	200	X	X	X	X
GIGANITE	1000	X	-	-	-
HARNIUM	200	X	X	X	X
SOLDONIUM	1000	X	-	-	-
GAMOTITE	200	X	X	X	X
ZEPOTITE	1000	X	-	-	-
SOURAL	200	X	X	X	X
SPERAL	1000	X	-	-	-
ACENALINE	100	X	X	X	X
WENCELINE	300	X	X	X	X
APORALINE	900	X	-	-	-
NANOSILICA	200	X	X	X	X
HOT BERRY	50	X	X	X	X
COLD BERRY	50	X	X	X	X
SWEET BERRY	50	X	X	X	X
BITTER BERRY	50	X	X	X	X
STAMINA BERRY	50	X	X	X	X
TRANS ACID	100	X	X	X	X
METAMOR ACID	400	X	-	-	-
GRINDER BASE C	100	X	X	X	X
GRINDER BASE B	1000	X	-	-	-
PAR WOOD	200	X	X	-	-
NEU WOOD	200	X	-	X	-
MOT WOOD	200	X	-	-	X

[NOTE: 1-2 STAR ITEMS ARE NOT SHOWN, BUT ARE STILL FOR SALE]

[NEUDAIZ]
SHIKON ISLAND   BLOCK A-C

PARTNERS

NAME	LVL (Ethan's +...)	RACE	CLASS
1. Hyuga Ryght	+0	Human	Hunter
2. Maya Shidow	-2	Newman	Force
3. Mirei Mikuna	-4	Newman	Force

OBJECTIVES TO

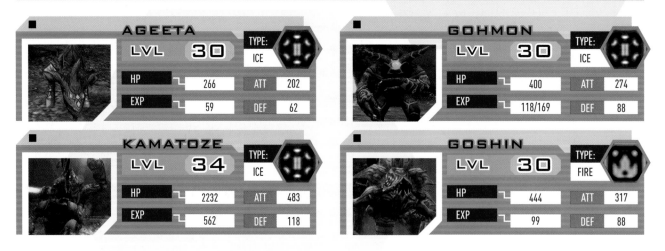

AGEETA		TYPE:	
LVL	30	ICE	
HP	266	ATT	202
EXP	59	DEF	62

GOHMON		TYPE:	
LVL	30	ICE	
HP	400	ATT	274
EXP	118/169	DEF	88

KAMATOZE		TYPE:	
LVL	34	ICE	
HP	2232	ATT	483
EXP	562	DEF	118

GOSHIN		TYPE:	
LVL	30	FIRE	
HP	444	ATT	317
EXP	99	DEF	88

1 TRIAL — CROSS THE SWAMP ON A FLOADER

The flyer will drop you at the banks of a vast swamp, which you can cross on a high-powered floader provided by your old friend Bruce. Before you hop on board, turn around and locate the Save Marker; the clock starts ticking as soon as you hop onto the floader, and the only way to reset the clock is to logout and reload your game.

The Communion has scattered orange explosive devices, some of which will estimate your speed and bearing and move to intercept you. The easiest way to avoid these moving mines is to ease off the accelerator as you approach, causing the mines to overshoot you. But don't worry if you misjudge the mine's trajectory—your floader can survive several direct hits, and the mines barely slow you down when you're traveling at regular speed. If you're aiming for an S-Rank, conserve HP early on so you'll have the freedom to blast through mines later.

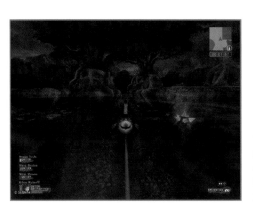

The time you lose dodging mines can be easily recouped by driving through the yellow speed boosts that float on the water's surface. However, you should hit the speed boosts only when you're facing the direction you want to go. If you've veered sharply to make a turn or dodge a mine (generally a poor idea), the boost will send you off course or into a wall.

Staying on course is the key to earning an S-Rank. Block A-1 is quite straightforward; there's only one fork near the end, where you'll want to make a hard left towards a moving mine. Block A-2 is far more confusing, but you can get through it quickly if you turn left whenever you have the option. Hang a hard left into the first speed boost (to the left of a moving mine) and continue northwest past a stationary mine, another speed boost, and two moving mines. Then straighten up and head due north to the exit. In Block A-3 you'll spot the first speed boost in the middle of three mines; hit it while you're facing northeast, then turn due north just before the second speed boost. Continue north all the way to the exit and your S-Rank prize.

TRIAL RANKING

CONDITIONS

1 CLEAR TIME 2:30 VALUE 1000pts
PENALTY -5 points per second late

RANKING INFORMATION

SCORE	RANK	MESETA	EXP	PRIZE
1000	S	10000	100	Innocent Pants
700 - 999	A	4000	70	-
400 - 699	B	1500	50	-
0 - 399	C	-	40	-

② GET REACQUAINTED WITH NEUDAIZ FAUNA

The beasts of the Shikon Islands are a familiar lot—you'll face burrowing Goshin, Barta-casting Gohmon, and hordes of Ageeta. But there are a few new twists: Gohmon are now led by two-eyed, orange-clawed Gohmon kings that will boost defense and restore lost HP for the underlings, and all-new giant Kamatoze enemies will add a layer of challenge.

When battling a Kamatoze at close range, circle it until you can get a shot at its side or flank, and then start swinging. But don't use Technics or Photon Arts that will lock you in place (such as the Spear's Dus Daggas or the 1-hand Sword's Gravity Strike) because you need to turn and run the instant you see ice crystals surrounding the Kamatoze. The crystals will continue to creep outward, dealing catastrophic damage to anyone in their path.

PARTNERS

NAME	LVL (Ethan's +...)	RACE	CLASS
1. Hyuga Ryght	+0	Human	Hunter
2. Maya Shidow	-2	Newman	Force
3. Mirei Mikuna	-4	Newman	Force

OBJECTIVES ③ TO ④

③ TRIAL   BRING DOWN THE ONMAGOUG

The Onmagoug is back for a rematch in Block C-1. Use the same strategy that you used in Chapter 5, targeting its wings in first-person mode, then battering it with 1-hand Sword combos when it falls. The only twist is that you have to protect Mirei, but it is unlikely that the Onmagoug's weak attacks will incapacitate her within a minute and a half. If you have trouble beating the Onmagoug within two cycles of attacks (which will be necessary to earn an S-Rank), load your Save File, turn around, and head back to Ohtoku City to upgrade your Sword and ranged weapons.

BOSS NINE
ONMAGOUG

BOSS

ONMAGOUG ●

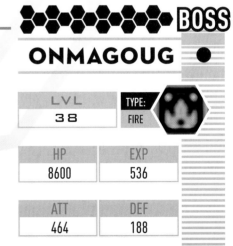

LVL	TYPE:
38	FIRE

HP	EXP
8600	536

ATT	DEF
464	188

TRIAL RANKING

③

③

RANKING INFORMATION

SCORE	RANK	MESETA	EXP	PRIZE
1000	S	10000	100	Double Saber
700 - 999	A	4000	70	-
400 - 699	B	1500	50	-
0 - 399	C	-	40	-

CONDITIONS

1 CLEAR TIME 1:30 VALUE 900pts
PENALTY -5 point per second late

MONSTERS

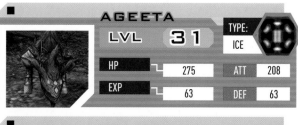

AGEETA
LVL **31**
TYPE: ICE

HP	275	ATT	208
EXP	63	DEF	63

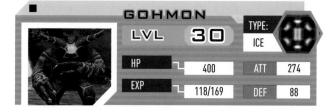

GOHMON
LVL **30**
TYPE: ICE

HP	400	ATT	274
EXP	118/169	DEF	88

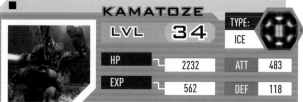

KAMATOZE
LVL **34**
TYPE: ICE

HP	2232	ATT	483
EXP	562	DEF	118

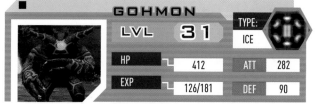

GOHMON
LVL **31**
TYPE: ICE

HP	412	ATT	282
EXP	126/181	DEF	90

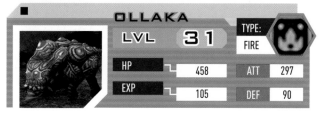

OLLAKA
LVL **31**
TYPE: FIRE

HP	458	ATT	297
EXP	105	DEF	90

GOSHIN
LVL **31**
TYPE: FIRE

HP	458	ATT	327
EXP	105	DEF	90

④ ## FACE TOUGHER FOES IN BLOCK D

The difficulty ramps up a bit in the three maps of Block D, where you'll face larger groups of high-level monsters. Ollaka have returned to the rotation, but they're among the easiest foes you'll face, and can easily be slain at melee range if you circle behind or beside them. It's the Kamatoze that will give you the most trouble, as they now appear in pairs or accompanied by other foes. Despite the threat the Kamatoze pose, you should always take out the lesser monsters first.

GETTING STARTED

STORY MODE

FREE MISSIONS

NETWORK MODE

After revealing the key in the eastern room in Block D-2, keep exploring. You'll find a Warp behind a tree in the northeast corner, and it's the only way to reach the island with the item containers.

[NEUDAIZ]
SHIHON ISLAND   OLD HAHURA TEMPLE

PARTNERS

NAME	LVL (Ethan's +...)	RACE	CLASS
1. Hyuga Ryght	+0	Human	Hunter
2. Maya Shidow	-2	Newman	Force
3. Mirei Mikuna	-4	Newman	Force

OBJECTIVES ⑤ TO ⑧

⑤   CLEAR THE TEMPLE DEFENSES

The Old Hakura Temple is defended by mechanical Bysha that behave much like Chapter 6's Gohma Dilla. Zonde-series Technics and plasma Photon Arts will finally come in handy here, as either will deal heavy damage to these ground-based foes. Melee fighters should use the Photon Arts of a 1-hand Sword, Twin Blade, or Claw weapon to pop foes up into the air. (This is something that almost always works on the Bysha and can preempt all of their attacks.) But melee fighters will have to worry about the old Gohma Dilla explosion trick—prepare to run when you see the tell-tale blue circles radiating from a Bysha.

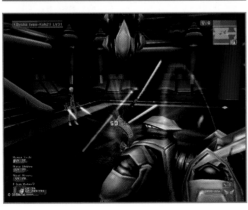

The difference between the two Bysha types is that the Otsu32 can also use a long-range flamethrower to fry distant targets. Rangers should be able to strafe out of the way, but Forces will be hamstrung by their Technic casting time, and may want to move in and attempt to pre-empt the attacks with melee strikes instead.

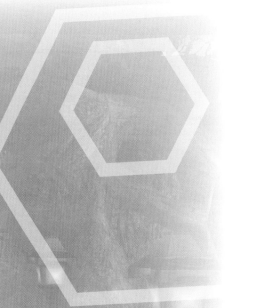

⑥ PICK UP A REAL HAND GUN

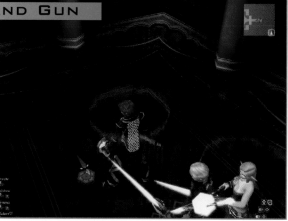

When you enter Block A-2, head east and keep going in that direction until you find a large room with several Bysha and a locked door. When you clear the room, use the key to unlock the door, and you'll find a dead end with a few chests. One of the chests always contains a Real Hand Gun, a silly but effective sidearm that any class can use. Equip it quickly (and link Plasma Hit!), as smashing the box will spawn a squad of Bysha.

MONSTERS

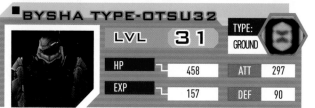

BYSHA TYPE-KOH21

LVL	**31**	TYPE: GROUND
HP	458	ATT	297
EXP	157	DEF	90

BYSHA TYPE-OTSU32

LVL	**31**	TYPE: GROUND
HP	458	ATT	297
EXP	157	DEF	90

BYSHA TYPE-OTSU32

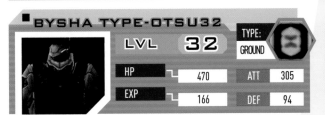

LVL	32		TYPE: GROUND
HP	470	ATT	305
EXP	166	DEF	94

ARMED SERVANT (OZUNA)

LVL	31		TYPE: --
HP	412	ATT	282
EXP	126	DEF	90

ARMED SERVANT (TAGUBA)

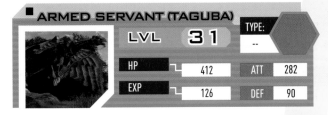

LVL	31		TYPE: --
HP	412	ATT	282
EXP	126	DEF	90

RAID DOHGI'S OFFICE

The hall in the northeast corner of Block A-2 leads to Dohgi's Office, where Mirei will pull up his files and uncover the truth about his organization. Explore the office thoroughly to turn up a Save Marker and Heal Spot, and put both to good use. When you exit, you'll find the southern hallway is now open, but the path is guarded by Armed Servants. These foes come in two flavors: Taguba blast you with offensive spells like Barta, while Ozuna have no attack capability but can heal their allies and cast spells to weaken your party. Unfortunately, there isn't any easy way to tell them apart from a distance, so you'll have to get close enough to read the data box in the corner to tell who is who.

⑧ TRIAL — DISMANTLE DOHGI'S WAR MACHINE

If you battle the Adahna Degahna head on, you're in for a long and grueling fight. Its attacks are easy enough to dodge, but its frequent dashes and warps will force you to spend much of the fight chasing it across a vast battlefield. Furthermore, its regenerative abilities will erase much of the damage you inflict. Fortunately, you can prevent all of that—the trick is to charge at the Adahna Degahna as soon as the battle begins (or if you miss that opportunity, after it warps) and get directly behind it and between its treads. This is a safe spot where you'll be immune to most of its attacks, and if you move along with it while attacking its flank constantly, you can prevent it from using any of its evasive moves. Long Swords like the Breaker make the best weapons, as they have a wide enough swing to hit Adahna Degahna in several places even after it runs out of PP. If you're not a Hunter (and you don't have one in your party) burn through the PP of each of your melee weapons in turn. Ranged weapons and Wands aren't much use here, but an attack boost from a Shifta Technic or an Agtaride will make it all the easier to earn an S-Rank.

BOSS TEN
ADAHNA DEGAHNA

BOSS

ADAHNA DEGAHNA ●

LVL	TYPE:
38	LIGHT

HP	EXP
5960	5160

ATT	DEF
526	250

TRIAL RANKING

CONDITIONS

1 CLEAR TIME **2:30** VALUE **1000pts**
PENALTY -5 points per second late

RANKING INFORMATION ⑧

SCORE	RANK	MESETA	EXP	PRIZE
1000	S	10000	100	Twin Real Handgun
700 - 999	A	4000	70	-
400 - 699	B	1500	50	-
0 - 399	C	-	40	-

CHAPTER 8

IN MELLVORE'S WAKE

MISSION: IN THE RUINS

CHAPTER OBJECTIVES

- ☐ TRIAL: Exterminate the SEED-forms
- ☐ Check in with Pete and Lumia
- ① ☐ Slay the Mellvore tunnel beasts
- ② ☐ Battle the plant defenders
- ③ ☐ Flip the nine control switches
- ④ ☐ Prepare for the boss battle
- ⑤ ☐ TRIAL: Exterminate SEED-Vitace
- ⑥ ☐ TRIAL: Rendezvous with Tomrain
- ⑦ ☐ Receive your new assignment
- ⑧ ☐ Search for the Gates of Denikaya
- ⑨ ☐ TRIAL: Destroy the De Ragnus

[GUARDIANS COLONY] **FOOD PLANT**

PARTNERS

	NAME	LVL (Ethan's +...)	RACE	CLASS
1.	Leogini S. Berafort	+2	Beast	Hunter
2.	Tonnio Rhima	+1	Beast	Hunter

TRIAL EXTERMINATE THE SEED-FORMS

This chapter will plunge you into a trial, mere seconds after the chapter title screen. You're stuck with all the same gear you had at the end of Chapter 7, so dig up a weapon that still has some PP and go to town on the invaders of the Linear Line. But be forewarned; at level 35, even Pannon have the power to give Ethan a beating. In fact, now that they're heavily enhanced by Technics, the Pannon are the deadliest enemies in the first two blocks! Fortunately, the only factor on which you'll be judged here is time, so don't worry about scouring every nook and cranny for enemies. Just run for the exits as soon as the keys appear.

You'll meet up with Leo and Tonnio in Block A-2, and together you'll need to collect a key in each of the four rooms before you can unlock the door to Block A-3. That's where you'll battle the first of three SEED-Vance enemies—they're vulnerable to the same tactics you've used to beat them in the past, but hacking through their 2,740 HP will take some time. Whatever your class, battle the SEED-Vance at melee range (ideally with Photon Arts like Rising Strike) so Leo and Tonnio will get into the action too.

MONSTERS

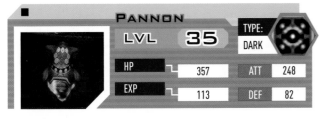

PANNON
LVL **35**
TYPE: DARK
| HP | 357 | ATT | 248 |
| EXP | 113 | DEF | 82 |

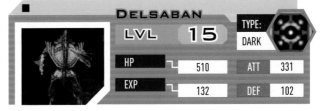

DELSABAN
LVL **15**
TYPE: DARK
| HP | 510 | ATT | 331 |
| EXP | 132 | DEF | 102 |

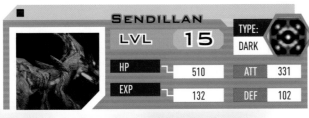

SENDILLAN
LVL **15**
TYPE: DARK
| HP | 510 | ATT | 331 |
| EXP | 132 | DEF | 102 |

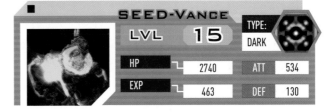

SEED-VANCE
LVL **15**
TYPE: DARK
| HP | 2740 | ATT | 534 |
| EXP | 463 | DEF | 130 |

TRIAL RANKING

CONDITIONS

1 CLEAR TIME 8:00 VALUE 1000pts
PENALTY -5 points per second late

RANKING INFORMATION

SCORE	RANK	MESETA	MP	PRIZE
1000	S	7500	110	Scape Doll
700 - 999	A	3000	80	-
400 - 699	B	1500	60	-
0 - 399	C	-	50	-

CHECK IN WITH PETE AND LUMIA

After completing your mission, return home to clear your inventory and catch up with the news. Pete will bring you up to speed on what happened between Chapters 7 and 8, and point out the new Free Missions that are available to you. When you're ready to get back to business, head upstairs to Guardians HQ to speak with Lucaim Nav and the Guardians President. They'll introduce you to your new partner, Lou, and order the pair of you to Mellvore immediately. Lou will leave before you, and you'll find her waiting at the Parum PPT Port with Maya Shidow in tow. Accept Lou's Partner Card and add both to your party, which will allow you to select the "In the Ruins" mission from the Holtes City Flyer Base.

Go to the underground facility in Old Mellvore City in order to cooperate with Tomrain in an experiment concerning A-photons.

Required		
1	Lou	
2	Maya	

LOC	Old Mellvore City	Party	3/3

[HOLTES CITY]
SHOP REPORT

Only G.R.M. is offering a significant stock update in this chapter, but the few new toys behind the weapon shop counter should give Hunters and Rangers plenty to get excited about. You may have won a Double Saber in the last chapter, but only now can you buy its Tornado Dance Photon Art. The Double Saber isn't great solo, but its unique Photon Art tranforms Ethan into a human torpedo that can hit stationary bosses for incredible amounts of damage. The Ranger toy is the Laser Cannon, a slow two-handed gun that blasts through foes, allowing you to hit each enemy in a line or damage large foes at multiple points.

ITEM SHOP

ITEMS	COST
MONOMATE	30
DIMATE	150
TRIMATE	1000
SOL ATOMIZER	100
MOON ATOMIZER	500
PHOTON CHARGE	1500
GRINDER C+1	300
GRINDER C+2	800
GRINDER C+3	1500
GRINDER B+1	3000
GRINDER B+2	6000
GRINDER B+3	10000
DAMAGE TRAP	50
BURN TRAP	100
FREEZE TRAP	120
DAMAGE TRAP G	600
BURN TRAP G	750
FREEZE TRAP G	750

ARMOR SHOP *GRM*

ARMOR	COST	DEF	EVA	SLOTS	ELEMENTS	DFP
STELLALINE	5500	52	85	1	ELECTRIC-10%	7
MEGALINE	18000	70	113	2	-	10
BUSTERLINE	5000	50	84	1	-	7
ZEETLINE	19000	65	110	2	-	10

[NOTE: 1-2 STAR ITEMS ARE NOT SHOWN, BUT ARE STILL FOR SALE]

UNITS	COST	ATT	ACC
PERPA / POWER	2500	14	0
PERPA / HIT	2000	0	10
MEGA / POWER	13000	20	0

[NOTE: 1 STAR ITEMS ARE NOT SHOWN, BUT ARE STILL FOR SALE]

[NOTE: PURPLE TEXT DENOTES THAT THIS IS NEW TO THE SHOP.]

WEAPON SHOP
GRM

MELEE WEAPONS	COST	PP	ATT	ACC	ELEMENTS	ATP
BREAKER	3800	172	250	80	GROUND-16%	97 (LONG SWORD)
DOUBLE SABER	21000	197	178	102	-	150 (DOUBLE BLADE)
TWIN BUSTER	3300	180	104	80	-	97 (TWIN BLADES)

RANGED WEAPONS	COST	PP	ATT	ACC	ELEMENTS	ATA
BLASTER	3000	285	266	36	-	26 (RIFLE)
SHOOTER	9000	323	357	58	-	39 (RIFLE)
LASER CANNON	21000	357	581	53	-	39 (CANNON)
AUTOGUN	3900	142	98	34	-	26 (HANDGUN)
GREASEGUN	2800	147	22	16	-	26 (MACHINEGUN)
REPEATER	9500	166	30	28	-	39 (MACHINEGUN)

[NOTE: 1-2 STAR ITEMS ARE NOT SHOWN, BUT ARE STILL FOR SALE]

DISC SHOPS

[NOTE: G.C. = GUARDIANS COLONY // PAR = PARUM // NEU = NEUDAIZ // MOT = MOATOOB]

DISCS	COST	ATTACHES TO	G.C.	PAR	NEU	MOT
TORNADO BREAK	500	LONG SWORD	X	X	X	X
BOGGA ZUBBA	6000	KNUCKLES	X	X	X	X
DUS DAGGAS	2500	SPEAR	X	X	X	X
TORNADO DANCE	15000	DOUBLE BLADE	-	X	-	-
RISING CRUSH	500	TWIN BLADES	X	X	X	X
RENKAI BUYOU-ZAN	480	TWIN DAGGERS	X	X	X	X
BUKUU RENSEN-GA	14000	TWIN CLAWS	X	X	X	X
RISING STRIKE	350	1-HAND BLADE	X	X	X	X
SHUNBU SHOUREN-ZAN	450	DAGGER	X	X	X	X
SHOUSEN TOTSUZAN-GA	14000	CLAW	X	X	X	X
BURNING SHOT	3000	RIFLE	X	X	X	X
FROZEN SHOT	3000	RIFLE	X	X	X	X
PLASMA SHOT	3000	RIFLE	X	X	X	X
GRAV SHOT	3000	RIFLE	X	X	X	X
BARADA BANGA	4000	SHOTGUN	X	X	X	X
BARADA RIGA	4000	SHOTGUN	X	X	X	X
BARADA INGA	4000	SHOTGUN	X	X	X	X
BARADA DIGA	4000	SHOTGUN	X	X	X	X
ENSEI-SOU	3000	BOW	X	X	X	X
REISEI-SOU	3000	BOW	X	X	X	X
RAISEI-SOU	3000	BOW	X	X	X	X

DISCS	COST	ATTACHES TO	G.C.	PAR	NEU	MOT
JISEI-SOU	3000	BOW	X	X	X	X
BURNING PRISM	10000	LASER CANNON	-	X	-	-
FROZEN PRISM	10000	LASER CANNON	-	X	-	-
PLASMA PRISM	10000	LASER CANNON	-	X	-	-
GRAV PRISM	10000	LASER CANNON	-	X	-	-
TWIN BURN	400	TWIN HANDGUN	X	X	X	X
TWIN FREEZE	400	TWIN HANDGUN	X	X	X	X
TWIN PLASMA	400	TWIN HANDGUN	X	X	X	X
TWIN GRAV	3000	TWIN HANDGUN	X	X	X	X
BURNING HIT	400	HANDGUN	X	X	X	X
FROZEN HIT	400	HANDGUN	X	X	X	X
PLASMA HIT	400	HANDGUN	X	X	X	X
GRAV HIT	3000	HANDGUN	X	X	X	X
YAK BANGA	7000	CROSSBOW	X	X	X	X
YAK RIGA	7000	CROSSBOW	X	X	X	X
YAK INGA	7000	CROSSBOW	X	X	X	X
YAK DIGA	7000	CROSSBOW	X	X	X	X
BURNING FURY	3000	MACHINEGUN	X	X	X	X
FROZEN FURY	3000	MACHINEGUN	X	X	X	X
PLASMA FURY	3000	MACHINEGUN	X	X	X	X
GRAV FURY	3000	MACHINEGUN	X	X	X	X

[NOTE: TECHNICS ARE ALSO FOR SALE, BUT NO NEW ADDITIONS APPEAR SINCE THE PREVIOUS CHAPTER]

SYNTHESIS SHOPS

[NOTE1: G.C. = GUARDIANS COLONY // PAR = PARUM // NEU = NEUDAIZ // MOT = MOATOOB]
[NOTE2: 1-3 STAR ITEMS ARE NOT SHOWN, BUT ARE STILL FOR SALE]

BOARDS	COST	G.C.	PAR	NEU	MOT
[B] DOUBLE SABER	10000	X	X	-	-
[B] MISAKI	3500	X	-	X	-
[B] JITSEEN	5000	X	X	-	-
[B] REPEATER	2500	X	X	-	-
[B] VULLSEYE	8000	X	X	-	-
[B] LASER CANNON	5000	X	X	-	-
[B] BAYBARI	8000	X	-	X	-
[B] SHIGGA BIGUL	2500	X	-	-	X
[B] REAL HAND GUN	8000	X	-	-	-

BOARDS	COST	G.C.	PAR	NEU	MOT
[B] BEAMGUN	5000	X	X	-	-
[B] REAL TWIN H. GUN	10000	X	-	-	-
[B] SLYROD	3000	X	-	X	-
[B] MEGALINE	2500	X	X	-	-
[B] GIGALINE	8000	X	X	-	-
[B] ME-SENBA	2500	X	-	X	-
[B] RABOL MEGA	2500	X	-	-	X
[B] RABOL GIGA	8000	X	-	-	X
[B] TRIMATE	50	X	X	X	X

SHOPS CONTINUED ▶

GETTING STARTED
STORY MODE
FREE MISSIONS
NETWORK MODE

SYNTHESIS SHOPS

[NOTE: G.C. = GUARDIANS COLONY // PAR = PARUM // NEU = NEUDAIZ // MOT = MOATOOB]

MATERIALS	COST	G.C.	PAR	NEU	MOT	MATERIALS	COST	G.C.	PAR	NEU	MOT
PHOTON	300	X	X	X	X	WENCELINE	300	X	X	X	X
EL-PHOTON	800	X	X	X	X	APORALINE	900	X	X	X	X
IM-PHOTON	800	X	X	X	X	NANOSILICA	200	X	X	X	X
BAN-PHOTON	500	X	X	X	X	HOT BERRY	50	X	X	X	X
RAY-PHOTON	500	X	X	X	X	COLD BERRY	50	X	X	X	X
ZON-PHOTON	500	X	X	X	X	SWEET BERRY	50	X	X	X	X
DI-PHOTON	500	X	X	X	X	BITTER BERRY	50	X	X	X	X
CARLIAN	200	X	X	X	X	STAMINA BERRY	50	X	X	X	X
PEPARIAN	1000	X	X	X	X	TRANS ACID	100	X	X	X	X
MEGANITE	200	X	X	X	X	METAMOR ACID	400	X	X	X	X
GIGANITE	1000	X	X	X	X	GRINDER BASE C	100	X	X	X	X
HARNIUM	200	X	X	X	X	GRINDER BASE B	1000	X	X	X	X
SOLDONIUM	1000	X	X	X	X	PAR WOOD	200	X	X	-	-
GAMOTITE	200	X	X	X	X	PAR ASH	750	X	X	-	-
ZEPOTITE	1000	X	X	X	X	MOT WOOD	200	X	-	-	X
SOURAL	200	X	X	X	X	MOT ASH	750	X	-	-	X
SPERAL	1000	X	X	X	X	NEU WOOD	200	X	-	X	-
ACENALINE	100	X	X	X	X	NEU ASH	750	X	-	X	-

[PARUM]
UNDERGROUND PASSAGE/PLANT

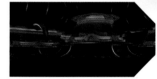

PARTNERS

NAME	LVL (Ethan's +...)	RACE	CLASS
1. Lou	-2	CAST	Hunter
2. Maya Shidow	-2	Newman	Force
3. Kou Taragi	+0	Human	Ranger

OBJECTIVES ① TO ⑤

---

① SLAY THE MELLVORE TUNNEL BEASTS

Your final party member, Kou Taragi, will join you at the outskirts of Mellvore. Together you'll have to battle your way through an underground tunnel to reach a well-protected A-photon plant.

Electric-type foes are common in this chapter, so you can get an edge by linking Diga-series Technics and Grav Photon Arts to your Wands and ranged weapons. The only real threat in the first block is the Jarba, a two-legged monster that can cast Megid and throw a mean right hook. Use quick melee attacks to prevent it from executing special attacks, and stay behind it or to the left in order to keep out of punching range.

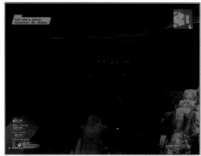

The Jarba often strike in dark rooms that are off the main path, and battling them with limited vision isn't easy. Run around the perimeter looking for the yellow and green glowing lights of item boxes, one of which conceals a light switch. But if you don't care about minor items and experience points, you can simply turn around and leave, as the dark rooms never contain anything essential.

MONSTERS

JARBA

LVL	**37**	TYPE:	FIRE
HP	1340	ATT	522
EXP	632	DEF	127

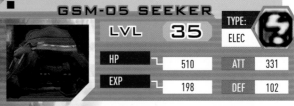

GSM-05 SEEKER

LVL	**35**	TYPE:	ELEC
HP	510	ATT	331
EXP	198	DEF	102

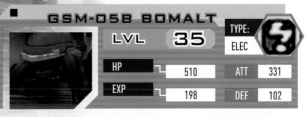

GSM-05B BOMALT

LVL	**35**	TYPE:	ELEC
HP	510	ATT	331
EXP	198	DEF	102

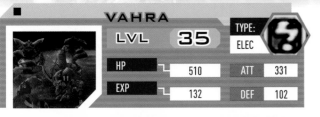

VAHRA

LVL	**35**	TYPE:	ELEC
HP	510	ATT	331
EXP	132	DEF	102

SPECIAL OPS (SOLDA)

LVL	**35**	TYPE:	--
HP	918	ATT	530
EXP	184	DEF	102

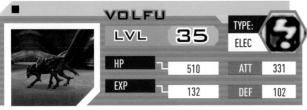

VOLFU

LVL	**35**	TYPE:	ELEC
HP	510	ATT	331
EXP	132	DEF	102

SPECIAL OPS (ASSAULT)

LVL	**35**	TYPE:	--
HP	510	ATT	364
EXP	132	DEF	102

GETTING STARTED

STORY MODE

FREE MISSIONS

NETWORK MODE

2   BATTLE THE PLANT DEFENDERS

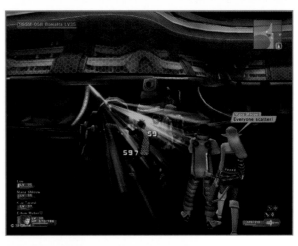

You'll find the A-Photon plant In Block A-2, but you'll have to destroy its automated defenses before Dr. Taragi can begin his experiments. The GSM behave similarly to the Gohma Dilla and Bysha machines of past chapters, radiating blue circles before they perform an energy discharge and self-destructing when they die. Seekers can also use their mounted turrets to blast distant Forces and Rangers, but have little defense against melee fighters (provided they use quick attacks instead of lengthy combos, so they can turn and run when necessary). The Bomalta have powerful short-range attacks, but are completely at the mercy of Rangers and Forces. Figure out which version you're fighting, and plan your tactics accordingly!

The door will lock behind you when you enter Block B-1, and you won't be able to return to town for supplies until you reach Block C. Block B-1 and B-2 each contain nine switches you must flip before you can proceed. They're easy to find in Block B-1, but you'll need to travel systematically through Block B-2 to locate all the switches in the second set. (Try following either the right or left wall throughout the entire installation.)

As a general rule you'll always spawn a pack of foes when you approach a switch on the ground level, but the upper-level switches are completely unguarded. The plant defenses include both GSM and Special Ops troops, which also come in two varieties. Trump either one by using whichever weapon they don't; quick melee attacks will keep the Solda from getting off a Rifle shot, and bullet volleys will keep the Assault types from getting within Claw range. When the defenders are GSM-05b Bomalta, back up to a ramp and cut loose with Technics while the Bomalta struggle to reach you.

④ PREPARE FOR THE BOSS BATTLE

When all the switches have been flipped in Block B-2, the final wave of enemies will appear in the northwest corner of the map. Kill them all to receive the key that unlocks the barrier in front of the teleporter at the end of the northern path. That teleporter will take you to an unguarded trio of item containers, one of which often contains a new 1-hand sword called the Jitseen. After claiming the treasure, proceed through one more enemy-filled room to reach the door to Block C-1. A Save Marker and Heal Spot are ahead, and if you want a Photon Charge or a weapons upgrade, you can now return to Holtes City to get it.

⑤ TRIAL EXTERMINATE SEED-VITACE

MONSTERS

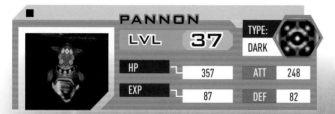

PANNON

LVL	37	TYPE: DARK
HP	357	ATT	248
EXP	87	DEF	82

DELSABAN

LVL	37	TYPE: DARK
HP	510	ATT	331
EXP	146	DEF	102

This trial begins with an onslaught of Delsaban and Pannon foes, and the SEED-Vitace boss will only appear when the room is clear. While it resembles SEED-Vance, it won't fall for the same tricks, and its extremely damaging attacks are much harder to dodge. To battle it safely you can dodge its attacks and fire ranged weapons and Technics from a safe distance, but your ranking will suffer for it.

To earn an S-Rank in this battle you'll need to claim victory within one minute while preventing Kou Taragi from fainting. The easiest way to do this is to head back to Holtes City, switch to a Hunter class, and pick up a Double Saber, the Tornado Dance Photon Art, and the Regrant Technic. As soon as the battle begins, rush into the midst of the monsters and hold down the Regrant button to clear the room of foes before the conversation even ends! When the SEED-Vitace appears, exclusively attack it with Tornado Dance, which can't be disrupted by the SEED-Vitace's attacks. Tornado Dance will kill the SEED-Vitace so quickly that you won't need to worry about Dr. Taragi's welfare!

BOSS

BOSS TEN
SEED-VITACE

SEED-VITACE

LVL	TYPE:
55	DARK

HP	EXP
3790	1449

ATT	DEF
738	179

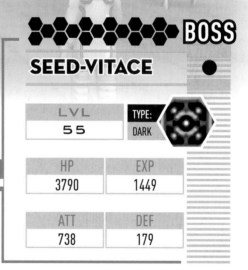

TRIAL RANKING ⑤

CONDITIONS

1. **CLEAR TIME 1:00 VALUE 900pts**
   PENALTY -5 points per second late

2. **DR. TARAGI FAINTS 0 VALUE 100pts**
   PENALTY -100 points per time Dr. Taragi faints

RANKING INFORMATION

SCORE	RANK	MESETA	MP	PRIZE
1000	S	7500	110	Innocent Jacket
700 - 999	A	3000	80	-
400 - 699	B	1500	60	-
0 - 399	C	-	50	-

LAKE DENES RELIC

PARTNERS

NAME	LVL (Ethan's +...)	RACE	CLASS
1. Lou	-2	CAST	Hunter
2. Maya Shidow	-2	Newman	Force
3. Kou Taragi	+0	Human	Ranger
4. Kanal Tomrain	-3	Human	Civilian

OBJECTIVES ⑥ TO ⑨

⑥ TRIAL RENDEZVOUS WITH TOMRAIN

Return to town for a PP recharge after the boss fight, as an even tougher trial awaits in the Relics. Those seeking an S-Rank will need both weapons that can clear a crowd quickly (like the Ranger Shotgun or a Hunter Long Sword) and lots of fast melee weapons to unload on the many Jarba that appear in the challenge. The Jarba can now cast Resta to heal themselves, so you'll need to rely on continuous melee attacks to do any permanent damage. But don't jump the gun—Jarba are immune for the first few seconds after they appear, so any PP spent before you have a red crosshair lock will be wasted.

MONSTERS

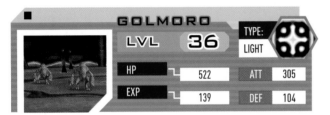

GOLMORO
LVL **36** TYPE: LIGHT

HP	522	ATT	305
EXP	139	DEF	104

BADIRA
LVL **36** TYPE: FIRE

HP	365	ATT	254
EXP	83	DEF	83

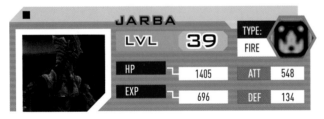

JARBA
LVL **39** TYPE: FIRE

HP	1405	ATT	548
EXP	696	DEF	134

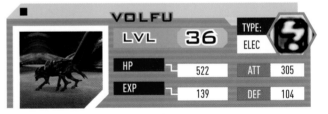

VOLFU
LVL **36** TYPE: ELEC

HP	522	ATT	305
EXP	139	DEF	104

TRIAL RANKING ⑥

RANKING INFORMATION

CONDITIONS

1 CLEAR TIME 10:00 VALUE 600pts
PENALTY -1 point per second late

2 ENEMIES 72 VALUE 300pts
PENALTY -5 points per enemy missed

3 DR. TARAGI FAINTS 0 VALUE 100pts
PENALTY -100 points per time Dr. Taragi faints

SCORE	RANK	MESETA	MP	PRIZE
1000	S	7500	110	Grinder A+4
700 - 999	A	3000	80	-
400 - 699	B	1500	60	-
0 - 399	C	-	50	-

⑦ RECEIVE YOUR NEW ASSIGNMENT

The trial ends when, after battling through two straight blocks, you reach Dr. Tomrain's team at the Power Control Room. Lou will stay here with Dr. Taragi, while Ethan and Maya are charged with leading Dr. Tomrain through two more blocks to the Gates of Denikaya. You can buy a few items from Bruce before you go, but there's no need to constrain yourself to his limited stock when Holtes City is just a doorway away.

WEAPON SHOP — Bruce's

MELEE WEAPONS	COST	PP	ATT	ACC	ELEMENTS	ATP
DOUBLE SABER	21000	197	178	102	-	150 (DOUBLE BLADE)

RANGED WEAPONS	COST	PP	ATT	ACC	ELEMENTS	ATA
LASER CANNON	21000	357	581	53	-	39 (CANNON)

ITEM SHOP

ITEMS	COST
MONOMATE	30
DIMATE	150
TRIMATE	1000
SOL ATOMIZER	100
MOON ATOMIZER	500
PHOTON CHARGE	1500

MONSTERS CONTINUED

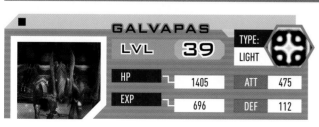

GALVAPAS
LVL **39**
TYPE: LIGHT
HP 1405 | ATT 475
EXP 696 | DEF 112

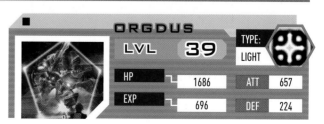

ORGDUS
LVL **39**
TYPE: LIGHT
HP 1686 | ATT 657
EXP 696 | DEF 224

As you might imagine, Dr. Tomrain isn't much of a fighter, but he's pretty smart about fleeing from dangerous situations. And since this isn't a trial, who cares what happens to him anyway?

The usual batch of Relics foes will give way to a few surprises. First is Galvapos, a giant quadriped with a wide variety of attacks. Fortunately you can see its ranged attack coming a mile away (it charges up energy and rears up before using it) so even Technic-users will have plenty of time to dodge after casting Megid Technics. That Technic will be just as useful against the Svaltus-like Orgdus who appear towards the end of Block B-2.

⑨ TRIAL   DESTROY THE DE RAGNUS

The two-headed De Ragnus breathes fire from one mouth and ice from the other. Its sides are heavily armored, so set up camp under its neck or behind its tail, both places where you can deal heavy damage and the De Ragnus has trouble targeting you. To effectively strike its neck, use a Photon Art like Rising Crush or Rising Strike. If you can't hit upwards regularly, stick with the tail, which is harder to hit but usually remains within standard weapons range. Melee weapons are your best choice here, but Rangers can do some damage with a Shotgun and Forces can hit the head effectively with the Gizonde Technic. When the De Ragnus takes to the sky, switch to a gun and blast its head for a bit of extra damage.

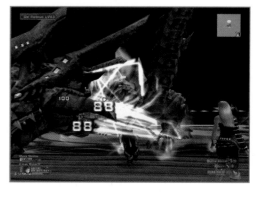

BOSS ELEVEN
DE RAGNUS

Maya Shidow
LV 39

Ethan Waber
LV 41
HP 506/937

To get an S-Rank, use Shifta and Zodial Technics before you enter the room, then go straight for the De Ragnus's neck and unleash a constant stream of Photon Arts. If you can hit it consistently, you can kill it before it takes to the sky. When it moves away from you, approach it from the fire side so you don't risk getting frozen and losing time while you're encased in a block of ice.

DE RAGNUS   ● BOSS

LVL	TYPE:
43	--

HP	EXP
9740	235

ATT	DEF
278	106

TRIAL RANKING

CONDITIONS

1 CLEAR TIME 2:00 VALUE 1000pts
PENALTY -5 points per second late

RANKING INFORMATION

SCORE	RANK	MESETA	MP	PRIZE
1000	S	7500	110	Asami-zashi
700 - 999	A	3000	80	-
400 - 699	B	1500	60	-
0 - 399	C	-	50	-

CHAPTER 9

HOT S.O.S.

CHAPTER OBJECTIVES

☐ Help Lou search for Lou

☐ Prepare for a long journey

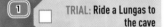

MISSION: SEARCH FOR LOU

① ☐ TRIAL: Ride a Lungas to the cave

② ☐ Battle the Zoona of East Kugu Cave

③ ☐ Raid the Block A-2 treasure room

④ ☐ Slay the beasts of the open desert

⑤ ☐ Reveal Block B-2's secret passage

⑥ ☐ Answer Lou's distress beacon

⑦ ☐ TRIAL: Race to the Landeel

⑧ ☐ TRIAL: Destroy Magas Maggahna

[NEUDAIZ] OHTOKU CITY

PARTNERS

NONE

HELP LOU SEARCH FOR LOU

You begin Chapter 9 on Neudaiz, immediately after the events of Chapter 8. Head home and talk to Pete for an update about recent events, then visit Clyez City's Guardians HQ for a mission briefing. There you'll meet a new Lou, who will join you on a mission to rescue the other Lou. The action takes place in the Kugu Desert, so hop a shuttle to Moatoob and connect with your team there.

PREPARE FOR A LONG JOURNEY

As in Chapter 4, you will not have the option of returning to town between Blocks, so make sure you have all the recovery items, Photon Charges, and weapons you'll need. The shops in Moatoob have plenty of great stuff for Hunters and Forces, but Rangers may want to consider a quick trip to Parum to upgrade their gear. After you finish shopping and add Leo, Lou, and Tonnio to your party, head to the Flyer Base and sign up for the "Search for Lou" mission.

Party

MISSION: SEARCH FOR LOU

The Lou unit captured by the Endrum Collective is emitting a distress signal from within the East Kugu Desert. Take another Lou unit and search the area.

Required
1 Lou
2 Leo
3 Tonnio

NOTE: Cannot return during mission.

LOC   East Kugu Desert   **Party**   4/4

SHOP REPORT

The shop updates in Chapter 9 will surely take a toll on your wallet. The priciest items are the new sets of armor available everywhere, and the costs climb even higher if you purchase the powerful new units available at GRM and Tenora Works. Of special note is GRM's Mega/Stamina unit, the first unit to fit into the rarely used "Extra" slot. It won't be cheap, but with the Rabol Patte armor sold at Tenora Works, you can now equip three units at once!

Tenora Works offers plenty of great weapon upgrades for Hunters, including the Electric-infused Mukrudi Spear, the Soda Caliba Long Sword and the Alseva Drada Twin Blades. Rangers will find better stock at GRM, where they can pick up a Vullseye Rifle or Gatling Machine Gun. They can also add dark and light to their elemental arsenals by picking up Dark and Rising Photon Arts for any ranged weapon. Yohmei hasn't updated their stock much, so Forces will have to settle for the 1-hand Swords, Daggers and Handguns available on Moatoob. Before you spring for a Seva Dreda 1-hand Sword, consider buying [B] Durandal machinery (the GRM equivalent) and making one yourself. You'll probably have to buy several materials for it, but it will be cheaper overall and you can infuse it with any element you like by using such elemental photons as the newly available Gra-photon (light) and Megi-photon (dark).

ARMOR SHOP — GRM

ARMOR	COST	DEF	EVA	SLOTS	ELEMENTS	DFP
STELLALINE	5500	52	85	1	ELECTRIC-10%	7
MEGALINE	18000	70	113	2	-	10
GIGALINE	38000	88	137	2	FIRE-15%	11
CRESLINE	38000	88	137	0	-	17
BUSTERLINE	5000	50	83	1	-	7
ZEETLINE	19000	65	110	2	-	10

[NOTE: 1-2 STAR ITEMS ARE NOT SHOWN, BUT ARE STILL FOR SALE]

UNITS	COST	ATT	ACC
PERPA / POWER	2500	14	0
PERPA / HIT	2000	0	10
MEGA / POWER	13000	20	0
MEGA / STAMINA	15000	0	0

[NOTE: 1 STAR ITEMS ARE NOT SHOWN, BUT ARE STILL FOR SALE]

ARMOR SHOP — Yohmei

ARMOR	COST	DEF	EVA	SLOTS	ELEMENTS	DFP
STA-SENBA	5500	50	87	1	LIGHT-8%	7
ME-SENBA	18000	67	116	2	-	10
GI-SENBA	38000	85	140	2	ICE-16%	11
REIHA-SENBA	5500	48	85	1	-	7

[NOTE: PURPLE TEXT DENOTES THAT THIS IS NEW TO THE SHOP.]

SHOPS CONTINUED ▸

ARMOR SHOP — Tenora Works

ARMOR	COST	DEF	EVA	SLOTS	ELEMENTS	DFP
RABOL STELLA	5000	53	83	1	DARK-10%	7
RABOL MEGA	18000	73	110	2	-	10
RABOL GIGA	38000	91	134	2	GROUND-15%	11
RABOL MIDRA	5500	52	82	1	-	7
RABOL PATTE	38000	89	133	3	-	11

UNITS	COST	DEF	EVA
STELLA / GUARD	2800	18	0
STELLA / LEGS	2800	0	18
MEGA / WALL	17000	+14	+14
MEGA / RAINBOW	17000	+0	+0

WEAPON SHOP — GRM

MELEE WEAPONS	COST	PP	ATT	ACC	ELEMENTS	ATP
BREAKER	3800	172	250	80	GROUND-16%	97 (LONG SWORD)
DOUBLE SABER	21000	197	178	102	-	150 (DOUBLE BLADE)
TWIN BUSTER	3300	180	104	80	-	97 (TWIN BLADES)

RANGED WEAPONS	COST	PP	ATT	ACC	ELEMENTS	ATA
BLASTER	3000	285	266	36	-	26 (RIFLE)
SHOOTER	9000	323	357	58	-	39 (RIFLE)
VULLSEYE	26000	342	444	58	-	51 (RIFLE)
LASER CANNON	21000	357	581	53	-	39 (CANNON)
AUTOGUN	3900	142	98	34	-	26 (HANDGUN)
GREASEGUN	2800	147	22	16	-	26 (MACHINEGUN)
REPEATER	9500	166	30	28	-	39 (MACHINEGUN)
GATLING	27500	176	37	28	-	51 (MACHINEGUN)

[NOTE: 1-2 STAR ITEMS ARE NOT SHOWN, BUT ARE STILL FOR SALE]

WEAPON SHOP — Tenora Works

MELEE WEAPONS	COST	PP	ATT	ACC	ELEMENTS	ATP
SODA BREKKA	3600	172	275	72	-	97 (LONG SWORD)
SODA CALIBA	29000	207	460	95	-	202 (LONG SWORD)
GUDDA BRANA	5500	165	150	77	-	97 (KNUCKLES)
GUDDA WAYA	9500	187	201	98	-	150 (KNUCKLES)
MUKPAT	3500	175	259	72	-	97 (SPEAR)
MUKRUDI	25000	210	432	94	ELEC-22%	202 (SPEAR)
ALSEVA BATA	3800	180	115	72	-	97 (TWIN BLADES)
ALSEVA DRADA	26000	216	192	94	-	202 (TWIN BLADES)
ALDAGA STEG	3750	195	75	72	ELEC-23%	97 (TWIN DAGGERS)
ALDAGA RIPPA	25550	234	125	95	-	202 (TWIN DAGGERS)
SEVA SATA	3200	127	209	75	-	97 (1-HAND BLADE)
SEVA DRADA	24000	153	348	96	-	202 (1-HAND BLADE)
DAGA STEG	3000	135	137	76	ELEC-23%	97 (DAGGER)
DAGA RIPPA	245000	162	229	97	-	202 (DAGGER)

WEAPON SHOP   *Tenora Works*   [CONTINUED]

RANGED WEAPONS	COST	PP	ATT	ACC	ELEMENTS	ATA
SHIGGA WADDA	5700	307	55	19	-	26 (SHOTGUN)
SHIGGA BIGUL	10000	348	74	41	-	39 (SHOTGUN)
ARB OGA	5400	187	120	24	-	26 (TWIN HANDGUN)
ARB BIGA	25500	225	200	46	-	51 (TWIN HANDGUN)
B'DUKI OGA	3800	142	108	24	-	10 (HANDGUN)
B'DUKI BE	24500	171	181	46	-	32 (HANDGUN)
CUBO UPINDE	8800	163	168	43	-	39 (CROSSBOW)

FORCE WEAPONS	COST	PP	TECH	ELEMENTS	TP
W'GANBA	3000	180	209	-	62 (WAND)
W'GACAN	25500	216	348	-	125 (WAND)

DISC SHOPS

[NOTE: G.C. = GUARDIANS COLONY // PAR = PARUM // NEU = NEUDAIZ // MOT = MOATOOB]

DISCS	COST	ATTACHES TO	G.C.	PAR	NEU	MOT
TORNADO BREAK	500	LONG SWORD	X	X	X	X
BOGGA ZUBBA	6000	KNUCKLES	X	X	X	X
DUS DAGGAS	2500	SPEAR	X	X	X	X
TORNADO DANCE	15000	DOUBLE BLADE	-	X	-	-
RISING CRUSH	500	TWIN BLADES	X	X	X	X
RENKAI BUYOU-ZAN	480	TWIN DAGGERS	X	X	X	X
BUKUU RENSEN-GA	14000	TWIN CLAWS	X	X	X	X
RISING STRIKE	350	1-HAND BLADE	X	X	X	X
SHUNBU SHOUREN-ZAN	450	DAGGER	X	X	X	X
SHOUSEN TOTSUZAN-GA	14000	CLAW	X	X	X	X
BURNING SHOT	3000	RIFLE	X	X	X	X
FROZEN SHOT	3000	RIFLE	X	X	X	X
PLASMA SHOT	3000	RIFLE	X	X	X	X
GRAV SHOT	3000	RIFLE	X	X	X	X
RISING SHOT	12000	RIFLE	-	X	-	-
DRAK SHOT	12000	RIFLE	-	X	-	-
BARADA BANGA	4000	SHOTGUN	X	X	X	X
BARADA RIGA	4000	SHOTGUN	X	X	X	X
BARADA INGA	4000	SHOTGUN	X	X	X	X
BARADA DIGA	4000	SHOTGUN	X	X	X	X
BARADA YOGA	12000	SHOTGUN	-	-	-	X
BARADA MEGIGA	12000	SHOTGUN	-	-	-	X
ENSEI-SOU	3000	BOW	X	X	X	X
REISEI-SOU	3000	BOW	X	X	X	X
RAISEI-SOU	3000	BOW	X	X	X	X
JISEI-SOU	3000	BOW	X	X	X	X
YOUSEI-SOU	12000	BOW	-	-	X	-
INSEI-SOU	12000	BOW	-	-	X	-
BURNING PRISM	10000	LASER CANNON	X	X	X	X
FROZEN PRISM	10000	LASER CANNON	X	X	X	X
PLASMA PRISM	10000	LASER CANNON	X	X	X	X
GRAV PRISM	10000	LASER CANNON	X	X	X	X
RISING PRISM	12000	LASER CANNON	-	X	-	-
DARK PRISM	12000	LASER CANNON	-	X	-	-
TWIN BURN	400	TWIN HANDGUN	X	X	X	X
TWIN FREEZE	400	TWIN HANDGUN	X	X	X	X
TWIN PLASM	400	TWIN HANDGUN	X	X	X	X
TWIN GRAV	3000	TWIN HANDGUN	X	X	X	X
TWIN RISING	12000	TWIN HANDGUN	-	-	-	X
TWIN DARK	12000	TWIN HANDGUN	-	-	-	X
BURNING HIT	400	HANDGUN	X	X	X	X
FROZEN HIT	400	HANDGUN	X	X	X	X
PLASMA HIT	400	HANDGUN	X	X	X	X
GRAV HIT	3000	HANDGUN	X	X	X	X
RISING HIT	12000	HANDGUN	-	-	-	X
DARK HIT	12000	HANDGUN	-	-	-	X
YAK BANGA	7000	CROSSBOW	X	X	X	X
YAK RIGA	7000	CROSSBOW	X	X	X	X
YAK INGA	7000	CROSSBOW	X	X	X	X
YAK DIGA	7000	CROSSBOW	X	X	X	X
YAK YOGA	12000	CROSSBOW	-	-	-	X
YAK MEGIGA	12000	CROSSBOW	-	-	-	X
BURNING FURY	3000	MACHINEGUN	X	X	X	X
FROZEN FURY	3000	MACHINEGUN	X	X	X	X
PLASMA FURY	3000	MACHINEGUN	X	X	X	X
GRAV FURY	3000	MACHINEGUN	X	X	X	X
RISING FURY	12000	MACHINEGUN	X	-	-	-
DARK FURY	12000	MACHINEGUN	X	-	-	-

[NOTE: TECHNICS ARE ALSO FOR SALE, BUT NO NEW ADDITIONS APPEAR SINCE THE PREVIOUS CHAPTER]

SHOPS CONTINUED

[NOTE: G.C. = GUARDIANS COLONY // PAR = PARUM // NEU = NEUDAIZ // MOT = MOATOOB]

BOARDS	COST	G.C.	PAR	NEU	MOT
[B] DURANDAL	10000	X	X	-	-
[B] DOUBLE SABER	10000	X	X	-	-
[B] ASSINO-ZASHI	11000	X	-	-	-
[B] MISAKI	3500	X	-	X	-
[B] GUDDA RIBAT	8000	X	-	-	-
[B] MUKRUDI	8000	X	-	-	X
[B] JITSEEN	5000	X	X	-	-
[B] REPEATER	2500	X	X	-	-
[B] VULLSEYE	8000	X	X	-	-
[B] LASER CANNON	5000	X	X	-	-
[B] BAYBARI	8000	X	-	X	-
[B] SHIGGA BIGUL	2500	X	-	-	X
[B] REAL HAND GUN	8000	X	-	-	-
[B] BEAMGUN	5000	X	X	-	-
[B] REAL TWIN H.GUN	10000	X	-	-	-
[B] SLYROD	3000	X	-	X	-
[B] MEGALINE	2500	X	X	-	-
[B] GIGALINE	8000	X	X	-	-
[B] ME-SENBA	2500	X	-	X	-
[B] GI-SENBA	8000	X	-	X	-
[B] RABOL MEGA	2500	X	-	-	X
[B] RABOL GIGA	8000	X	-	-	X
[B] TRIMATE	50	X	X	X	X

CONVERTERS	COST	G.C.	PAR	NEU	MOT
[B] ORE C. 3 > 4	400	X	X	X	X
[B] ORE C.4 > 5	800	X	X	-	-
[B] ORE C. 5 > 6	1200	X	X	-	-
[B] METAL CONV. C > B	100	X	X	X	X
[B] METAL CONV. B > A	1500	X	X	X	X
[B] WOOD CONV. C > B	200	X	X	X	X
[B] WOOD CONV. B >A	1500	X	X	X	X

MATERIALS	COST	G.C.	PAR	NEU	MOT
PHOTON	300	X	X	X	X
EL-PHOTON	800	X	X	X	X
IM-PHOTON	800	X	X	X	X
BAN-PHOTON	500	X	X	X	X
RAY-PHOTON	500	X	X	X	X
ZAN-PHOTON	500	X	X	X	X
DI-PHOTON	500	X	X	X	X
GRA-PHOTON	800	X	-	-	-
MEGI-PHOTON	800	X	-	-	-
CARLIAN	200	X	X	X	X
PEPARIAN	1000	X	X	X	X
MEGANITE	200	X	X	X	X
GIGANITE	1000	X	X	X	X
HARNIUM	200	X	X	X	X
SOLDONIUM	1000	X	X	X	X
GAMOTITE	200	X	X	X	X
ZEPOTITE	1000	X	X	X	X
SOURAL	200	X	X	X	X
SPERAL	1000	X	X	X	X
ACENALINE	100	X	X	X	X
WENCELINE	300	X	X	X	X
APORALINE	900	X	X	X	X
DIANALINE	2500	X	-	-	-
NANOSILICA	200	X	X	X	X
NANOCARBON	1000	X	-	-	-
HOT BERRY	50		X	X	X
COLD BERRY	50		X	X	X
SWEET BERRY	50		X	X	X
BITTER BERRY	50		X	X	X
STAMINA BERRY	50		X	X	X
TRANS ACID	100		X	X	X
METAMOR ACID	400		X	X	X
GRINDER BASE C	100		X	X	X
GRINDER BASE B	1000		X	X	X
PAR WOOD	200	X	-	-	-
PAR ASH	750	X	-	-	-
MOT WOOD	200	-	-	-	X
MOT ASH	750	-	-	-	X
NEU WOOD	200	-	-	X	-
NEU ASH	750	-	-	X	-

[MOATOOB]
EAST HUGU DESERT - PART 1

PARTNERS

NAME	LVL (Ethan's +...)	RACE	CLASS
1. Lou	-2	CAST	Hunter
2. Leogini S. Berafort	+2	Beast	Hunter
3. Tonnio Rhima	+1	Beast	Hunter

OBJECTIVES [1] TO [3]

[1] TRIAL — RIDE A LUNGAS TO THE CAVE

When your flyer crashes, you'll be forced to improvise. Do as Tonnio suggests and catch a Lungas by approaching it and pressing the "confirm" button. You can now ride the Lungas through two blocks of desert, aiming for the cave at the west end of Block A-4. Your Lungas will lose HP as you ride it, but if you torch the trees in the desert you'll find items that will restore 30 HP to your mount. Be vigilant about keeping the HP of your Lungas high; if it hits zero you'll have to walk all the way back to the start of the trial to find another one. To reach your destination without getting turned around, always take the paths that are blocked by brush (which the Lungas can destroy).

MONSTERS

VANDA
LVL	40	TYPE: FIRE
HP	574	ATT 373
EXP	170	DEF 114

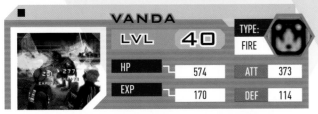

NAVAL
LVL	40	TYPE: GROUND
HP	402	ATT 280
EXP	102	DEF 91

KOG NADD
LVL	45	TYPE: LIGHT
HP	3536	ATT 536
EXP	840	DEF 151

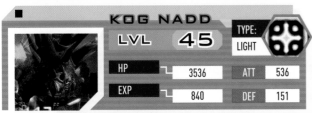

ZOONA
LVL	45	TYPE: FIRE
HP	444	ATT 536
EXP	315	DEF 126

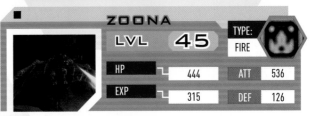

TRIAL RANKING

CONDITIONS

1 CLEAR TIME 6:00 VALUE 700pts
PENALTY -1 point per second late

2 ENEMIES 21 VALUE 300pts
PENALTY -15 points per enemy missed

RANKING INFORMATION

SCORE	RANK	MESETA	MP	PRIZE
1000	S	10000	120	Grinder A+5
700 - 999	A	4000	90	-
400 - 699	B	1500	70	-
0 - 399	C	-	60	-

As you travel you'll encounter small packs of Vanda, who will use claw swipes and Diga Technics to damage both Ethan and the Lungas. If there are only one or two of them you can claim a quick victory by using the Lungas's flame breath, but when you see a larger group you should dismount and battle them on foot. This will keep the Lungas safe (in fact, it will regenerate HP while you're away) and allow you to kill the Vanda more quickly. You'll need to slay all 21 of the Vanda to earn an S-Rank, but all are on the main path and easy to find.

② BATTLE THE ZOONA OF EAST KUGU CAVE

The next segment of your journey will take you through the East Kugu Cave. Here you'll encounter more Vanda (including lords), Ground-type Navals and a few powerful Kog Nadd. The deadliest of the bunch may be the Zoona, winged creatures who resemble Shagreece but attack more and descend into standard weapon range less often. Rangers may need to switch to a first-person view to get a clear shot, but Hunters with a wide array of Photon Arts may have some effective melee options. Photon Arts like Rising Strike, Rising Crush, Bukuu Rensen-ga (for Twin Claws) and Spinning Break (an S-Rank prize from Leo) all have the ability to hit flying targets above you. Forces can fry the Zoona by using Gizonde when they're directly below their target.

③ RAID THE BLOCK A-2 TREASURE ROOM

When you get the #1 Key in the northern section of Block A-2, don't use it right away. Instead proceed south to an apparent dead end, where you'll find the #3 Key behind a rock formation. You won't need it to proceed, but the #3 Key can be used in the southern section of the block to open a gate to six unguarded treasure chests. One often holds the Dual Slasher weapon, an ice-infused Double Blade that will provide a nice damage bonus against the Vanda and Zoona monsters here.

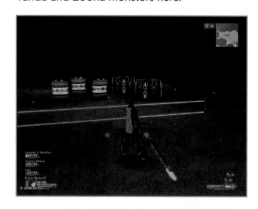 

[MOATOOB]
EAST HUGU DESERT - PART 2

PARTNERS

NAME	LVL (Ethan's +...)	RACE	CLASS
1. Lou	-2	CAST	Hunter
2. Leogini S. Berafort	+2	Beast	Hunter

OBJECTIVES ④ TO ⑥

④ SLAY THE BEASTS OF THE OPEN DESERT

The open desert holds plenty of challenges, beginning with an Endrum ambush as soon as the Vol Brothers event ends. Charge at the trio of Special Ops agents and incapacitate them with quick melee weapon attacks. When those three die you'll be left with only the native fauna, but they're not any easier; you'll face higher-level Vanda and sand-burrowing Bul Buna that behave similarly to the Goshin of past missions.

MONSTERS

VANDA

LVL	41	TYPE: FIRE
HP	586	ATT 380
EXP	178	DEF 116

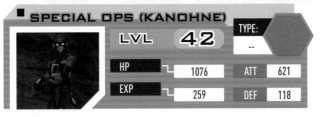

SPECIAL OPS (KANOHNE)

LVL	42	TYPE: --
HP	1076	ATT 621
EXP	259	DEF 118

BIL DE VEAR

LVL	41	TYPE: GROUND
HP	2344	ATT 570
EXP	712	DEF 162

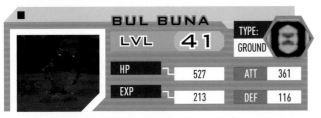

BUL BUNA

LVL	41	TYPE: GROUND
HP	527	ATT 361
EXP	213	DEF 116

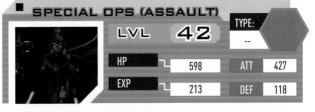

SPECIAL OPS (ASSAULT)

LVL	42	TYPE: --
HP	598	ATT 427
EXP	213	DEF 118

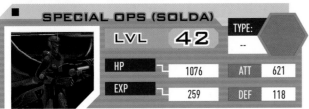

SPECIAL OPS (SOLDA)

LVL	42	TYPE: --
HP	1076	ATT 621
EXP	259	DEF 118

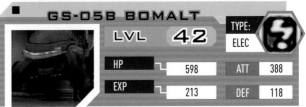

GS-05B BOMALT

LVL	42	TYPE: ELEC
HP	598	ATT 388
EXP	213	DEF 118

GETTING STARTED

STORY MODE

FREE MISSIONS

NETWORK MODE

At the top of the food chain sits the Bil de Vear, a mighty biped with a stunning array of attacks. Shooting it with ranged weapons will just leave you at the receiving end of a leaping dive or high-speed tackle, so stay close and try to circle around the Bil de Vear to strike at its back or left side with Photon Arts. Like most bipedal enemies, the Bil de Vear is a righty and can't do much with its left arm.

5 REVEAL BLOCK B-2'S SECRET PASSAGE

Defeating the enemies in the first room of Block B-2 will reveal a key that opens the door to the east. There you'll find the key to the north gate of the first room, as well as a suspicious incongruity between the auto-map and the actual terrain. Dust off your goggles and point them between the trees in the northeast corner of the room to reveal a weak point that you can attack with any weapon. Knocking the boulder aside will reveal a vast, unguarded area with a few containers.

6 ANSWER LOU'S DISTRESS BEACON

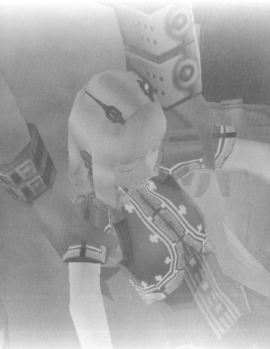

You'll find the missing Lou at the end of Block B, but will still have to battle through another block to reach Tonnio and Liina. Block C is a short one, consisting of only a single map of two enemy-filled rooms, but instead of the usual desert creatures you'll face the tougher GSM bots and Special Ops units you faced in Chapter 8's underground plant. Eliminate the soldiers quickly, then back away from the GSM-05b Bomalta units and blast them with Technics. A Photon Charger is just ahead, so don't worry about conserving PP.

[MOATOOB]
EAST HUGU DESERT - PART 3

PARTNERS

NAME	LVL (Ethan's +...)	RACE	CLASS
1. Lou	-2	CAST	Hunter
2. Tonnio Rhima	+1	Beast	Hunter
3. Liina Sukaya	+1	Beast	Hunter

OBJECTIVES 7 TO 8

(7) TRIAL — RACE TO THE LANDEEL

Despite Lou's insistence that you get to the Landeel as quickly as possible, you'll still need to take out every single enemy in two blocks to earn an S-Rank. You'll also have to ensure the safety of Lou, which is a little tougher than it has been in past escort missions, since she's a frontline fighter and does not shrink from combat. The biggest potential threat are the Vanda, who can take her from full health to near death with a long blast of fire breath. Photon Arts like Rising Crush and Tornado Break that let you wade into the midst of a pack of Vanda and damage them all are the best way to prevent flame attacks while quickly eradicating the Vanda. Technics work too, but you'll need to wade into the fray if you want to get Tonnio and Liina into the action.

MONSTERS

Each Block has a teleporter, and while the first one is pointless (it will only send you to a different part of the map, forcing you to backtrack to kill the enemies you missed), using the teleporter in Block 2 is a necessary step towards earning an S-Rank. You'll find the teleporter to the right in the luminescent cave beyond the first locked door, but do not enter it until you have cleared both that room and the next one of enemies. Otherwise, after killing a few enemies on a small island, you'll be warped beyond the second locked door and you will never have a chance to kill those foes.

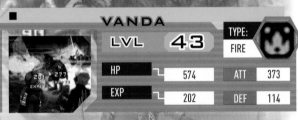

VANDA — LVL 43 — TYPE: FIRE
| HP | 574 | ATT | 373 |
| EXP | 202 | DEF | 114 |

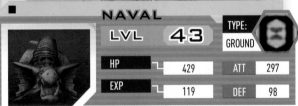

NAVAL — LVL 43 — TYPE: GROUND
| HP | 429 | ATT | 297 |
| EXP | 119 | DEF | 98 |

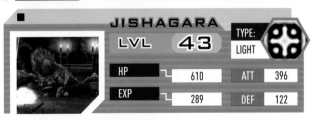

JISHAGARA — LVL 43 — TYPE: LIGHT
| HP | 610 | ATT | 396 |
| EXP | 289 | DEF | 122 |

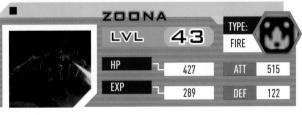

ZOONA — LVL 43 — TYPE: FIRE
| HP | 427 | ATT | 515 |
| EXP | 289 | DEF | 122 |

TRIAL RANKING

CONDITIONS

1 CLEAR TIME 9:00 VALUE 600pts
PENALTY -1 point per second late

2 ENEMIES 76 VALUE 300pts
PENALTY -5 points per enemy missed

3 LOU FAINTS 0 VALUE 100pts
PENALTY -100 points per time
Lou faints

RANKING INFORMATION

SCORE	RANK	MESETA	MP	PRIZE
1000	S	10000	120	Vullseye
700 - 999	A	4000	90	-
400 - 699	B	1500	70	-
0 - 399	C	-	60	-

⑧ TRIAL — DESTROY MAGAS MAGGAHNA

Magas is very similar to the Adahna Degahna boss you fought in Chapter 7, but a few key differences make this a much tougher fight. There isn't an exploitable safe point behind it, and you can no longer prevent its teleportation by dealing constant damage. The Magas Maggahna has weak points at its base, arms, and chest. The base is by far the easiest target to hit, but if you damage it too much it will break away, and you'll have to finish off the boss by picking another target (the arms, for instance, which are also pretty easy to handle).

S-Rank seekers will once again want to use the Shifta-enhanced Tornado Dance Photon Art as their primary mode of attack. The trick is to attack the arms whenever you have an opportunity; if you focus your hits on the base you'll end up destroying it prematurely and will then have to waste a great deal of time chasing Magas and waiting for it to lower its arms. One arm is usually prone while the other attacks, so strike at the vulnerable arm whenever you can and only switch to the base when both arms are out of range. This is a tough one, but worth it—the Tero / HP Restore S-Rank prize will make the rest of the game a whole lot easier.

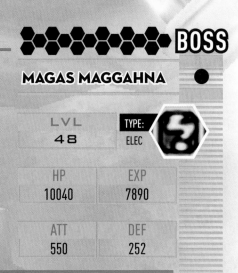

■■■■■■■ **BOSS**

MAGAS MAGGAHNA ●

LVL	TYPE:
48	ELEC

HP	EXP
10040	7890

ATT	DEF
550	252

BOSS TWELVE
MAGAS MAGGAHNA

TRIAL RANKING

RANKING INFORMATION

CLEAR TIME **2:00** VALUE **1000**pts
PENALTY **-5** points per second late

SCORE	RANK	MESETA	MP	PRIZE
1000	S	10000	120	Tero / HP Restore
700 - 999	A	4000	90	-
400 - 699	B	1500	70	-
0 - 399	C	-	60	-

GETTING STARTED

STORY MODE

FREE MISSIONS

NETWORK MODE

RITE OF DIVINATION

MISSION: DIVINATION ESCORT

[MOATOOB] DAGORA CITY

PARTNERS

NONE

SPEAK WITH THE GUARDIANS PRESIDENT

This mission begins at the Moatoob Guardians HQ, where your team from Chapter 9 will be debriefed and dispersed. Return home to check in with Pete, then pay a visit to Guardians HQ. The President himself will brief you on your new assignment: visit the Communion temple on Neudaiz and convince the Maiden to help you locate the Neudaiz confinement system.

SECURE THE SUPPORT OF THE COMMUNION

You'll find the Communion headquarters next door to the PPT Spaceport, in the large building with the strange pink arc around the door. The Communion leader won't cooperate, but the Maiden will, so the mission is on! You'll meet half your team at the destination site, so all you need to do is add Lou to your party and head to to the Ohtoku City Flyer Base.

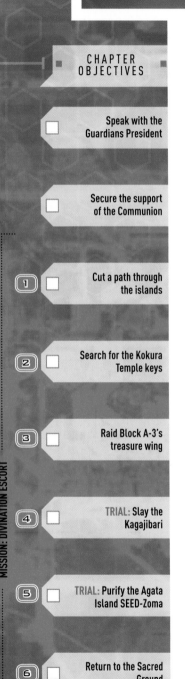

MISSION: DIVINATION ESCORT

In order to locate the confinement system, Karen will attempt a divination on the Sacred Grounds. Protect her during this time.

Required	1 Lou 1

LOC	Agata Islands	Party	2/2

SHOP REPORT

You'll find several strange new units like Giga / Skill PP Save on store shelves, but many have drawbacks that outweigh their benefits. Consider carefully before you drop 25K on an item that may do more harm than good. One unit you won't regret buying is the HP-regenerating Safety Heart, although anyone who won a Tero / HP Restore unit from Chapter 9's boss won't need it.

Your Meseta would be better spent on weapons, as you can now buy a five-star version of any weapon you desire. GRM's Maser Cannon and Yohmei's Go-Misaki Claw are huge upgrades over their last iterations, and many of the new weapons have strong ice, fire, or dark photons.

Forces may have a hard time deciding between a new Rod and the powerful Megid-series Technics that are now sold in Neudaiz. A good Rod filled with conventional fire and ice Technics will be much more useful than dark Technics in this chapter, but it's hard to say no to that HP-draining Megiverse Technic...

[NOTE: PURPLE TEXT DENOTES THAT THIS IS NEW TO THE SHOP.]

ARMOR SHOP — GRM

ARMOR	COST	DEF	EVA	SLOTS	ELEMENTS	DFP
MEGALINE	18000	70	113	2	-	10
GIGALINE	38000	88	137	2	FIRE-15%	11
CRESLINE	38000	88	137	0	-	17
ZEETLINE	19000	65	110	2	-	10

UNITS	COST	ATT	ACC
MEGA / POWER	13000	20	0
GIGA / SKILL PP SAVE	25000	-200	-100
GIGA / BULLET PP SAVE	25000	-200	-100
MEGA / STAMINA	15000	0	0
SAFETY HEART	38000	0	0

[NOTE: 1-3 STAR ITEMS ARE NOT SHOWN, BUT ARE STILL FOR SALE]

ARMOR SHOP — Yohmei

ARMOR	COST	DEF	EVA	SLOTS	ELEMENTS	DFP
ME-SENBA	18000	67	116	2	-	10
GI-SENBA	38000	85	140	2	ICE-16%	11

UNITS	COST	TECH	MENT
ME / QUICK	8000	-14	0
GI / SMART	25000	0	0
GI / MAGIC	25000	28	12
ELECTRO HEART	23000	0	0

[NOTE: 1-3 STAR ITEMS ARE NOT SHOWN, BUT ARE STILL FOR SALE]

SHOPS CONTINUED ••••••••••••••••••▶

WEAPON SHOP — GRM

MELEE WEAPONS	COST	PP	ATT	ACC	ELEMENTS	ATP
CALIBUR	30000	207	418	102	ICE-21%	202 (LONG SWORD)
DOUBLE SABER	21000	197	178	102	-	150 (DOUBLE BLADE)
BONE DANCE	27000	208	222	102	-	202 (DOUBLE BLADE)
DUAL SLASHER	27000	216	174	102	ICE-21%	202 (TWIN BLADES)
DURANDAL	27000	153	317	105	ICE-21%	202 (1-HAND SWORD)

RANGED WEAPONS	COST	PP	ATT	ACC	ELEMENTS	ATA
SHOOTER	9000	323	357	58	-	39 (RIFLE)
VULLSEYE	26000	342	444	58	-	51 (RIFLE)
LASER CANNON	21000	357	581	53	-	39 (CANNON)
MASER CANNON	27000	378	723	53	-	51 (CANNON)
REPEATER	9500	166	30	28	-	39 (MACHINEGUN)
GATLING	27500	176	37	28	-	51 (MACHINEGUN)

[NOTE: 1-3 STAR ITEMS ARE NOT SHOWN, BUT ARE STILL FOR SALE]

WEAPON SHOP — Yohmei

MELEE WEAPONS	COST	PP	ATT	ACC	ELEMENTS	ATP
CLAYMAUD	11000	215	302	96	-	150 (LONG SWORD)
PARZANATA	10000	218	284	96	-	150 (SPEAR)
HALBENATA	26000	231	353	96	FIRE-25%	202 (SPEAR)
RYO-PALASRA	10000	224	126	96	-	150 (TWIN BLADES)
RYO-SAGAZASHI	9500	243	82	96	FIRE-25%	150 (TWIN DAGGERS)
ASSINO-ZASHI	25000	257	102	96	-	202 (TWIN DAGGERS)
RYO-MISAKI	11500	233	156	96	-	150 (TWIN CLAWS)
MIJIN-MISAKI	30000	247	193	96	DARK-22%	202 (TWIN CLAWS)
PALASRA	9000	158	229	97	-	150 (1-HAND BLADE)
SAKANO-ZASHI	8800	168	151	98	-	150 (DAGGER)
RIPA-ZASHI	25000	178	188	98	FIRE-25%	202 (DAGGER)
MISAKI	9000	162	266	96	-	150 (CLAW)
GA-MISAKI	27000	210	462	96	DARK-22%	202 (CLAW)

RANGED WEAPONS	COST	PP	ATT	ACC	ELEMENTS	ATA
RIKALBARI	9000	387	413	46	-	39 (BOW)
BAYBARI	25000	409	513	46	-	51 (BOW)
RYO-LOUKTORE	9800	233	132	48	-	39 (TWIN HANDGUN)
RYO-BETATORE	25000	247	164	48	-	39 (TWIN HANDGUN)
LOUKTORE	8500	177	119	48	-	39 (HANDGUN)
BETATORE	25000	188	148	48	-	51 (HANDGUN)

FORCE WEAPONS	COST	PP	TECH	ELEMENTS	TP
SLYROD	11000	411	266	-	92 (ROD)
HAJIROD	31000	435	331	-	125 (ROD)
SEPTARA	9500	224	229	-	92 (WAND)
CANARA	27000	237	285	-	125 (WAND)

[NOTE: 1-3 STAR ITEMS ARE NOT SHOWN, BUT ARE STILL FOR SALE]

WEAPON SHOP   *Tenora Works*

MELEE WEAPONS	COST	PP	ATT	ACC	ELEMENTS	ATP
SODA CALIBA	29000	207	460	95	-	202 (LONG SWORD)
GUDDA WAYA	9500	187	201	98	-	150 (KNUCKLES)
GUDDA RIBAT	26000	198	250	98	ELEC-22%	202 (KNUCKLES)
MUKRUDI	25000	210	432	94	-	202 (SPEAR)
ALSEVA DRADA	26000	216	192	94	-	202 (TWIN BLADES)
ALDAGA RIPPA	25550	234	125	94	-	202 (TWIN DAGGERS)
SEVA DRADA	24000	153	348	96	-	202 (1-HAND BLADE)
DAGA RIPPA	24500	162	229	97	-	202 (DAGGER)

RANGED WEAPONS	COST	PP	ATT	ACC	ELEMENTS	ATA
SHIGGA BIGUL	10000	348	74	41	-	39 (SHOTGUN)
SHIGGA AMZA	27000	369	91	41	-	51 (SHOTGUN)
ARB BIGA	25500	225	200	46	-	51 (TWIN HANDGUN)
B'DUKI BE	24500	171	181	46	-	32 (HANDGUN)
CUBO UPINDE	8800	163	168	43	-	39 (CROSSBOW)
CUBO DUNGA	25000	172	209	43	-	39 (CROSSBOW)

FORCE WEAPONS	COST	PP	TECH	ELEMENTS	TP
W'GACAN	25500	216	348	-	125 (WAND)

DISC SHOPS

[NOTE: PHOTON ARTS ARE ALSO FOR SALE, BUT NO NEW ADDITIONS APPEAR SINCE THE PREVIOUS CHAPTER]
[NOTE: G.C. = GUARDIANS COLONY // PAR = PARUM // NEU = NEUDAIZ // MOT = MOATOOB]

DISCS	COST	ATTACHES TO	G.C.	PAR	NEU	MOT	DISCS	COST	ATTACHES TO	G.C.	PAR	NEU	MOT
FOIE	1000	WAND / STAFF	X	X	X	X	DIGA	450	WAND / STAFF	X	X	X	X
RAFOIE	3500	WAND / STAFF	X	X	X	X	RADIGA	3500	WAND / STAFF	X	X	X	X
DAMFOIE	4500	WAND / STAFF	X	X	X	X	DAMDIGA	4500	WAND / STAFF	X	X	X	X
GIFOIE	8000	WAND / STAFF	X	X	X	X	GIDIGA	8000	WAND / STAFF	X	X	X	X
SHIFTA	2500	WAND / STAFF	X	X	X	X	NOSDIGA	4500	WAND / STAFF	X	X	X	X
JELLEN	3500	WAND / STAFF	X	X	X	X	DIZAS	35000	WAND / STAFF	-	-	X	-
BARTA	1000	WAND / STAFF	X	X	X	X	RESTA	1000	WAND / STAFF	X	X	X	X
RABARTA	3500	WAND / STAFF	X	X	X	X	GIRESTA	9800	WAND / STAFF	X	X	X	X
DAMBARTA	4500	WAND / STAFF	X	X	X	X	REVERSER	3000	WAND / STAFF	X	X	X	X
GIBARTA	8000	WAND / STAFF	X	X	X	X	REGRANT	14000	WAND / STAFF	X	X	X	X
DEBAND	2500	WAND / STAFF	X	X	X	X	RENTIS	35000	WAND / STAFF	-	-	X	-
ZALURE	1500	WAND / STAFF	X	X	X	X	RETIER	4000	WAND / STAFF	X	X	X	X
ZONDE	1000	WAND / STAFF	X	X	X	X	MEGID	450	WAND / STAFF	X	X	X	X
RAZONDE	3500	WAND / STAFF	X	X	X	X	RAMEGID	3500	WAND / STAFF	X	X	X	X
GIZONDE	8000	WAND / STAFF	X	X	X	X	DAMMEGID	4500	WAND / STAFF	X	X	X	X
NOSZANDE	4500	WAND / STAFF	X	X	X	X	NOSMEGID	8000	WAND / STAFF	X	X	X	X
ZODIAL	4000	WAND / STAFF	X	X	X	X	MEGIVERSE	35000	WAND / STAFF	-	-	X	-
ZOLDEEL	1500	WAND / STAFF	X	X	X	X	MEGISTAR	35000	WAND / STAFF	-	-	X	-

SYNTHESIS SHOPS

[NOTE: 1-4 STAR ITEMS ARE NOT SHOWN, BUT ARE STILL FOR SALE]
[NOTE: G.C. = GUARDIANS COLONY // PAR = PARUM // NEU = NEUDAIZ // MOT = MOATOOB]

BOARDS	COST	G.C.	PAR	NEU	MOT	BOARDS	COST	G.C.	PAR	NEU	MOT
[B] DURANDAL	10000	X	X	-	-	[B] GIGALINE	8000	X	X	-	-
[B] ASSINO-ZASHI	11000	X	-	-	-	[B] TERALINE	12000	X	X	-	-
[B] GUDDA RIBAT	8000	X	-	-	-	[B] GI-SENBA	8000	X	-	X	-
[B] MUKRUDI	8000	X	-	-	X	[B] TE-SENBA	12000	X	-	X	-
[B] VULCAN	11000	X	X	-	-	[B] RABOL GIGA	8000	X	-	-	X
[B] VULLSEYE	8000	X	X	-	-	[B] RABOL TERO	12000	X	-	-	X
[B] BAYBARI	8000	X	-	X	-	[B] TRIMATE	50	X	X	X	X
[B] SHIGGA STAM	11000	X	-	-	X						

PARTNERS

NAME	LVL (Ethan's +...)	RACE	CLASS
1. Lou	-2	CAST	Hunter
2. Kanal Tomrain	-3	Human	Civilian
3. Karen Erra	+3	Newman	Hunter

OBJECTIVES ① TO ④

① CUT A PATH THROUGH THE ISLANDS

There's no need to travel covertly this time, so the flyer will take you directly to Agata Island. There you'll meet your team of Kanal and Karen, and the four of you will have to battle through three straightforward blocks. The foes are all species you've fought before, but with a few enhancements. The Ollaka and Ageeta now have Lords in their midst that can deal more damage, but they're still not capable of putting up much opposition. The bigger threat is the Olgohmon who have a wider, faster and far deadlier version of Barta than the standard Gohmon. Even Rangers will have trouble dodging the rivers of ice, so characters of all classes should draw a 1-hand Sword and take the battle to them at close range. Save your Wand or Rod PP for the Kamatoze, who are much more vulnerible to Technics.

MONSTERS

AGEETA

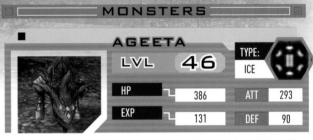

LVL	46	TYPE: ICE
HP	386	ATT 293
EXP	131	DEF 90

OLGOHMON

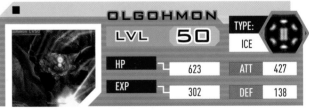

LVL	50	TYPE: ICE
HP	623	ATT 427
EXP	302	DEF 138

KAMATOZE

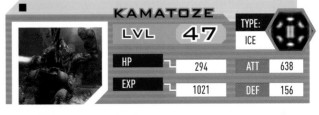

LVL	47	TYPE: ICE
HP	294	ATT 638
EXP	1021	DEF 156

2   SEARCH FOR THE KOKURA TEMPLE KEYS

The Kokura Temple has fallen into the icy clutches of the SEED. You won't have to deal with any SEED-Zoma yet, but you will have to fight through the Ologhmon, Ageeta and ice-variant Ollaka that have made a home here. You'll also have to contend with some very unconventional block layouts. In Block A-2, head north from the entrance to a central hallway that has teleporters at two or three ends. Take them in either order, since both lead to the #1 keys that open the east door back in the first room of the map.

3   RAID BLOCK A-3'S TREASURE WING

Most of the action in Block A-3 takes place in a three-room wing in the northwest corner of the map. After you claim the second key in the room on the right, head upstairs and run along the catwalk to the west. There you'll find a container that often contains a Vulcan Machine Gun. If you won the Rising Fury Photon Art in an earlier map, link it up now, since it will prove to be a useful weapon against the new dark-type Dilnazen foes that prowl this block. When using ranged tactics, move perpendicular to the Dilnazen so it won't be able to tackle you. At close range, use Rising Strike (at level 11 or higher) to leap above its counterattacks as you damage it.

MONSTERS CONTINUED

OLLAKA

LVL	46	TYPE: ICE
HP	644	ATT	418
EXP	219	DEF	128

DILNAZEN

LVL	48	TYPE: DARK
HP	2672	ATT	651
EXP	980	DEF	185

DILNAZEN

LVL	49	TYPE: DARK
HP	2720	ATT	663
EXP	1016	DEF	190

OLLAKA

LVL	48	TYPE: ICE
HP	668	ATT	434
EXP	236	DEF	122

When you finally reach the Sacred Ground, you'll find a mysterious creature waiting. You'll battle with only Karen by your side, but protecting her is not one of the battle's objectives. For the easiest victory, back away from Kagajibari and blast it with long-range weapons and Technics, ideally Megid. You need to stand farther away than you usually would so you can avoid its own Technics, including the life-draining Megiverse. (The Kagajibari will retaliate with Technics of the same type you use against it.) Fortunately aiming shouldn't be a problem, since it will either walk slowly towards you or tussle with Karen. Hunters without effective long-range options should barrel into the Kagajibari with Tornado Dance. You'll take a few hits, but using conventional hit-and-run tactics to avoid damage will make it difficult to win the trial in under two minutes.

BOSS THIRTEEN
KAGAJIBARI

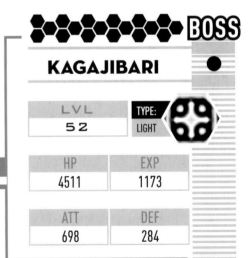

BOSS

KAGAJIBARI

LVL	TYPE:
52	LIGHT

HP	EXP
4511	1173

ATT	DEF
698	284

TRIAL RANKING

CLEAR TIME 2:00 VALUE 1000pts
PENALTY -5 points per second late

RANKING INFORMATION

SCORE	RANK	MESETA	MP	PRIZE
1000	S	10000	130	Gudda Breba
700 - 999	A	4000	100	-
400 - 699	B	1500	80	-
0 - 399	C	-	70	-

④

[NEUDAIZ]
AGITA ISLAND BLOCKS B-D

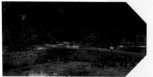

PARTNERS

	NAME	LVL (Ethan's +...)	RACE	CLASS
1.	Lou	-2	CAST	Hunter

OBJECTIVES 5 TO 7

5 TRIAL — PURIFY THE AGATA ISLAND SEED-ZOMA

The SEED have landed in Agata Island, and as the color of the horizon suggests, you'll be facing the fire Zoma, not the ice kind. Save your game and prep your action palette with the Goggles and the Photon Eraser, as well as a Wand full of ice Technics and as many ice-infused weapons as you can dig up. You'll be facing hordes of fire-breathing Gohmon here, so you'll want to either be a quick-firing Ranger with ice-type bullets or a Hunter with a good Photon Art on an ice weapon like the Dual Slasher. Forces who hope to score an S-Rank may need to return to HQ for a class change (the door to Ohtoku City is right across from the Save Marker).

MONSTERS

AGEETA

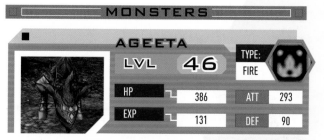

LVL	46	TYPE: FIRE
HP	386	ATT	293
EXP	131	DEF	90

GOHMON

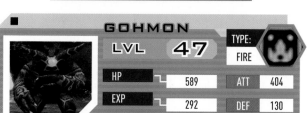

LVL	47	TYPE: FIRE
HP	589	ATT	404
EXP	292	DEF	130

SEED-VITACE

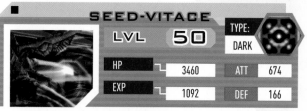

LVL	50	TYPE: DARK
HP	3460	ATT	674
EXP	1092	DEF	166

KAGAJIBARA

LVL	49	TYPE: LIGHT
HP	4284	ATT	663
EXP	1053	DEF	272

YG01U BUGGES

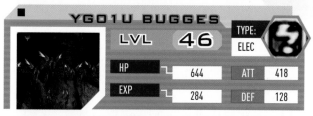

LVL	46	TYPE: ELEC
HP	644	ATT	418
EXP	284	DEF	128

GSM-05M TIRENTOS

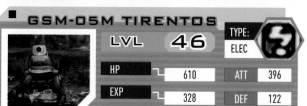

LVL	46	TYPE: ELEC
HP	610	ATT	396
EXP	328	DEF	122

GRINNA BETE C

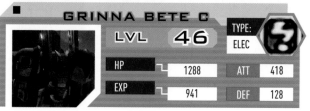

LVL	46	TYPE: ELEC
HP	1288	ATT	418
EXP	941	DEF	128

GETTING STARTED

STORY MODE

FREE MISSIONS

NETWORK MODE

This trial won't try to trick you the way purification Free Missions do—it will merely try to overwhelm you with difficult foes. All of the monsters and SEED-Zoma will be directly on your path, so there's no need to waste time shooting chests to trigger monster waves or hunting for out-of-the-way nooks. As in the first SEED purification trial, you can save a bit of time by identifying the blewmes first and then hoping your partner will purify them while you battle attackers.

The enemies here include both high-level SEED-Vitace and Kagajibara enemies, usually backed-up by Gohmon and Ageeta. Wipe out the weaker foes with Photon Arts like Rising Strike that will keep you moving (so you can't be targeted easily by ranged attacks), then switch to Tornado Dance and home in on the big guys. You'll take some hard hits, so keep Dimate and Sol Atomizers at the ready; you'll earn plenty more recovery items by killing the SEED-Zoma.

TRIAL RANKING

CONDITIONS	RANKING INFORMATION					
		SCORE	RANK	MESETA	MP	PRIZE
1 CLEAR TIME 16:00 VALUE 700pts PENALTY -1 point per second late		1000	S	10000	130	Grinder S+4
		700 - 999	A	4000	100	-
2 ENEMIES 57 VALUE 300pts		400 - 699	B	1500	80	-
PENALTY -5 points per enemy missed		0 - 399	C	-	70	-

⑤

⑥ ◢ **RETURN TO SACRED GROUND**

At the end of the trial you'll find yourself in Block C-1, where you'll enjoy a respite provided by a Heal Spot, a Save Marker, and Bruce's shop. There isn't a Photon Charger, but Photon Charge items are quite plentiful in the chests of this area. You can also buy them from Bruce, who has augmented his supply of healing items with every new weapon that appeared on store shelves this chapter. With a boss ahead, now might be a good time to upgrade that Double Saber to a Bone Dance.

Block C-1 forks in two directions. The path to the left will take you back to the Sacred Ground, where you can challenge this mission's boss. The path to the right leads to Block D-1, a dead end that's full of enemies. If you want to farm for Meseta or Exp. Points before the boss fight, that's the direction to travel.

Both paths are packed with new enemies. Slay the YG01U BUGGES quickly, before they can suck the life out of Ethan and Lou with their Megiverse Technics. Keep moving as you battle the GSM units and Grinna Bete C so they can't get a bead on you with their ranged weapons; neither is much of a threat once you get within melee range.

⑦ TRIAL   SAVE KAREN FROM THE SEED-MAGASHI

The SEED-Magashi is maddeningly spry, teleporting away in the midst of your Photon Arts and skillfully side-stepping your attacks. Be ever ready to turn and run if you're battling at mid-range with Technics, as the Magashi will promptly tackle distant foes. Rangers will have more time to see the tackle coming and dodge it, and can potentially do more damage if they have a good weapon with a "rising" (light-type) Photon Art.

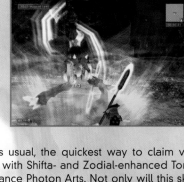

BOSS FOURTEEN
SEED-MAGASHI

As usual, the quickest way to claim victory is with Shifta- and Zodial-enhanced Tornado Dance Photon Arts. Not only will this skill do lots of damage quickly, but the combo will often end by knocking the Magashi onto his back. Hit him once or twice while he's down, but back away without hanging around too long, or he'll nail you with a spin kick every time. That Shifta/Zodial Wand is a good thing to keep handy, because some of the Magashi's attacks can cause penalties to your attack and defense scores. But Shifta will turn that red arrow right-side up and allow you to deal as much damage as possible whenever you connect with a combo.

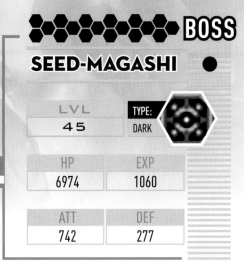

⬡⬡⬡⬡⬡⬡ BOSS

SEED-MAGASHI ⬤

LVL	TYPE:
45	DARK

HP	EXP
6974	1060

ATT	DEF
742	277

TRIAL RANKING

⑦

CLEAR TIME 2:00 VALUE 1000pts
PENALTY -5 points per second late

RANKING INFORMATION

SCORE	RANK	MESETA	MP	PRIZE
1000	S	10000	120	Te / PP Generate
700 - 999	A	4000	90	-
400 - 699	B	1500	70	-
0 - 399	C	-	60	-

GETTING STARTED   STORY MODE   FREE MISSIONS   NETWORK MODE

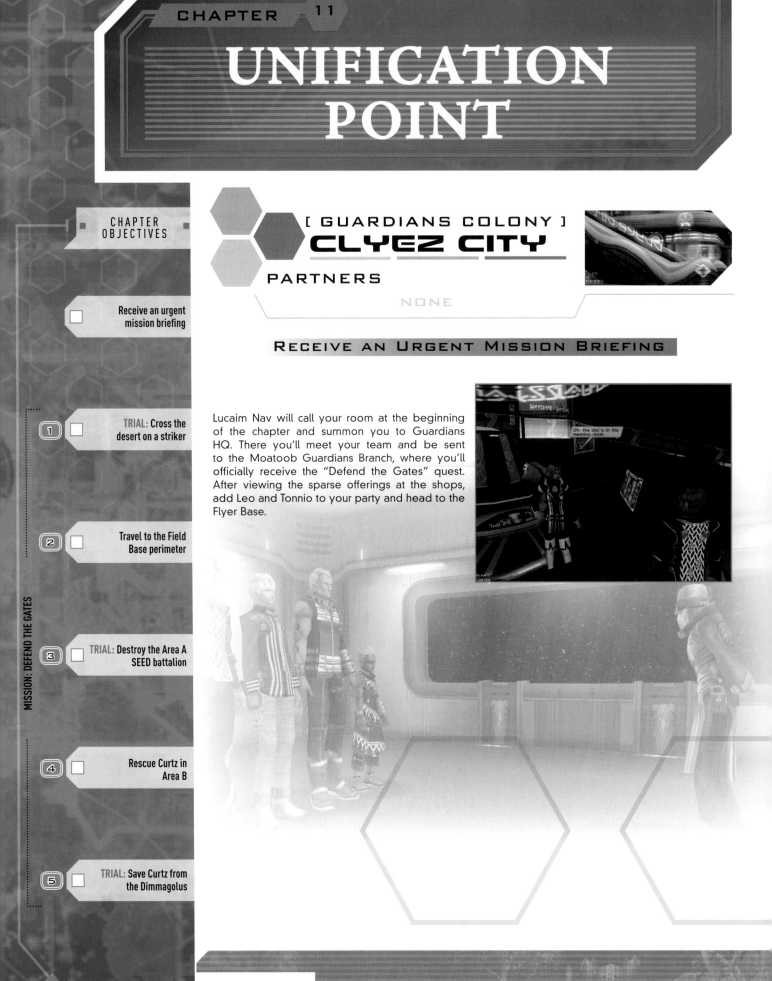

CHAPTER 11

UNIFICATION POINT

CHAPTER
OBJECTIVES

☐ Receive an urgent
mission briefing

MISSION: DEFEND THE GATES

1 ☐ TRIAL: Cross the
desert on a striker

2 ☐ Travel to the Field
Base perimeter

3 ☐ TRIAL: Destroy the Area A
SEED battalion

4 ☐ Rescue Curtz in
Area B

5 ☐ TRIAL: Save Curtz from
the Dimmagolus

[GUARDIANS COLONY]
CLYEZ CITY
PARTNERS

NONE

RECEIVE AN URGENT MISSION BRIEFING

Lucaim Nav will call your room at the beginning of the chapter and summon you to Guardians HQ. There you'll meet your team and be sent to the Moatoob Guardians Branch, where you'll officially receive the "Defend the Gates" quest. After viewing the sparse offerings at the shops, add Leo and Tonnio to your party and head to the Flyer Base.

MISSION: DEFEND THE GATES

Ensure success for the unification point by defending the Confinement System.

Required 1 Leo   2 Tonnio

LOC West Kugu Desert

Party 3/3

Only Rangers will really get excited about this chapter's Shop update. They can pick up a Falcon Rifle, Hikauri Bow, and Shigga Stam Shotgun if they don't mind taking an interplanetary shopping tour. Since you can't fight every battle at long range, a Mukarad Spears may come in handy as well. Hunters should consider the Spears and Gudda Greta Knuckles, but may want to spend their Meseta at the Armor and Synthesis Shops instead. You'll face plenty of dark-type monsters in the future, so Tenora Works' Rabol Tero is by far the best of the new Line Shields.

At the Synthesis Shop, Hunters can buy a [B] Ascalon board and any missing ingredients, and use them to synthesize a powerful new Long Sword. (If you don't have two Upteline you can buy a new Ore Convertor 5 > 6 and make it out of Marseline.) The board allows you to insert a photon of your choice in the photon slot, and using Ban-photons to make a flaming Ascalon will give S-Rank-seeking Hunters a huge boost later in this chapter.

SHOP REPORT

[NOTE: PURPLE TEXT DENOTES THAT THIS IS NEW TO THE SHOP.]

ARMOR SHOP — GRM

ARMOR	COST	DEF	EVA	SLOTS	ELEMENTS	DFP
MEGALINE	18000	70	113	2	-	10
GIGALINE	38000	88	137	2	FIRE-15%	11
TEROLINE	45000	106	159	2	ELECTRIC-15%	13
CRESLINE	38000	88	137	0	-	17
ZEETLINE	19000	65	110	2	-	10

UNITS	COST	ATT	ACC
MEGA / POWER	13000	20	0
GIGA / SKILL PP SAVE	25000	-200	-100
GIGA / BULLET PP SAVE	25000	-200	-100
MEGA / STAMINA	15000	0	0
SAFETY HEART	380000	0	0

[NOTE: 1-3 STAR ITEMS ARE NOT SHOWN, BUT ARE STILL FOR SALE]

ARMOR SHOP — Yohmei

ARMOR	COST	DEF	EVA	SLOTS	ELEMENTS	DFP
ME-SENBA	18000	70	113	2	-	10
GI-SENBA	38000	88	137	2	FIRE-15%	11
TE-SENBA	45000	103	153	2	LIGHT-18%	13

UNITS	COST	TECH	MENT
ME / QUICK	8000	-14	0
GI / SMART	25000	0	0
GI / MAGIC	25000	28	12
ELECTRO HEART	23000	0	0

[NOTE: 1-3 STAR ITEMS ARE NOT SHOWN, BUT ARE STILL FOR SALE]

SHOPS CONTINUED ••••••••••••••••••▶

BASIC TRAINING   STORY MODE   NETWORK MODE   FREE MISSIONS

ARMOR SHOP — Tenora Works

ARMOR	COST	DEF	EVA	SLOTS	ELEMENTS	DFP
RABOL MEGA	18000	73	110	2	-	10
RABOL GIGA	38000	91	134	2	GROUND-15%	11
RABOL TERO	45000	109	156	2	DARK-17%	13
RABOL PATTE	38000	89	133	3	-	11
RABOL DANGA	45000	107	154	2	-	13

UNITS	COST	DEF	EVA
MEGA / WALL	17000	+14	+14
MEGA / RAINBOW	17000	+0	+0
GIGA / STAMINA	23000	+0	+0

[NOTE: 1-3 STAR ITEMS ARE NOT SHOWN, BUT ARE STILL FOR SALE]

WEAPON SHOP — GRM

MELEE WEAPONS	COST	PP	ATT	ACC	ELEMENTS	ATP
CALIBUR	30000	207	418	102	ICE-21%	202 (LONG SWORD)
BONE DANCE	27000	208	222	102	-	202 (DOUBLE BLADE)
DUAL SLASHER	27000	216	174	102	ICE-21%	202 (TWIN BLADES)
DURANDAL	27000	153	317	105	ICE-21%	202 (1-HAND BLADE)

RANGED WEAPONS	COST	PP	ATT	ACC	ELEMENTS	ATA
VULLSEYE	26000	342	444	58	-	51 (RIFLE)
FALCON	31000	261	531	58	-	63 (RIFLE)
MASER CANNON	27000	378	723	53	-	51 (CANNON)
GATLING	27500	176	37	28	-	51 (MACHINEGUN)
VULCAN	31500	186	44	28	-	63 (MACHINEGUN)

[NOTE: 1-3 STAR ITEMS ARE NOT SHOWN, BUT ARE STILL FOR SALE]

WEAPON SHOP — Yohmei

MELEE WEAPONS	COST	PP	ATT	ACC	ELEMENTS	ATP
HALBENATA	26000	231	353	96	FIRE-25%	202 (SPEAR)
ASSINO-ZASHI	25000	257	102	96	-	202 (TWIN DAGGERS)
MIJIN-MISAKI	30000	247	193	96	DARK-22%	202 (TWIN CLAWS)
RIPA-ZASHI	25000	178	188	98	FIRE-25%	202 (DAGGER)
GA-MISAKI	27000	210	462	96	DARK-22%	202 (CLAW)

RANGED WEAPONS	COST	PP	ATT	ACC	ELEMENTS	ATA
BAYBARI	25000	409	513	46	-	51 (BOW)
HIKAURI	39000	432	614	46	-	63 (BOW)
RYO-BETATORE	25000	247	164	48	-	39 (TWIN HANDGUN)
BETATORE	25000	188	148	48	-	51 (HANDGUN)

FORCE WEAPONS	COST	PP	TECH	ELEMENTS	TP
HAJIROD	31000	435	331	-	125 (ROD)
CANARA	27000	237	285	-	125 (WAND)

[NOTE: 1-4 STAR ITEMS ARE NOT SHOWN, BUT ARE STILL FOR SALE]

WEAPON SHOP — Tenora Works

MELEE WEAPONS	COST	PP	ATT	ACC	ELEMENTS	ATP
SODA CALIBA	29000	207	460	95	-	202 (LONG SWORD)
GUDDA RIBAT	26000	198	250	98	-	202 (KNUCKLES)
GUDDA GRETA	32000	209	299	98	LIGHT-19%	250 (KNUCKLES)
MUKRUDI	25000	210	432	94	ELEC-22%	202 (SPEAR)
MUKARAD	33000	222	517	94	-	250 (SPEAR)
ALSEVA DRADA	26000	216	192	94	-	202 (TWIN BLADES)
ALDAGA RIPPA	25550	234	125	94	-	202 (TWIN DAGGERS)
SEVA DRADA	24000	153	348	96	-	202 (1-HAND BLADE)
DAGA RIPPA	24500	162	229	97	-	202 (DAGGER)

RANGED WEAPONS	COST	PP	ATT	ACC	ELEMENTS	ATA
SHIGGA AMZA	27000	369	91	41	-	51 (SHOTGUN)
SHIGGA STAM	32000	389	109	41	-	51 (SHOTGUN)
ARB BIGA	25500	255	200	46	-	51 (TWIN HANDGUN)
B'DUKI BE	24500	171	181	46	-	32 (HANDGUN)
CUBO DUNGA	25000	172	209	43	-	39 (CROSSBOW)

FORCE WEAPONS	COST	PP	TECH	ELEMENTS	TP
W'GACAN	25500	216	348	-	125 (WAND)

[NOTE: 1-4 STAR ITEMS ARE NOT SHOWN, BUT ARE STILL FOR SALE]

SYNTHESIS SHOPS

[NOTE1: G.C. = GUARDIANS COLONY // PAR = PARUM // NEU = NEUDAIZ // MOT = MOATOOB]
[NOTE2: 1-4 STAR ITEMS ARE NOT SHOWN, BUT ARE STILL FOR SALE]

BOARDS	COST	G.C.	PAR	NEU	MOT	BOARDS	COST	G.C.	PAR	NEU	MOT
[B] DURANDAL	10000	X	X	-	-	[B] GIGALINE	8000	X	X	-	-
[B] ASCALAN	11000	X	X	-	-	[B] TEROLINE	12000	X	X	-	-
[B] ASSINO-ZASHI	11000	X	-	X	-	[B] HARDLINE	15500	X	X	-	-
[B] SAVA-ZASHI	14000	X	-	X	-	[B] GI-SENBA	8000	X	-	X	-
[B] GUDDA RIBAT	8000	X	-	-	X	[B] TE-SENBA	12000	X	-	X	-
[B] MUKRUDI	8000	X	-	-	X	[B] HAR-SENBA	15500	X	-	X	-
[B] VULCAN	11000	X	X	-	-	[B] RABOL GIGA	8000	X	-	-	-
[B] VULLSEYE	8000	X	X	-	-	[B] RABOL TERO	12000	X	-	-	X
[B] DUAL RAILGUN	11000	X	X	-	-	[B] RABOL HARD	15500	X	-	-	X
[B] BAYBARI	8000	X	-	X	-	[B] TRIMATE	50	X	X	X	X
[B] SHIGGA STAM	11000	X	-	-	X						

WEST HUGU DESERT

PARTNERS

NAME	LVL (Ethan's +...)	RACE	CLASS
1. Lou	-2	CAST	Hunter
2. Leogini S Berafort	+2	Beast	Hunter
3. Tonnio Rhima	+1	Beast	Hunter

OBJECTIVES ① TO ②

① TRIAL — CROSS THE DESERT ON A STRIKER

Leave the Lungas saddle at home, since you'll be crossing the Kugu desert in a mighty Striker tank that can blast through foes and boulders alike. 3:30 is the time to beat, and there's plenty of slack, so you can afford to take things slowly and plot your course. When there seem to be multiple ways to travel, pause and turn the camera to find the sparkling yellow light that indicates a destructible boulder. The passages they block are always on the correct route.

Hit the brakes when you see a foe, as they're much easier to battle from a distance than at close range (and they can do quite a bit of damage to your tank if they surround you). One blast from your cannon will kill anything, even a Bil de Vear, so there's no need to get out and fight on foot. The tank can only hold ten rounds of ammunition, but red ammo containers have been placed throughout the correct course and if you aim carefully instead of firing wildly, you'll always have more than enough ammo to get through.

MONSTERS

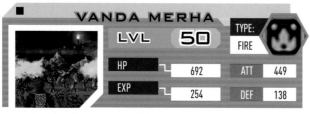

VANDA MERHA

LVL	50	TYPE: FIRE
HP	692	ATT 449
EXP	254	DEF 138

BIL DE VEAR

LVL	50	TYPE: GROUND
HP	2768	ATT 674
EXP	1016	DEF 193

NAVAL

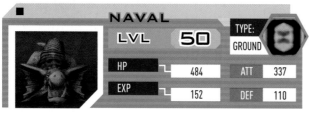

LVL	50	TYPE: GROUND
HP	484	ATT 337
EXP	152	DEF 110

DRUA GOHRA

LVL	54	TYPE: FIRE
HP	2976	ATT 725
EXP	1318	DEF 192

TRIAL RANKING

CONDITIONS

1. CLEAR TIME 3:30 VALUE 700pts
   PENALTY -5 points per second late

2. ENEMIES 12 VALUE 300pts
   PENALTY -5 points per enemy missed

RANKING INFORMATION

SCORE	RANK	MESETA	MP	PRIZE
1000	S	18000	140	Scape Doll
700 - 999	A	7000	110	-
400 - 699	B	3000	90	-
0 - 399	C	-	80	-

2 TRAVEL TO THE FIELD BASE PERIMETER

As you travel to the Field Base on foot, you'll encounter plenty of Vanda Mehra and Naval, as well as new Drua Gohra monsters. These giant lizards can breathe fire from their mouths and whip with their tails, but have no defense against attackers who strike at their sides. Use melee Photon Arts or Technics that end in a knockback effect, and you'll be able to get several free hits in while the Drua Gohra struggles to right itself.

The most dangerous foes are the Vanda, especially the packs that are lead by a shield- and helm-armored Vanda Mehra king. The grunts will form a tight circle around their leader, breathing fire in every direction while the leader boosts its troop with Shifta Technics. Breaking through their formation can be difficult, so blast them from a distance with ice Technics and ranged weapons.

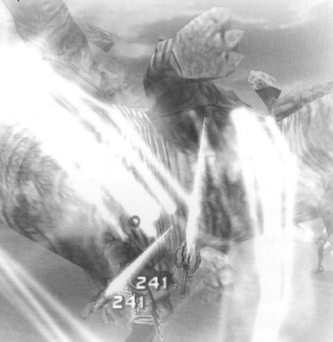

SYNTHESIS BOARDS IN THE DESERT...

There's a giant boulder at the east end of Block B-1, and you can reveal its weak spot with your goggles. Smash it away to reveal a small passage with three containers that usually hold recovery items.

Sol Atomizers are always a welcome find, but for once there's plenty of eye-popping stuff in the standard treasure containers. You're likely to find multiple boards for seven-star weapons, including the [B] Death Dancer (Twin Blades) and [B] Bulletmaster (Twin Handguns). But don't run back to your room to make 'em yet; the Bulletmaster requires five Kerseline materials and the Dead Dancer requires the same five Kerseline and five Stelnium to boot. Both of those materials cannot yet be purchased and can only be found from random enemy item drops, so never pass up a chance to kill a foe and take its stuff!

[MOATOOB]
THE PERIMETER

PARTNERS

NAME	LVL (Ethan's +...)	RACE	CLASS
1. Lou	-2	CAST	Hunter
2. Leogini S Berafort	+2	Beast	Hunter
3. Tonnio Rhima	+1	Beast	Hunter

OBJECTIVES 3 TO 5

3 TRIAL — DESTROY THE AREA A SEED BATTALION

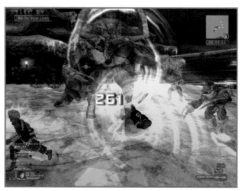

Forget scoring an S Rank—simply surviving this trial is a challenge! You'll face 150 monsters in two small areas, including Bil de Vear and Drua Gohra that appear in groups of up to three. Most of them are lower-level than the ones you fought in the last area, but they can easily overwhelm you by sheer numbers. Your one advantage is that all 150 are, without exception, ice-type. Forces should fill their best rod with four fire Technics (which will provide a 12% power boost), Rangers should link all of their weapons to "burning" Photon Arts, and Hunters should fill their action palette with as many fire-element weapons as they can find. If you don't have any on hand, return to Dagora City (via the open gate to the east). There you can purchase a Halbenata Spears at the weapon shop, and insert Ban-photons into weapon machinery boards to synthesize fire-element weapons of your own creation.

TRIAL RANKING

RANKING INFORMATION

	SCORE	RANK	MESETA	MP	PRIZE
	1000	S	18000	140	Grinder S+5
	700 - 999	A	7000	110	-
	400 - 699	B	3000	90	-
	0 - 399	C	-	80	-

CONDITIONS

1 CLEAR TIME 13:00 VALUE 1000pts
PENALTY -1 point per second late

B Ascalon
GRM (0)
PP 218/ 218
Att 500(1020)
Acc 102(176)
    80%
ATP req.: 250(500)

S-Rank seekers should bring along a Wand with Shifta and other stat boosters—it is well worth the time to cast stat-boosting Technics every few minutes. Use Photon Arts liberally and bring plenty of Photon Charges. Have a wide variety of weapons at your disposal so you can sweep the Naval with area-effect attacks, pick off the Vanda with ranged weapons, and go wild with melee combos (or spells like Damfoie) on the Bil de Vear and Drua Gohra. Even when you do everything right, a rare treasure will try to tempt you away from an S-Rank: there is a long, unguarded pit south of the entrance to the final room, and it ends at a trio of containers that always hold a seven-star Thunder Cannon weapon.

MONSTERS

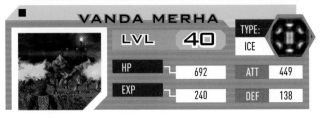

VANDA MERHA

		TYPE:
LVL	40	ICE
HP	692	ATT	449
EXP	240	DEF	138

BIL DE VEAR

		TYPE:
LVL	44	ICE
HP	2536	ATT	618
EXP	840	DEF	175

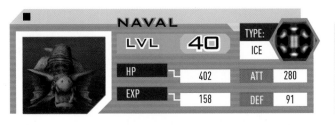

NAVAL

		TYPE:
LVL	40	ICE
HP	402	ATT	280
EXP	158	DEF	91

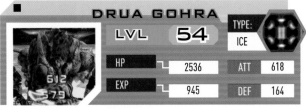

DRUA GOHRA

		TYPE:
LVL	54	ICE
HP	2536	ATT	618
EXP	945	DEF	164

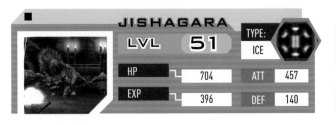

JISHAGARA

		TYPE:
LVL	51	ICE
HP	704	ATT	457
EXP	396	DEF	140

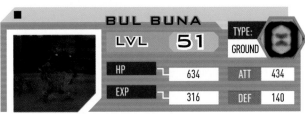

BUL BUNA

		TYPE:
LVL	51	GROUND
HP	634	ATT	434
EXP	316	DEF	140

GETTING STARTED

STORY MODE

FREE MISSIONS

NETWORK MODE

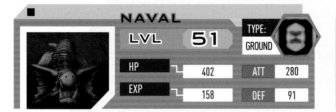

NAVAL

LVL **51**

TYPE: GROUND

| HP | 402 | ATT | 280 |
| EXP | 158 | DEF | 91 |

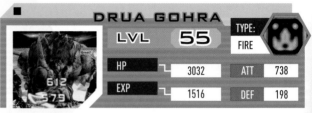

DRUA GOHRA

LVL **55**

TYPE: FIRE

| HP | 3032 | ATT | 738 |
| EXP | 1516 | DEF | 198 |

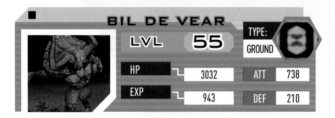

BIL DE VEAR

LVL **55**

TYPE: GROUND

| HP | 3032 | ATT | 738 |
| EXP | 943 | DEF | 210 |

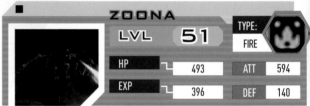

ZOONA

LVL **51**

TYPE: FIRE

| HP | 493 | ATT | 594 |
| EXP | 396 | DEF | 140 |

4 RESCUE CURTZ IN AREA B

Area A has been secured, but Area B lies in ruins and Curtz is among the fallen. Save, heal, and recharge; then head through the Area B door to save him. Your flaming weaponry will come in handy against the Jishagara you meet near the entrance, but as you proceed deeper into the base you'll want colder weapons to use against the powerful fire-type Zoona and Drua Gohra. You can get through Blocks B-1 and B-2 very quickly, but those in need of recovery items should stop short of the B-2 exit and proceed west, where they'll find key #2 in the possession of a Zoona flock. That key will open the locked door in the center of the map, which leads to a few monster-guarded item containers.

TRIAL ⑤   SAVE CURTZ FROM THE DIMMAGOLUS

The Dimmagolus is a cousin of the Onmagoug, and the same basic strategies will prove effective. Characters without strong long-range weaponry should head back to town to buy some, and Hunters may want to class-change to a Ranger for the duration of the battle. With a Shifta-boosted rifle, bow, or laser firing plasma bullets, a Ranger should be able to shred a Dimmagolus wing in a single shot.

The Dimmagolus begins the battle on terra firma, so charge at it as the opening conversation proceeds. If it takes to the sky before you can reach it, draw a ranged weapon and blast at the wings quickly, before it can attack. When the Dimmagolus hits the ground, use a good combo Photon Art; Rangers should use the Mukrudi Spears if they have it, as its electric photon is good for a few points of additional damage. When the Dimmagolus takes to the sky again, don't back up—you may be able to look straight up and hit its wings from below, sending it crashing back down for another melee combo.

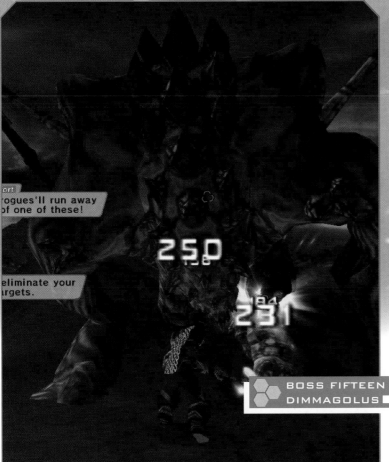

BOSS FIFTEEN
DIMMAGOLUS

⬡⬡⬡⬡⬡⬡⬡⬡➤ BOSS

DIMMAGOLUS ●

LVL	TYPE:
58	GROUND

HP	EXP
6974	1060

ATT	DEF
742	277

TRIAL RANKING

RANKING INFORMATION

SCORE	RANK	MESETA	MP	PRIZE
1000	S	18000	140	Mugungri
700 - 999	A	7000	110	-
400 - 699	B	3000	90	-
0 - 399	C	-	80	-

1 CLEAR TIME 1:30 VALUE 1000pts
PENALTY -5 points per second late

CHAPTER 12

LIFE CHOICES

CHAPTER OBJECTIVES

- [ ] Visit Curtz at the Alliance Military Base
- [ ] Search for Tylor at Dagora City
- [ ] Ask Rutsu for the anti-SEED shield
- 1 [ ] Ride the Landeel into the Hive
- 2 [ ] TRIAL: Find the distress call origin
- 3 [ ] Reunite and search for Dr. Taragi
- 4 [ ] Level-up in Block C's treasure loop
- 5 [ ] TRIAL: Stop the Carriguine
- 6 [ ] Stock up for the final battle
- 7 [ ] Raid the Central Control Room
- 8 [ ] Defeat Dulk Fakis: Round 1
- 9 [ ] Defeat Dulk Fakis: Round 2

MISSION: GUARDIAN'S CALLING

[GUARDIANS COLONY]
CLYEZ CITY
PARTNERS
NONE

VISIT CURTZ AT THE ALLIANCE MILITARY BASE

You've destroyed the SEED in the Gurhal system, but Maya and Hyuga remain trapped on a SEED vessel outside of the galaxy. The president isn't willing to help, but your friends are, and Leo and Tonnio will point you in the right direction when you storm out of Guardians HQ. You can find Curtz at the Alliance Military Force Headquarters in Holtes City's West District, but he'll decline your request for help. Fortunately, Lou will provide a new lead as you head back to Parum's PPT Spaceport.

SEARCH FOR TYLOR AT DAGORA CITY

You won't need to look far to get a lead on Tylor's whereabouts, as the first man you run into in Dagora City will blurt out a clue. Hang a right and walk to the end of town, where you'll find the Vol Brothers behind the counter of Gawik's pub. Liina will escort you to Tylor, but he won't agree to help unless you can secure an anti-SEED shield to protect his ship from the SEED.

ASK RUTSU FOR THE ANTI-SEED SHIELD

Your final stop is at the Communion Headquarters next to the PPT Spaceport in Ohtoku City. As usual, Rutsu will give you a chilly reception, and this time the Maiden isn't around to overrule him. But when you return to Clyez City, you'll find that somehow everything has fallen into place. A vessel and crew are waiting, and you can now accept the Guardian's Calling mission at the Space Dock of Clyez's City's 4th floor spaceport. There will be no returning to civilization after you sign up for this mission, so buy the best armor you can afford and procure a wide array of powerful weapons. Rangers and Forces should consider a class change to Hunter—while ranged tactics are quite effective against most of the Hive's monsters, powerful melee attacks are the key to beating the bosses at the end.

MISSION: GUARDIAN'S CALLING

Before the Alliance Military's offensive begins, rescue Maya, Hyuga, and the A-Photon researchers being held captive at the HIVE.

Required   No other characters permitted.

NOTE: Cannot return during mission.

LOC   The HIVE

Party   1/1

SHOP REPORT

[NOTE: PURPLE TEXT DENOTES THAT THIS IS NEW TO THE SHOP.]

Half a million meseta for one weapon!? Wow. Many of the weapon shops have skipped the A rank of weapons entirely and are selling super-expensive S-Rank weapons like the Two-headed Ragnus instead. You can do a dozen Free Missions to earn the cash, or you can settle for the incremental upgrades of new B-rank weapons like the Nightwalker double blade and Tomoirod rod. If you can afford it, a new set of armor and units may make a big difference in the battle to come, and between the three manufacturers you'll have a wide variety to choose from. The light-element Regrants Technic isn't new, but it's a must-buy for any class if you don't have it already.

If you're wondering what happened to the A-rank weapons, you'll find most of their boards at the synthesis shop. It won't be cheap, but you can now buy the materials you need to make any of them. You can't buy Kerseline directly, but you can make it with Ore Converters—to get five Kerseline, buy 20 Marseline, run it through a [B] Ore C. 5 > 6, then run the resulting Upteline through [B] Ore C. 6 > 7. Keep in mind that while the Force weapon boards like [B] Cometara have slots that don't require specific materials, if the items you insert aren't near the rarity level of the board, the recipe will fail. For items with flexible photon requirements, buy Gra-photons so you can make light-infused weapons that will be incredibly powerful in this chapter's mission. And of course, after investing so much money in materials, make sure to save your game before you attempt the synthesis.

ARMOR SHOP   GRM

ARMOR	COST	DEF	EVA	SLOTS	ELEMENTS	DFP
MEGALINE	18000	70	113	2	-	10
GIGALINE	38000	88	137	2	FIRE-15%	11
TEROLINE	45000	106	159	2	ELECTRIC-15%	13
HARDLINE	80000	124	181	3	FIRE-20%	15
CRESLINE	38000	88	137	0	-	17
ORPALINE	900000	154	261	2	-	15
ZEETLINE	19000	65	110	2	-	10

UNITS	COST	ATT	ACC
MEGA / POWER	13000	20	0
GIGA / SKILL PP SAVE	25000	-200	-100
GIGA / BULLET PP SAVE	25000	-200	-100
TERO / HIT	35000	0	20
TERO / ALL SAVE	35000	-200	-100
ORPA / POWER CHARGE	650000	150	0
MEGA / STAMINA	15000	0	0
SAFETY HEART	38000	0	0
TERO / HP RESTORE	60000	0	0

[NOTE: 1-3 STAR ITEMS ARE NOT SHOWN, BUT ARE STILL FOR SALE]

ARMOR SHOP   Yohmei

ARMOR	COST	DEF	EVA	SLOTS	ELEMENTS	DFP
ME-SENBA	18000	67	116	2	-	10
GI-SENBA	38000	85	140	2	ICE-16%	11
TE-SENBA	45000	103	153	2	LIGHT-18%	13
HAR-SENBA	80000	120	185	3	-	15
ORPA-SENBA	900000	149	265	2	-	21

UNITS	COST	TECH	MENT
ME / QUICK	8000	-14	0
GI / SMART	25000	0	0
GI / MAGIC	25000	28	12
TE / FORCE S	35000	28	-12
TE / TECH CHARGE	35000	82	0
ORPA / FORCE	650000	108	0
ELECTRO / HEART	23000	0	0
TE / PP GENERATE	60000	0	0

[NOTE: 1-3 STAR ITEMS ARE NOT SHOWN, BUT ARE STILL FOR SALE]

SHOPS CONTINUED

ARMOR SHOP — Tenora Works

ARMOR	COST	DEF	EVA	SLOTS	ELEMENTS	DFP
RABOL GIGA	38000	91	134	2	GROUND-15%	11
RABOL TERO	45000	109	156	2	DARK-17%	13
RABOL HARD	80000	128	177	3	-	15
RABOL ORPAD	900000	159	256	2	-	21
RABOL PATTE	38000	89	133	3	-	11
RABOL DANGA	45000	107	154	2	-	13

UNITS	COST	DEF	EVA
MEGA / WALL	17000	14	14
MEGA / RAINBOW	17000	0	0
TERO / RAINBOW	35000	0	0
TERO / WALL	35000	24	24
ORPAD / GUARD	650000	100	0
GIGA / STAMINA	23000	0	0
BLACK HEART	45000	0	0

[NOTE: 1-2 STAR ITEMS ARE NOT SHOWN, BUT ARE STILL FOR SALE]

ITEM SHOPS

ITEMS	COST	ITEMS	COST
MONOMATE	30	GRINDER A+1	5000
DIMATE	150	GRINDER A+2	10000
TRIMATE	1000	GRINDER A+3	15000
SOL ATOMIZER	100	GRINDER S+1	8000
MOON ATOMIZER	500	GRINDER S+2	16000
PHOTON CHARGE	1500	GRINDER S+3	32000
GRINDER C+1	300	DAMAGE TRAP	50
GRINDER C+2	800	BURN TRAP	100
GRINDER C+3	1500	FREEZE TRAP	120
GRINDER B+1	3000	DAMAGE TRAP G	600
GRINDER B+2	6000	BURN TRAP G	750
GRINDER B+3	10000	FREEZE TRAP G	750

WEAPON SHOP — GRM

MELEE WEAPONS	COST	PP	ATT	ACC	ELEMENTS	ATP
CALIBUR	30000	207	418	102	ICE-21%	202 (LONG SWORD)
ASCALAN	44000	218	500	102	-	250 (LONG SWORD)
BONE DANCE	27000	208	222	102	-	202 (DOUBLE BLADE)
NIGHTWALKER	40000	220	265	102	-	250 (DOUBLE BLADE)
DUAL SLASHER	27000	216	174	102	ICE-21%	202 (TWIN BLADES)
DUAL DURANDAL	41000	228	208	102	-	250 (TWIN BLADES)
TWO-HEADED RAGNUS	550000	288	315	143	FIRE-29%	347 (TWIN BLADES)
DURANDAL	27000	153	317	105	ICE-21%	202 (1-HAND BLADE)
FALCHIAN	36000	161	379	105	-	250 (1-HAND BLADE)
CRIMSON	500000	205	571	147	FIRE-29%	347 (1-HAND BLADE)

RANGED WEAPONS	COST	PP	ATT	ACC	ELEMENTS	ATA
VULLSEYE	26000	342	444	58	-	51 (RIFLE)
FALCON	31000	361	531	58	-	63 (RIFLE)
BLACKBULL	500000	456	799	98	-	78 (RIFLE)
MASER CANNON	27000	378	723	53	-	51 (CANNON)
THUNDER CANNON	40000	399	865	53	-	63 (CANNON)
DUAL RAILGUN	38000	237	217	56	-	63 (TWIN HANDGUN)
RAILGUN	36000	180	196	56	-	63 (HANDGUN)
VIPER	480000	228	296	96	-	78 (HANDGUN)
GATLING	27500	176	37	28	-	51 (MACHINEGUN)
VULCAN	31500	186	44	28	-	63 (MACHINEGUN)
MUZZLEFEVER	500000	235	68	48	-	78 (MACHINEGUN)

[NOTE: 1-4 STAR ITEMS ARE NOT SHOWN, BUT ARE STILL FOR SALE]

WEAPON SHOP   *Yohmei*

MELEE WEAPONS	COST	PP	ATT	ACC	ELEMENTS	ATP
HALBENATA	26000	231	353	96	FIRE-25%	202 (SPEAR)
ASSINO-ZASHI	25000	257	102	96	-	202 (TWIN DAGGERS)
TSISAVA-ZASHI	39000	271	122	96	-	250 (TWIN DAGGERS)
GIZAHAA-ZASHI	500000	343	184	136	-	347 (TWIN DAGGERS)
MIJIN-MISAKI	30000	257	193	96	DARK-22%	202 (TWIN CLAWS)
RAN-MISAKI	480000	330	1349	136	-	347 (TWIN CLAWS)
RIPA-ZASHI	25000	178	188	98	FIRE-25%	202 (DAGGER)
SAVA-ZASHI	36000	188	224	98	-	250 (DAGGER)
DEVA-ZASHI	490000	237	339	138	-	347 (DAGGER)
GA-MISAKI	27000	210	462	96	DARK-22%	202 (CLAW)
GIZA-MISAKI	500000	229	596	136	-	250 (CLAW)

RANGED WEAPONS	COST	PP	ATT	ACC	ELEMENTS	ATA
BAYBARI	25000	409	513	46	-	51 (BOW)
HIKAURI	39000	432	614	46	-	63 (BOW)
ULTERI	530000	546	925	136	-	78 (BOW)
RYO-BETATORE	25000	247	164	48	-	39 (TWIN HANDGUN)
BETATORE	25000	188	148	48	-	51 (HANDGUN)

FORCE WEAPONS	COST	PP	TECH	ELEMENTS	TP
HAJIROD	31000	435	331	-	125 (ROD)
TOMOIROD	50000	459	395	-	157 (ROD)
CANARA	27000	237	285	-	125 (WAND)
CROZARA	47000	250	341	-	157 (WAND)
URANSARA	520000	316	513	-	216 (WAND)

[NOTE: 1-4 STAR ITEMS ARE NOT SHOWN, BUT ARE STILL FOR SALE]

WEAPON SHOP   *Tenora Works*

MELEE WEAPONS	COST	PP	ATT	ACC	ELEMENTS	ATP
SODA CALIBA	29000	207	460	95	-	202 (LONG SWORD)
GUDDA RIBAT	26000	198	250	98	-	202 (KNUCKLES)
GUDDA GRETA	32000	209	299	98	LIGHT-19%	250 (KNUCKLES)
GUDDA SKELA	530000	264	452	136	DARK-27%	347 (KNUCKLES)
MUKRUDI	25000	210	432	94	ELEC-22%	202 (SPEAR)
MUKARAD	33000	222	517	94	-	250 (SPEAR)
MUKTRAND	540000	280	778	132	-	247 (SPEAR)
ALSEVA DRADA	26000	216	192	94	-	202 (TWIN BLADES)
ALDAGA RIPPA	25550	234	125	94	-	202 (TWIN DAGGERS)
SEVA DRADA	24000	153	348	96	-	202 (1-HAND BLADE)
DAGA RIPPA	24500	162	229	97	-	202 (DAGGER)

RANGED WEAPONS	COST	PP	ATT	ACC	ELEMENTS	ATA
SHIGGA AMZA	27000	369	91	41	-	51 (SHOTGUN)
SHIGGA STAM	32000	389	109	41	-	51 (SHOTGUN)
SHIGGA DESTA	500000	492	165	82	-	78 (SHOTGUN)
ARB BIGA	25500	225	200	46	-	51 (TWIN HANDGUN)
B'DUKI BE	24500	171	181	46	-	32 (HANDGUN)
CUBO DUNGA	25000	172	209	43	-	39 (CROSSBOW)
CUBO MAMBA	500000	230	376	84	-	78 (CROSSBOW)

FORCE WEAPONS	COST	PP	TECH	ELEMENTS	TP
W'GACAN	25500	216	348	-	125 (WAND)

[NOTE: 1-4 STAR ITEMS ARE NOT SHOWN, BUT ARE STILL FOR SALE]

SHOPS CONTINUED

GETTING STARTED

STORY MODE

FREE MISSIONS

NETWORK MODE

[NOTE: G.C. = GUARDIANS COLONY // PAR = PARUM // NEU = NEUDAIZ // MOT = MOATOOB]

BOARDS	COST	G.C.	PAR	NEU	MOT
[B] DURANDAL	10000	X	X	-	-
[B] ASCALON	11000	X	X	-	-
[B] ASSINO-ZASHI	11000	X	-	X	-
[B] SAVA-ZASHI	14000	X	-	X	-
[B] GUDDA RIBAT	8000	X	-	-	X
[B] MUKRUDI	8000	X	-	-	X
[B] HANZO	45000	X	X	-	-
[B] DEATH DANCER	45000	X	X	-	-
[B] SHINTSUKI-ZASHI	45000	X	-	X	-
[B] MUGUNGRI	45000	X	-	-	X
[B] VULCAN	11000	X	X	-	-
[B] VULLSEYE	8000	X	X	-	-
[B] DUAL RAILGUN	11000	X	X	-	-
[B] BAYBARI	8000	X	-	X	-
[B] SHIGGA STAM	11000	X	-	-	X
[B] ASSASSIN	45000	X	X	-	-
[B] BULLETMASTER	45000	X	X	-	-
[B] BEAM VULCAN	45000	X	X	-	-
[B] SHIGGA BOMA	45000	X	-	-	X
[B] COMETARA	45000	X	-	X	-
[B] GRANAROD	45000	X	-	X	-
[B] GIGALINE	8000	X	X	-	-
[B] TEROLINE	12000	X	X	-	-
[B] HARDLINE	15500	X	X	-	-
[B] GI-SENBA	8000	X	-	X	-
[B] TE-SENBA	12000	X	-	X	-
[B] HAR-SENBA	15500	X	-	X	-
[B] RABOL GIGA	8000	X	-	-	X
[B] RABOL TERO	12000	X	-	-	X
[B] RABOL HARD	15500	X	-	-	X
[B] TRIMATE	50	X	X	X	X
[B] GRINDER A	2500	X	X	X	X
[B] GRINDER S	5000	X	X	X	X

CONVERTERS	COST	G.C.	PAR	NEU	MOT
[B] ORE C. 3 > 4	400	X	X	X	X
[B] ORE C.4 > 5	800	X	X	X	X
[B] ORE C. 5 > 6	1200	X	X	X	X
[B] ORE C. 6 > 7	3000	X	X	X	X
[B] METAL CONV. C > B	200	X	X	X	X
[B] METAL CONV. B > A	1500	X	X	X	X
[B] WOOD CONV. C > B	200	X	X	X	X
[B] WOOD CONV. B > A	1500	X	X	X	X

MATERIALS	COST	G.C.	PAR	NEU	MOT
PHOTON	300	X	X	X	X
EL-PHOTON	800	X	X	X	X
IM-PHOTON	800	X	X	X	X
BAN-PHOTON	500	X	X	X	X
RAY-PHOTON	500	X	X	X	X
ZAN-PHOTON	500	X	X	X	X
DI-PHOTON	500	X	X	X	X
GRA-PHOTON	800	X	X	X	X
MEGI-PHOTON	800	X	X	X	X
CARLIAN	200	X	X	X	X
PEPARIAN	1000	X	X	X	X
SLATERIAN	4500	X	X	X	X
MEGANITE	200	X	X	X	X
GIGANITE	1000	X	X	X	X
TERANITE	4500	X	X	X	X
HARNIUM	200	X	X	X	X
SOLDONIUM	1000	X	X	X	X
STELNIUM	4500	X	X	X	X
GAMOTITE	200	X	X	X	X
ZEPOTITE	1000	X	X	X	X
CHICOTITE	4500	X	X	X	X
SOURAL	200	X	X	X	X
SPERAL	1000	X	X	X	X
ACENALINE	100	X	X	X	X
WENCELINE	300	X	X	X	X
APORALINE	900	X	X	X	X
DIANALINE	2500	X	X	X	X
MARSELINE	6000	X	X	X	X
NANOSILICA	200	X	X	X	X
NANOCARBON	1000	X	X	X	X
HOT BERRY	50	X	X	X	X
COLD BERRY	50	X	X	X	X
SWEET BERRY	50	X	X	X	X
BITTER BERRY	50	X	X	X	X
STAMINA BERRY	50	X	X	X	X
TRANS ACID	100	X	X	X	X
METAMOR ACID	400	X	X	X	X
ETHER ACID	800	X	X	X	X
GRINDER BASE C	100	X	X	X	X
GRINDER BASE B	1000	X	X	X	X
GRINDER BASE A	2500	X	X	X	X
GRINDER BASE S	5000	X	X	X	X
PAR WOOD	200	X	-	-	-
PAR ASH	750	X	-	-	-
PAR EBON	3000	X	-	-	-
MOT WOOD	200	X	-	-	X
MOT ASH	750	X	-	-	X
MOT EBON	750	X	-	-	X
NEU WOOD	200	X	-	X	-
NEU ASH	750	X	-	X	-
NEU EBON	750	X	-	X	-

[DEEP SPACE]
THE HIVE - BLOCK A

PARTNERS

NAME	LVL (Ethan's +...)	RACE	CLASS
1. Karen Erra	+3	Newman	Hunter

OBJECTIVES ① TO ②

---

①   RIDE THE LANDEEL INTO THE HIVE

Then it's me and Karen...

This mission begins aboard the Landeel, where you'll have to speak to all of your friends before the next event begins. When you arrive, the Guardians will split up into two teams, with Karen serving as Ethan's only partner. This mission's only non-boss trial will begin when you enter Block A-2, so boost yourself with Technics before you step through the door.

---

②   TRIAL   FIND THE DISTRESS CALL ORIGIN

The first rooms are populated by Deljaban and Bel Pannon, enhanced versions of the dark-type enemies that you fought in the Linear Line. They're far stronger and tougher than their predecessors, but their tactics haven't changed much. Wade in and clear them out with Photon Arts that knock them back or pop them up. Make the shield-wearing Lords the focus of your attacks, so they'll be too off-balance to cast Technics. When facing large groups, particularly of bouncy Bel Pannon, use the Regrants spell to clear the room without wasting a lot of time.

MONSTERS

DELJABAN

LVL	60	TYPE: DARK

| HP | 822 | ATT | 534 |
| EXP | 394 | DEF | 164 |

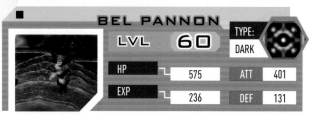

BEL PANNON

LVL	60	TYPE: DARK

| HP | 575 | ATT | 401 |
| EXP | 236 | DEF | 131 |

GAOZORAN

LVL	65	TYPE: DARK

| HP | 2038 | ATT | 546 |
| EXP | 1364 | DEF | 176 |

TRIAL RANKING

CONDITIONS

1 CLEAR TIME 7:00 VALUE 700pts
PENALTY -1 point per second late

2 ENEMIES 47 VALUE 300pts
PENALTY -5 points per enemy missed

RANKING INFORMATION

SCORE	RANK	MESETA	MP	PRIZE
1000	S	18000	150	Scape Doll
700 - 999	A	7000	120	-
400 - 699	B	3000	100	-
0 - 399	C	-	90	-

Small paths split off to the northeast and southeast in the third room of Block A-2. To kill all the enemies, you'll need to head to the end of the northeast path and destroy the chests there to generate a wave of foes. That wave will include the first Gaozoran, an enemy that poses a dire threat to both your wellbeing and your completion time. The Gaozoran will teleport to another part of the room after only a few melee hits, so Hunters should strike it only with combos (such as the Spears's Dus Daggas) that will score several hits before the target can get away. Rangers and Forces will have better results targeting it with ranged attacks, but will need to watch out for the dark-type Technics with which it returns fire.

[DEEP SPACE]
THE HIVE - BLOCK B-C

PARTNERS

NAME	LVL (Ethan's +...)	RACE	CLASS
1. Karen Erra	+3	Newman	Hunter
2. Hyuga Ryght	+0	Human	Hunter
3. Maya Shidow	-3	Newman	Force

OBJECTIVES ③ TO ⑤

③ REUNITE AND SEARCH FOR DR. TARAGI

The trial ends at Block A-3, where you'll discover that your friends are alive and well. Dr. Taragi remains missing, however, so you'll need to team up and continue your adventure. The enemies will get marginally tougher, but Hyuga and Maya will make things easier. Maya will cast Resta and a variety of stat-boosting Technics that will make a huge difference for your party, but you'll need to work hard to keep her alive during tough fights.

MONSTERS

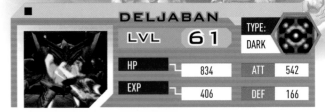

DELJABAN
LVL	61	TYPE: DARK
HP	834	ATT 542
EXP	406	DEF 166

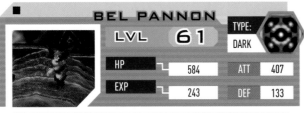

BEL PANNON
LVL	61	TYPE: DARK
HP	584	ATT 407
EXP	243	DEF 133

GAOZORAN
LVL	65	TYPE: DARK
HP	2038	ATT 546
EXP	1364	DEF 176

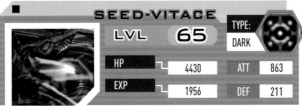

SEED-VITACE
LVL	65	TYPE: DARK
HP	4430	ATT 863
EXP	1956	DEF 211

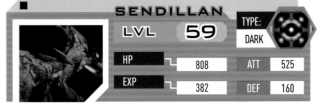

SENDILLAN
LVL	59	TYPE: DARK
HP	808	ATT 525
EXP	382	DEF 160

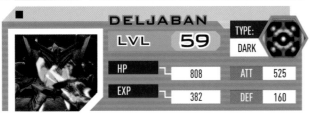

DELJABAN
LVL	59	TYPE: DARK
HP	808	ATT 525
EXP	382	DEF 160

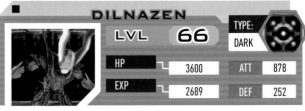

DILNAZEN
LVL	66	TYPE: DARK
HP	3600	ATT 878
EXP	2689	DEF 252

One such fight awaits in the first room of Block A-3, where a SEED-Vitace will join the usual suspects. It's still a sucker for Tornado Dance, fortunately, so Hunters can use that Photon Art to take it out of the fight before its tentacles can become a problem. When that room is clear, you can either head north to proceed or east to a treasure room. The treasure is a seven-star Hanzo Long Sword (no photon), but you'll need to fight three Gaozoran at once to get it.

4   LEVEL-UP IN BLOCK C'S TREASURE LOOP

Block A-4 contains a Save Marker and healer, and paths that head off in every direction. The path to proceed is to the north, where you'll fight a mini-boss in a short trial. If you aren't ready for that, you can follow the winding path to the east, where you'll eventually discover the entrance to Block C-1. This is an entirely optional area that ends in a treasure room filled with pods you can smash to reveal recovery items. The monsters tend to be lower-level than the ones in other regions of the Hive, making this an ideal area in which to earn experience points. The powerful Dilnazen do pose a threat, but if you can clear the room of other enemies and surround the Dilnazen, they won't be able to get any attacks in.

5   TRIAL   STOP THE CARRIGUINE

You'll find Dr. Taragi in the room north of the Save Marker. He'll give you the key that opens the west door, but you'll have to slay a Carriguine mini-boss before you'll be able to use it. The Carriguine will knock you away if you hang out at close range, and blast you with high-power Megid Technics if you strike from a distance. Using melee combos is the safest choice for both Ethan and Maya (who must be protected to earn an S-Rank), especially for Hunters and Rangers who may not have the Mental Powers to survive the Megid blasts. Repeated uses of Tornado Dance will lead to the quickest victory, but even Spears or Dagger combos can kill the Carriguine in under a minute if you boost them with Shifta.

TRIAL RANKING

CONDITIONS				

1   CLEAR TIME 1:00 VALUE 900pts
PENALTY -5 points per second late

2   MAYA FAINTS 0 VALUE 100pts
PENALTY -100 points per time Maya becomes incapacitated

RANKING INFORMATION

SCORE	RANK	MESETA	MP	PRIZE
1000	S	18000	150	Death Dancer
700 - 999	A	7000	120	-
400 - 699	B	3000	100	-
0 - 399	C	-	90	-

CARRIGUINE ●

LVL	TYPE:
60	DARK

BOSS SIXTEEN
CARRIGUINE

HP	EXP
11508	2836

ATT	DEF
587	246

[DEEP SPACE]

THE HIVE - CENTRAL CONTROL ROOM

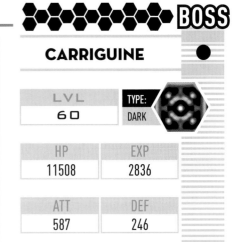

PARTNERS

NAME	LVL (Ethan's +...)	RACE	CLASS
1. Karen Erra	+3	Newman	Hunter
2. Leogini S Berafort	+2	Beast	Hunter
3. Tonnio Rhima	+1	Beast	Hunter

OBJECTIVES ⑥ TO ⑨

⑥ STOCK UP FOR THE FINAL BATTLE

When you return from your trial, you'll find Bruce waiting. In addition to selling most of the new B-rank weapons that were added to shops this chapter, he is now offering Agtaride, Defbaride, and Retaride items. Buy several and add them to your action palette; you can use them to boost your Attack, Defend, and Technic scores in the heat of battle, when it isn't practical to cast Shifta and the like. There aren't any Photon Chargers ahead, so buy as many Photon Charge items as you can fit in your inventory.

MONSTERS

DELJABAN

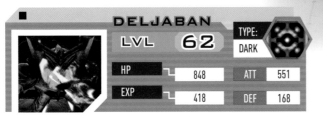

LVL	62	TYPE: DARK

HP	848	ATT	551
EXP	418	DEF	168

BEL PANNON

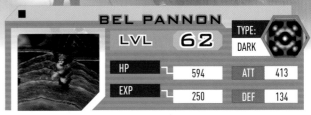

LVL	62	TYPE: DARK

HP	594	ATT	413
EXP	250	DEF	134

GAOZORAN

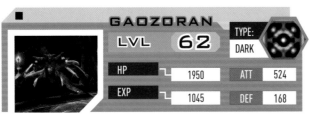

LVL	62	TYPE: DARK

HP	1950	ATT	524
EXP	1045	DEF	168

JUSNAGUN

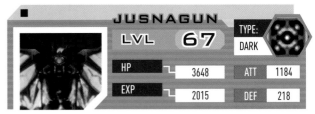

LVL	67	TYPE: DARK

HP	3648	ATT	1184
EXP	2015	DEF	218

7   RAID THE CENTRAL CONTROL ROOM

Head west from the Save Marker into Block B-2, where you'll be met by higher-level versions of the usual foes, as well as a new Jusnagun enemy. Unlike other winged creatures, Jusnagun rarely take flight, so you can battle them quite effectively with melee attacks. They have a lot of hit points to cut through, so be patient and avoid the temptation to spend a bunch of PP clearing the room. From the first room you can head northwest to a guarded treasure room (containing the usual random items) or southwest to reach the entrance to Block B-3. In Block B-3 you'll have a similar option, as you can head due north to Block B-4 or take a side path to the west and raid a few more treasure pods.

Save your game when you enter Block B-4. Then heal up, charge up, and cast your pre-boss Technics before you delve deeper into the room. There you'll be joined by Leo and Tonnio before the final boss battles begin.

8   DEFEAT DULK FAKIS: ROUND 1

While Dulk Fakis holds his position at the end of the platform, he'll run Ethan ragged by forcing him to dodge a bewildering array of attacks. You'll learn to identify the attacks by the color of energy that forms around Dulk Fakis before it strikes; a pink energy blast or orange fireball can be dodged by stepping to the sides, but you'll have to turn and run when you see the first signs of the purple death ray or the blue energy waves. When dodging the flood of blue energy, you'll have to flee to the opposite end of the platform, where the waves will dissipate just before they crash into the wall.

Between attacks, strike at Dulk Fakis's head with the usual anti-boss Photon Art combos. These will hit regularly at the beginning of the fight, but as the battle wears on, Dulk Fakis will protect himself with an energy shield more and more frequently. When you see him pop up, run away from the head to dodge the arm that will come crashing down soon after. Attack the arm with Photon Art combos as soon as he lands, but try to stay as close to the claw as possible so it will be easier to dodge when the arm attempts to sweep you away.

BOSS SEVENTEEN
DULK FAKIS

BOSS

DULK FAKIS

LVL	TYPE:
68	DARK

HP	EXP
21480	14790

ATT	DEF
657	286

9   DEFEAT DULK FAKIS: ROUND 2

In his second form, Dulk Fakis usually keeps his head above the fray, attacking with the strange creature at the tip of his tail. Focus your attacks on that creature's head and neck, where it's the most vulnerable. You can do far more damage if you can hit Dulk Fakis in his actual head, but he won't give you many opportunities. When Dulk Fakis turns upside down, rush in and blast the head with all the Photon Arts you can muster. After a few hits, Dulk Fakis will begin to spin like a coiling snake, leaving you with no viable targets. Step away from him and use ranged attacks or Photon Arts like Regrants to get a few points of damage in during this phase, or refresh your stat-boosting effects with Technics and items.

BOSS EIGHTEEN
DULK FAKIS

Dulk Fakis can use a wide variety of powerful Technics, but his deadliest attack summons a massive meteor that will devastate the entire battlefield; you'll know this attack is coming when Dulk Fakis leaves the battlefield and the camera pans back to focus on the incoming meteor. While you may no longer be able to see Ethan, you can still open menus and use items and Technics in your action palette. Refill your health to max before the meteor hits, then use Technics and items to boost your defenses. Have more healing items at the ready for after the meteor hits, as the impact will leave even high-level characters at the brink of death.

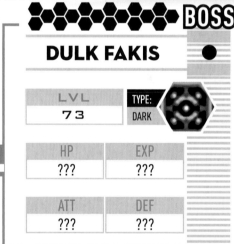

BOSS

DULK FAKIS

LVL	TYPE:
73	DARK

HP	EXP
???	???

ATT	DEF
???	???

Those who triumph over both versions of Dulk Fakis will earn the right to save their game after watching the ending. That Save File will put you back on Clyez City before you boarded the Landeel, but all your current items and levels will be preserved. You will also unlock a new mission in Extra Mode and a few new CAST voices that you can use in Extra Mode character creation!

OF LIGHT AND DARKNESS

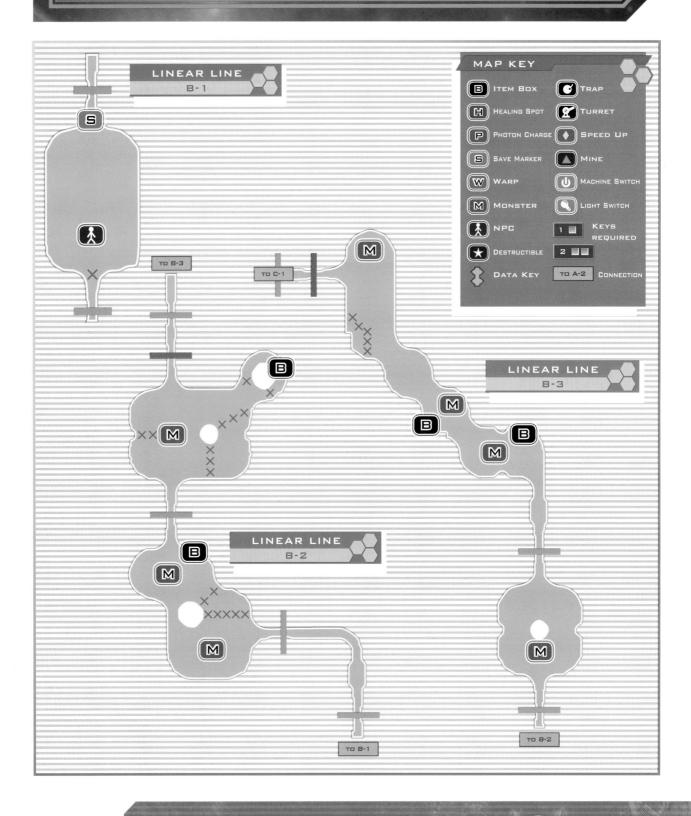

MAP KEY

B	Item Box		Trap
H	Healing Spot		Turret
P	Photon Charge		Speed Up
S	Save Marker		Mine
W	Warp		Machine Switch
M	Monster		Light Switch
	NPC	1	Keys Required
	Destructible	2	
	Data Key	TO A-2	Connection

LINEAR LINE B-1

LINEAR LINE B-3

LINEAR LINE B-2

TO B-3

TO C-1

TO B-1

TO B-2

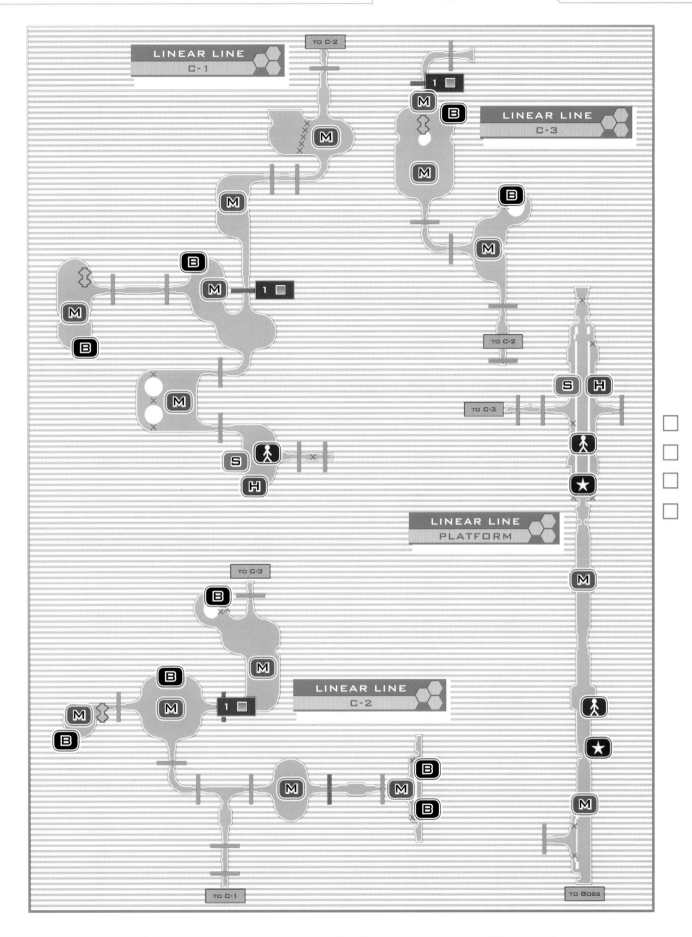

LINEAR LINE
C-1

TO C-2

LINEAR LINE
C-3

LINEAR LINE
PLATFORM

TO C-2

TO C-3

TO C-3

LINEAR LINE
C-2

TO C-1

TO BOSS

GETTING STARTED

STORY MODE

FREE MISSIONS

NETWORK MODE

TYPICAL LIVES

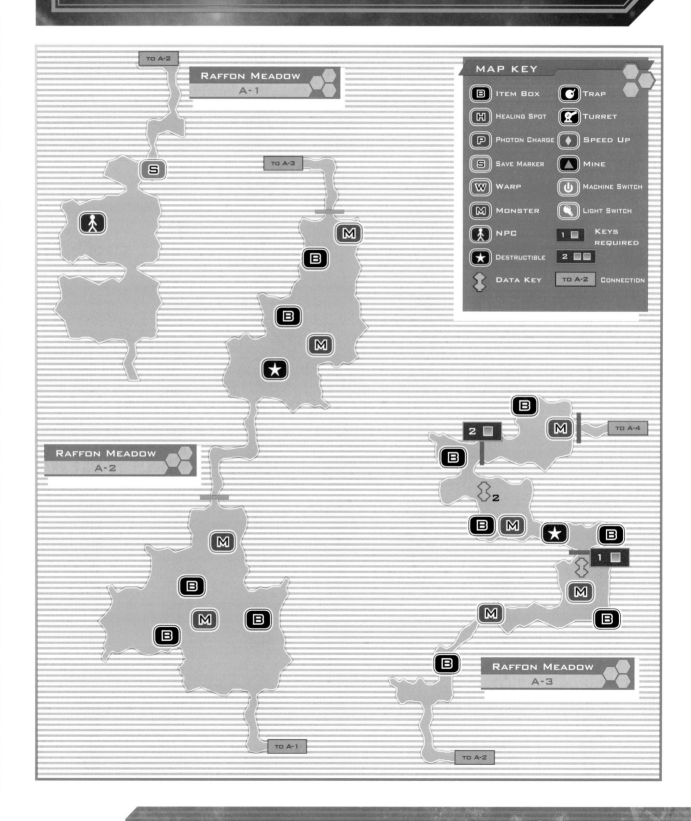

MAP KEY

B ITEM BOX	💣 TRAP
H HEALING SPOT	🔫 TURRET
P PHOTON CHARGE	◆ SPEED UP
S SAVE MARKER	▲ MINE
W WARP	⏻ MACHINE SWITCH
M MONSTER	🔦 LIGHT SWITCH
NPC	1 ▢ KEYS REQUIRED
★ DESTRUCTIBLE	2 ▢▢
⬡ DATA KEY	TO A-2 CONNECTION

RAFFON MEADOW A-1

RAFFON MEADOW A-2

RAFFON MEADOW A-3

TO A-2
TO A-3
TO A-4
TO A-1
TO A-2

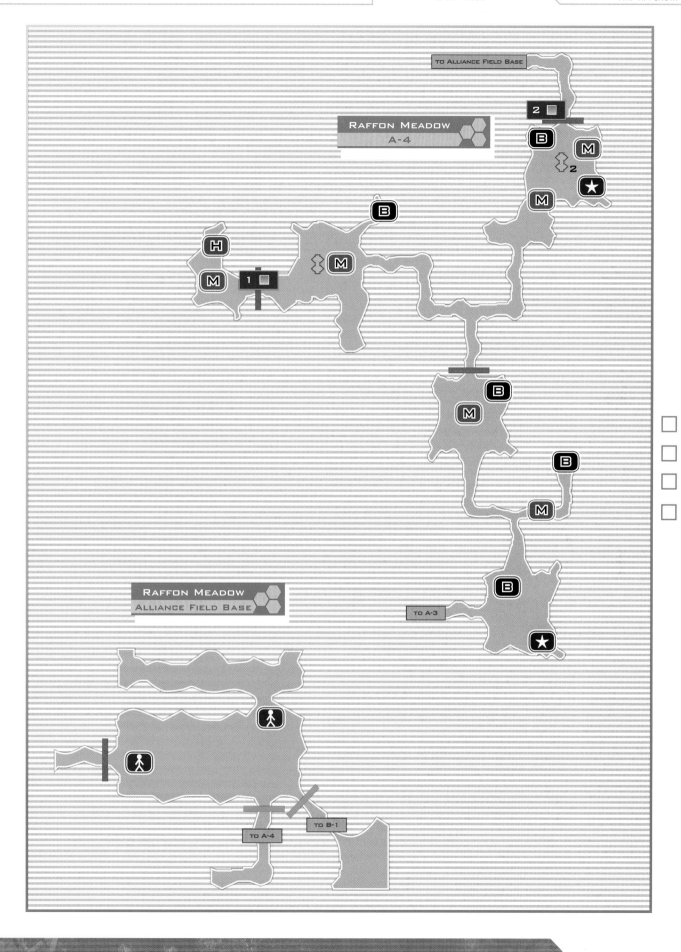

RAFFON MEADOW
A-4

TO ALLIANCE FIELD BASE

RAFFON MEADOW
ALLIANCE FIELD BASE

TO A-3

TO A-4   TO B-1

GETTING STARTED

STORY MODE

FREE MISSIONS

NETWORK MODE

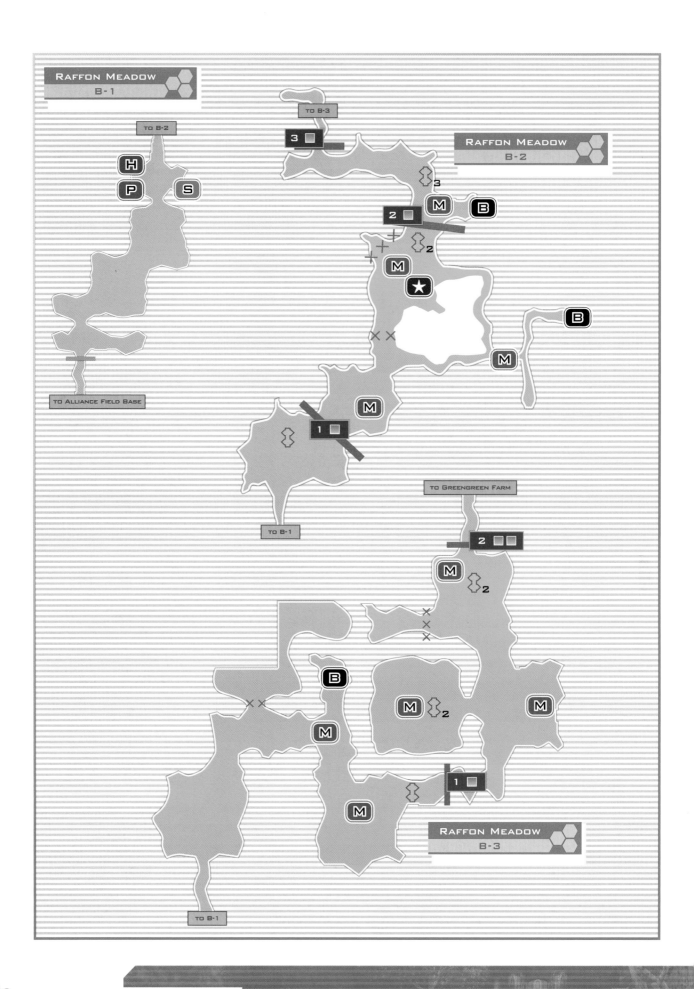

RAFFON MEADOW
B-1

TO B-2

H
P   S

TO ALLIANCE FIELD BASE

TO B-1

TO B-3

3

RAFFON MEADOW
B-2

3

M   B

2

2

M

★

B

M

M

1

TO GREENGREEN FARM

2

M

2

B

M

M

2

M

1

M

RAFFON MEADOW
B-3

TO B-1

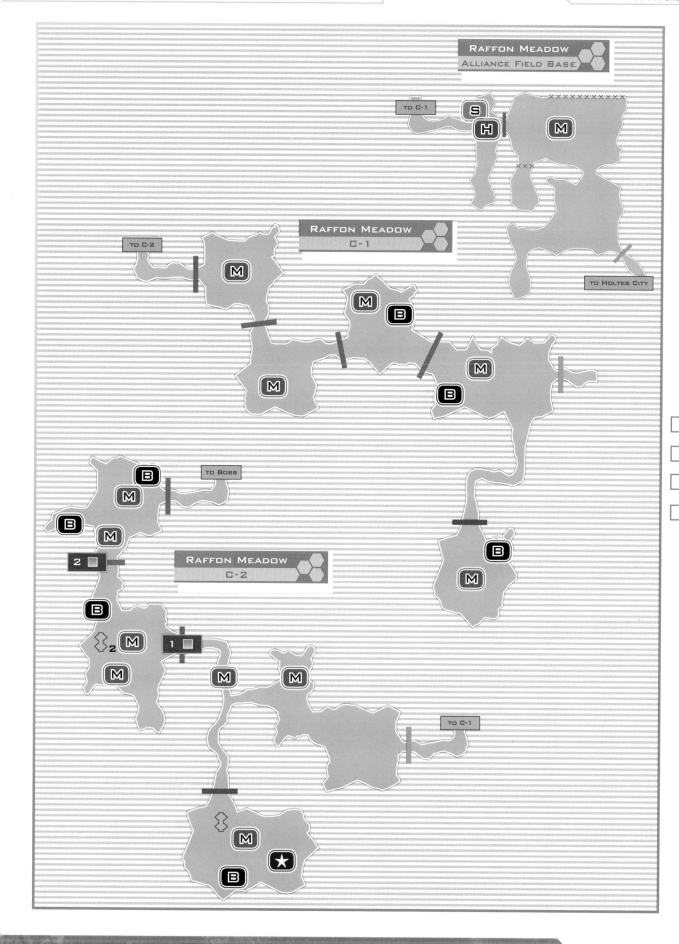

RAFFON MEADOW
ALLIANCE FIELD BASE

TO C-1

M

RAFFON MEADOW
C-1

TO C-2

M

TO HOLTES CITY

M

B

M

M

B

M

B

TO BOSS

B

M

M

B

2

RAFFON MEADOW
C-2

B

B

M

2

1

M

M

M

TO C-1

M

★

B

GETTING STARTED

STORY MODE

FREE MISSIONS

NETWORK MODE

RELICS

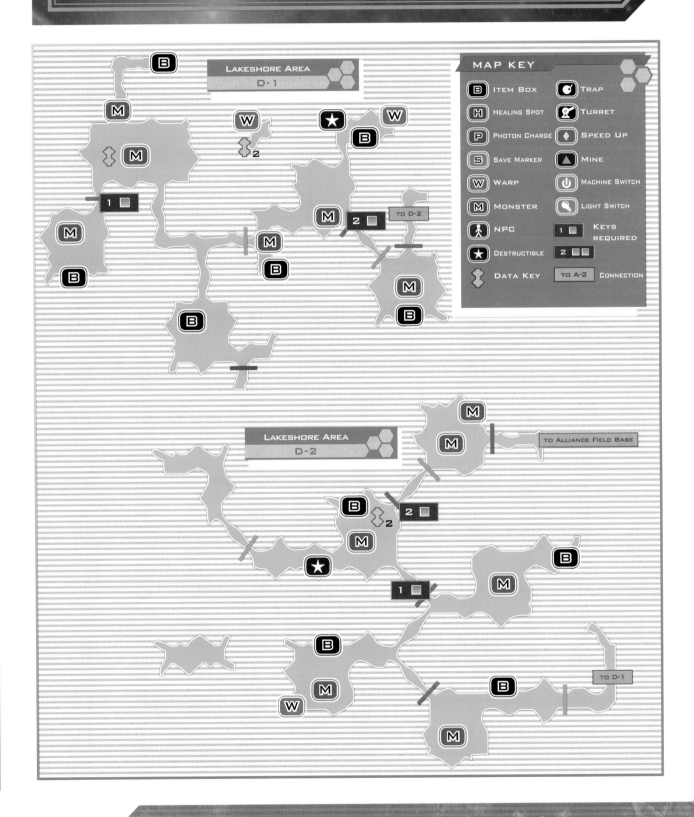

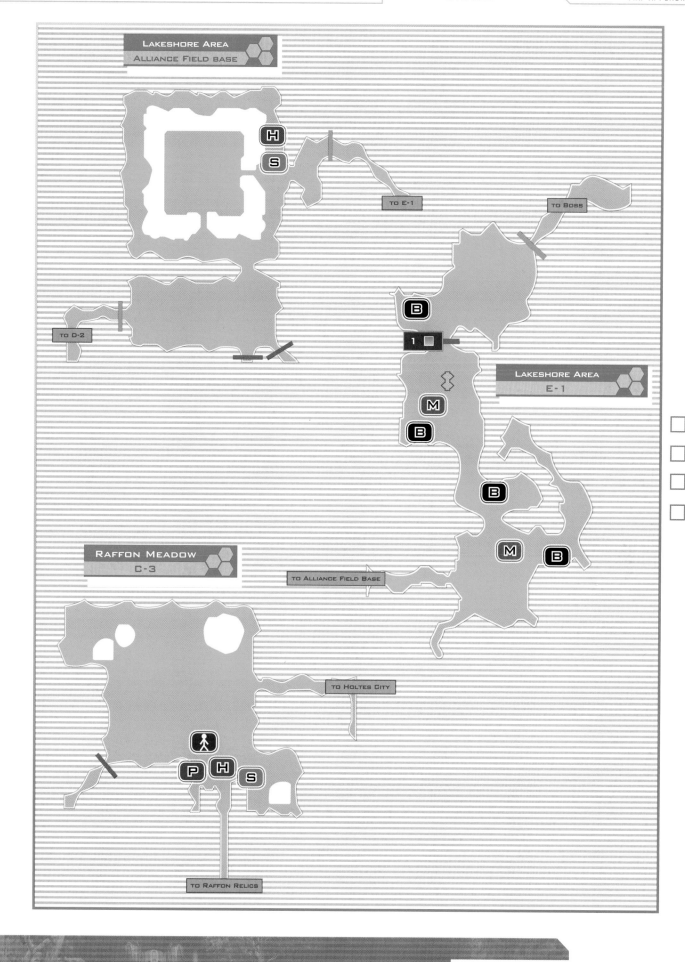

LAKESHORE AREA
ALLIANCE FIELD BASE

TO E-1

TO BOSS

TO D-2

LAKESHORE AREA
E-1

RAFFON MEADOW
C-3

TO ALLIANCE FIELD BASE

TO HOLTES CITY

TO RAFFON RELICS

GETTING STARTED

STORY MODE

FREE MISSIONS

NETWORK MODE

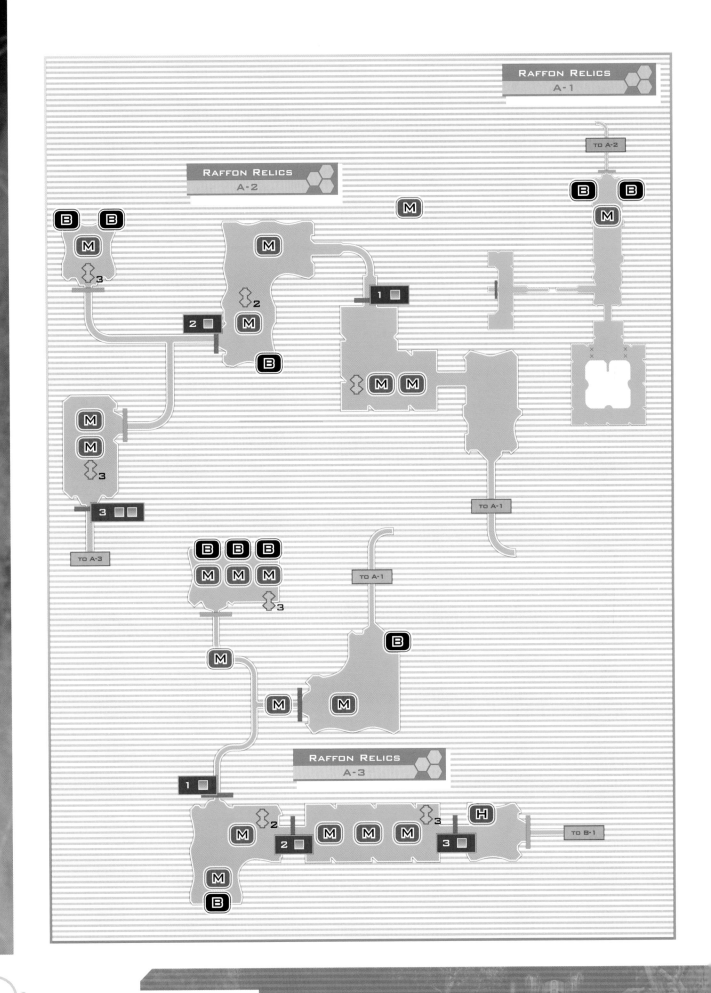

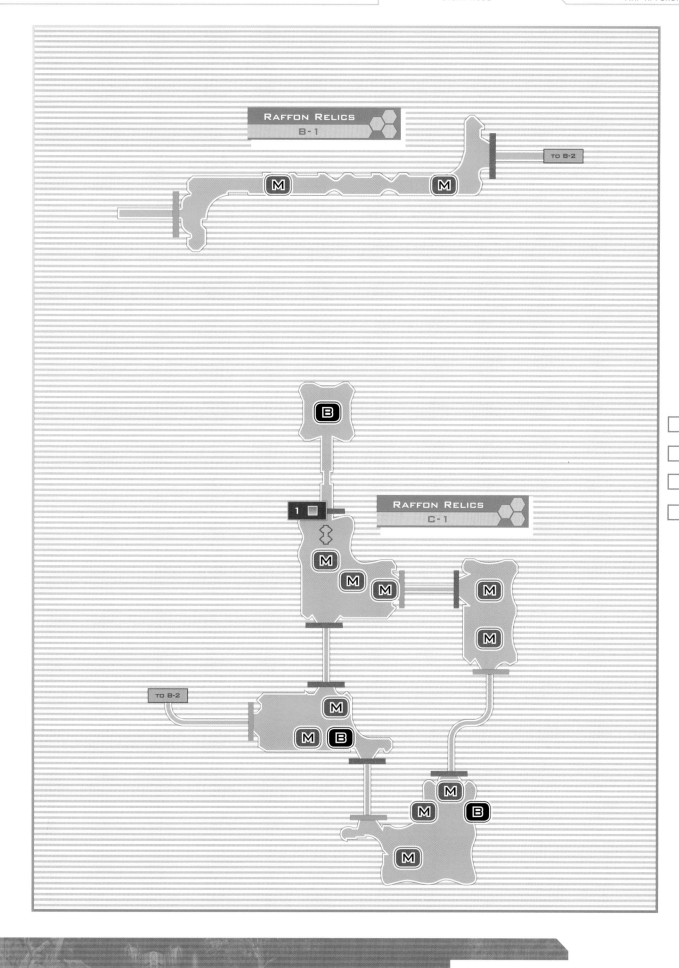

RAFFON RELICS
B-1

TO B-2

RAFFON RELICS
C-1

TO B-2

ROGUES

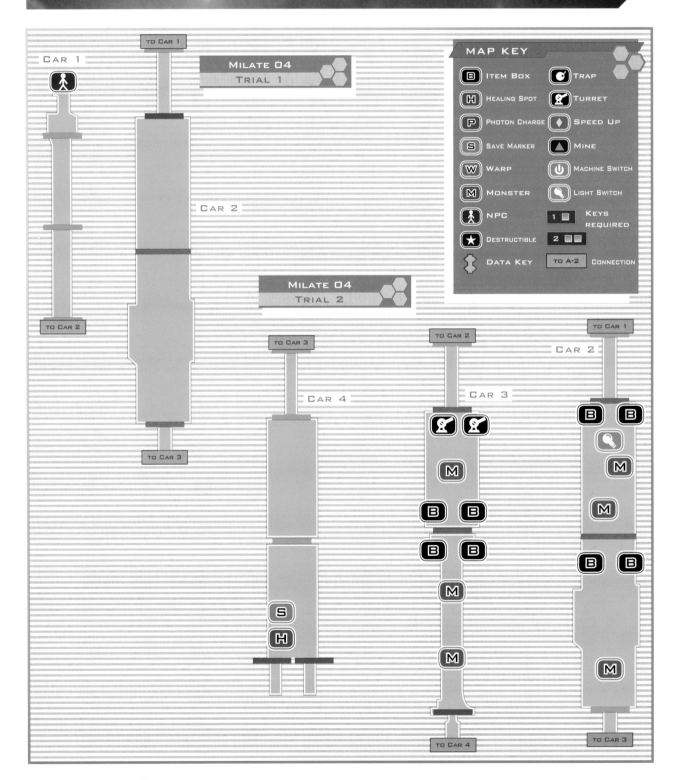

CAR 1

TO CAR 1

MILATE 04
TRIAL 1

MAP KEY

B	ITEM BOX	🎯	TRAP
H	HEALING SPOT	🔫	TURRET
P	PHOTON CHARGE	◆	SPEED UP
S	SAVE MARKER	▲	MINE
W	WARP	⏻	MACHINE SWITCH
M	MONSTER	🔧	LIGHT SWITCH
NPC		1 ▢	KEYS REQUIRED
★	DESTRUCTIBLE	2 ▢▢	
DATA KEY		TO A-2	CONNECTION

CAR 2

TO CAR 2

TO CAR 3

MILATE 04
TRIAL 2

TO CAR 3

TO CAR 2

CAR 2

TO CAR 1

CAR 4

CAR 3

B   B

🔫   🔫

🔧

M

M

B   B

B   B

M

B   B

B   B

M

S

M

H

M

TO CAR 4

TO CAR 3

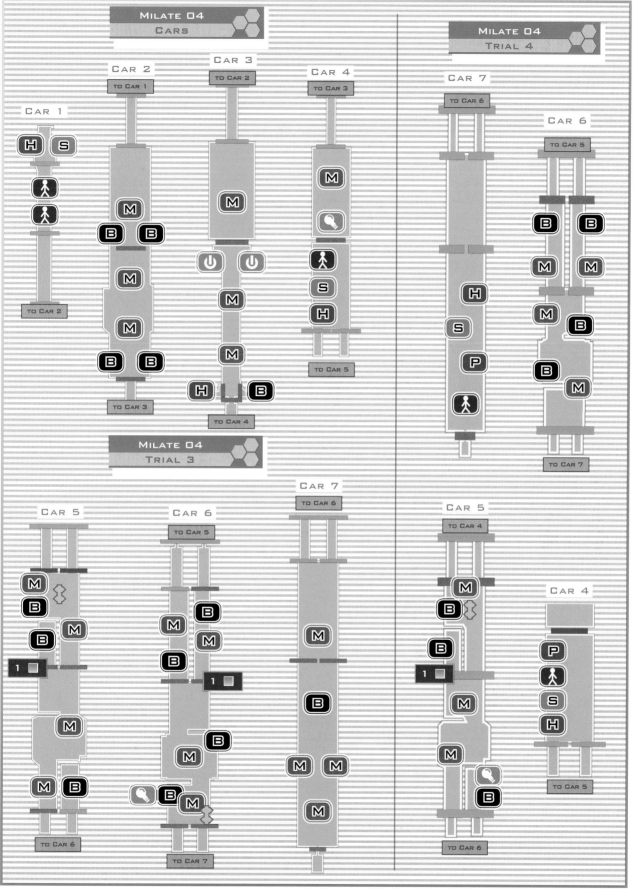

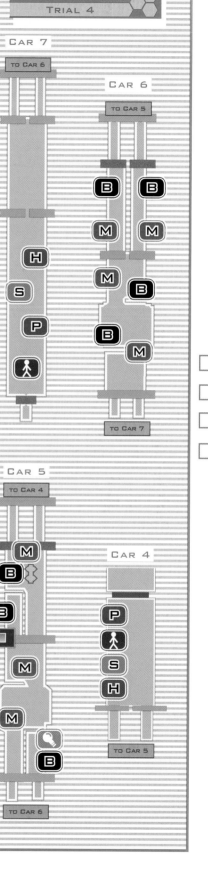

THE DIVINE MAIDEN

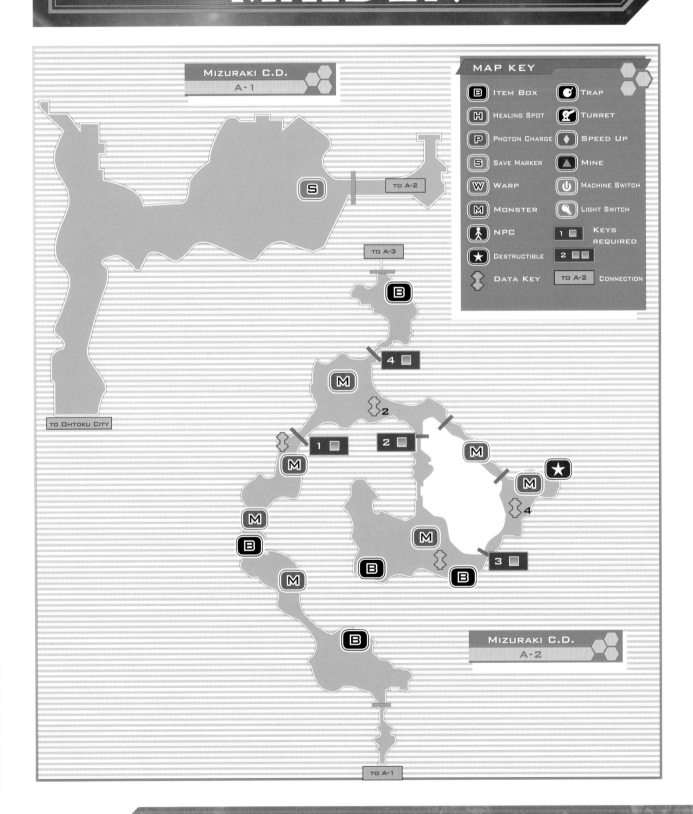

MIZURAKI C.D.
A-1

MAP KEY

B	ITEM BOX	**⊙**	TRAP
H	HEALING SPOT	**⚔**	TURRET
P	PHOTON CHARGE	**◆**	SPEED UP
S	SAVE MARKER	**▲**	MINE
W	WARP	**⏻**	MACHINE SWITCH
M	MONSTER	**🔑**	LIGHT SWITCH
🚶	NPC	**1 ▢**	KEYS REQUIRED
★	DESTRUCTIBLE	**2 ▢▢**	
⬦	DATA KEY	**TO A-2**	CONNECTION

TO A-2

TO A-3

TO OHTOKU CITY

MIZURAKI C.D.
A-2

TO A-1

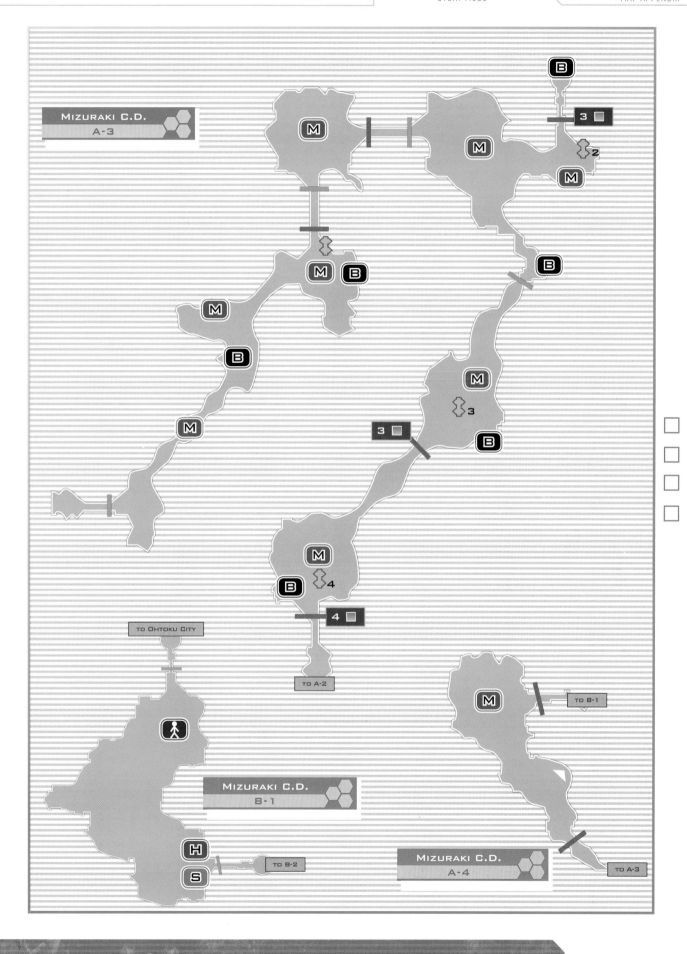

MIZURAKI C.D.
A-3

MIZURAKI C.D.
B-1

MIZURAKI C.D.
A-4

TO OHTOKU CITY

TO A-2

TO B-1

TO B-2

TO A-3

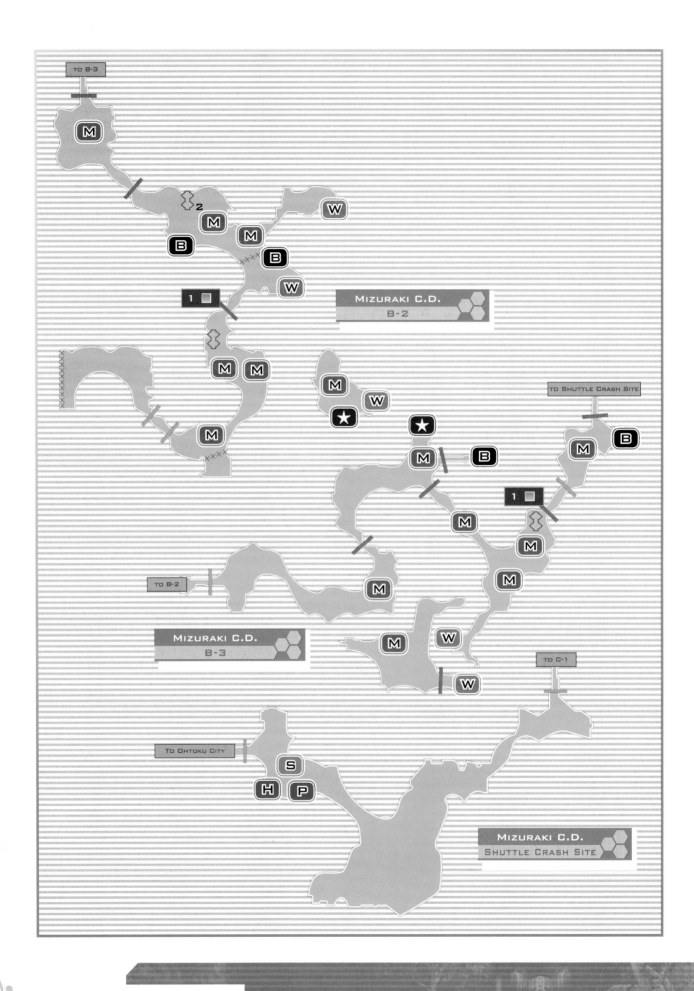

TO B-3

MIZURAKI C.D.
B-2

TO SHUTTLE CRASH SITE

TO B-2

MIZURAKI C.D.
B-3

TO C-1

TO OHTOKU CITY

MIZURAKI C.D.
SHUTTLE CRASH SITE

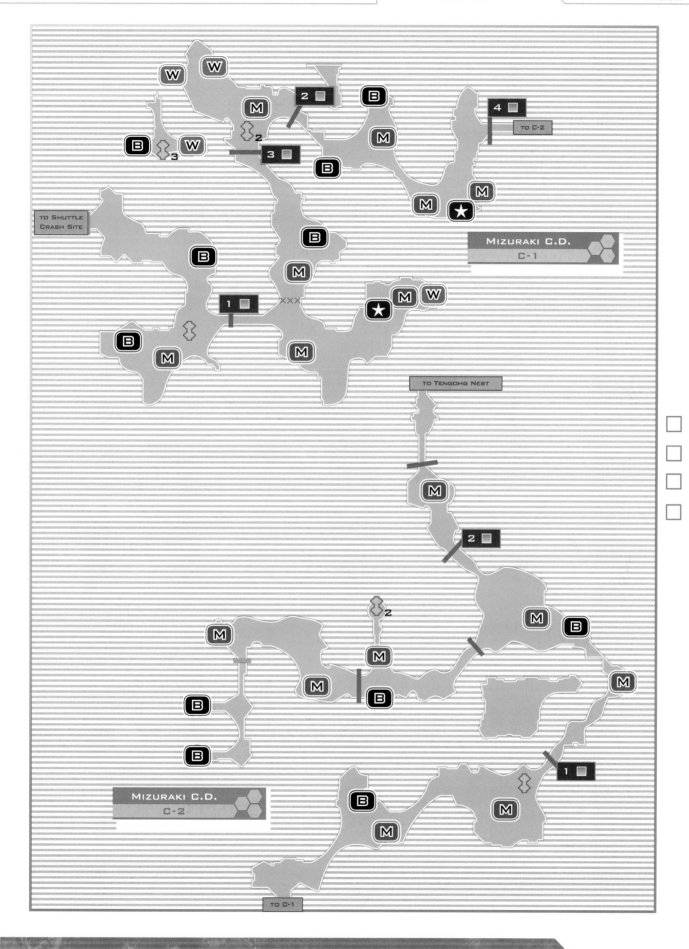

TO SHUTTLE
CRASH SITE

TO C-2

MIZURAKI C.D.
C-1

TO TENGOHG NEST

MIZURAKI C.D.
C-2

TO C-1

GETTING STARTED

STORY MODE

FREE MISSIONS

NETWORK MODE

CAPTIVES OF MOATOOB

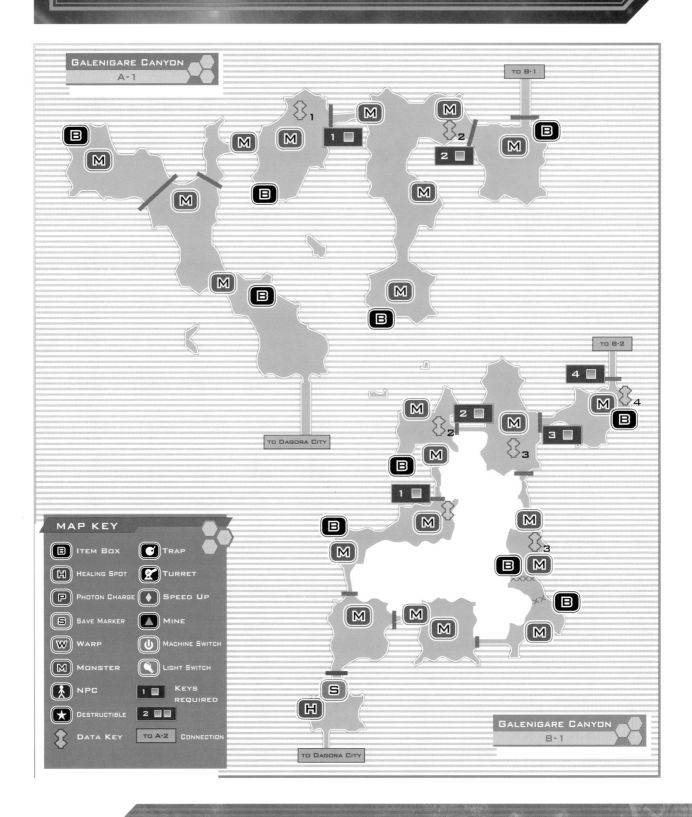

GALENIGARE CANYON
A-1

TO B-1

TO B-2

TO DAGORA CITY

MAP KEY

B	ITEM BOX	**C**	TRAP
H	HEALING SPOT	**X**	TURRET
P	PHOTON CHARGE	**◆**	SPEED UP
S	SAVE MARKER	**▲**	MINE
W	WARP	**U**	MACHINE SWITCH
M	MONSTER	**🔍**	LIGHT SWITCH
👤	NPC	**1** ☐	KEYS REQUIRED
★	DESTRUCTIBLE	**2** ☐☐	
⬡	DATA KEY	TO A-2	CONNECTION

GALENIGARE CANYON
B-1

TO DAGORA CITY

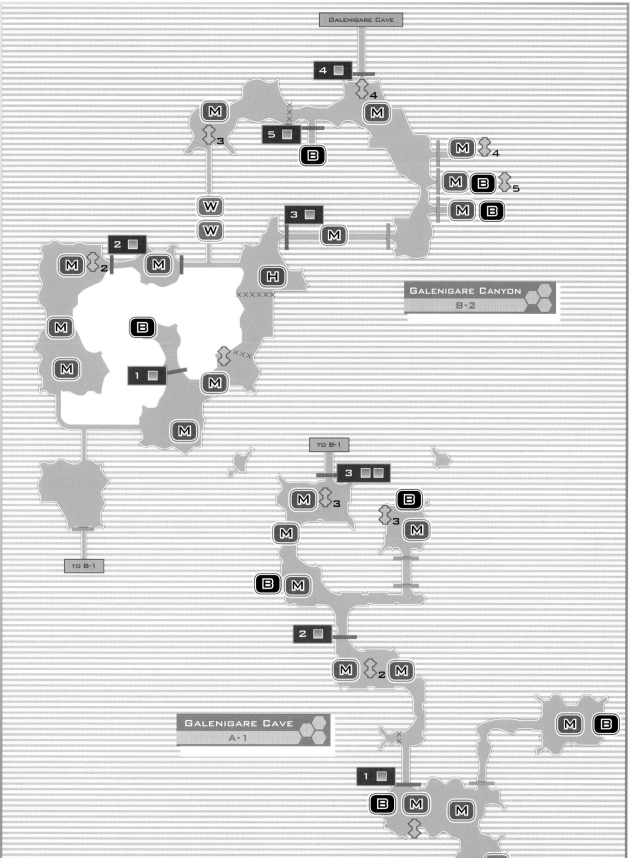

GALENIGARE CAVE

4

M

M

5

B

M

3

W

M 4

W

M B 5

3

M

M B

2

M M

H

GALENIGARE CANYON
B-2

M

B

M

1

M

M

TO B-1

3

M

3

B

M 3

TO B-1

B M

2

M 2 M

GALENIGARE CAVE
A-1

M B

1

B M M

H S

GETTING STARTED

STORY MODE

FREE MISSIONS

NETWORK MODE

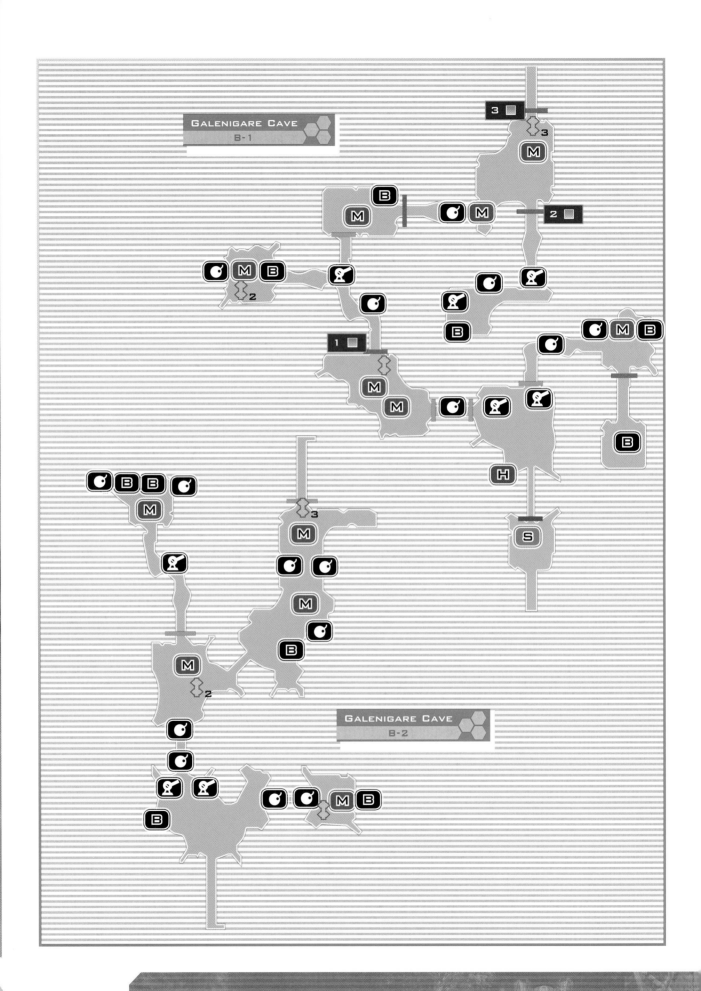

GALENIGARE CAVE
B-1

GALENIGARE CAVE
B-2

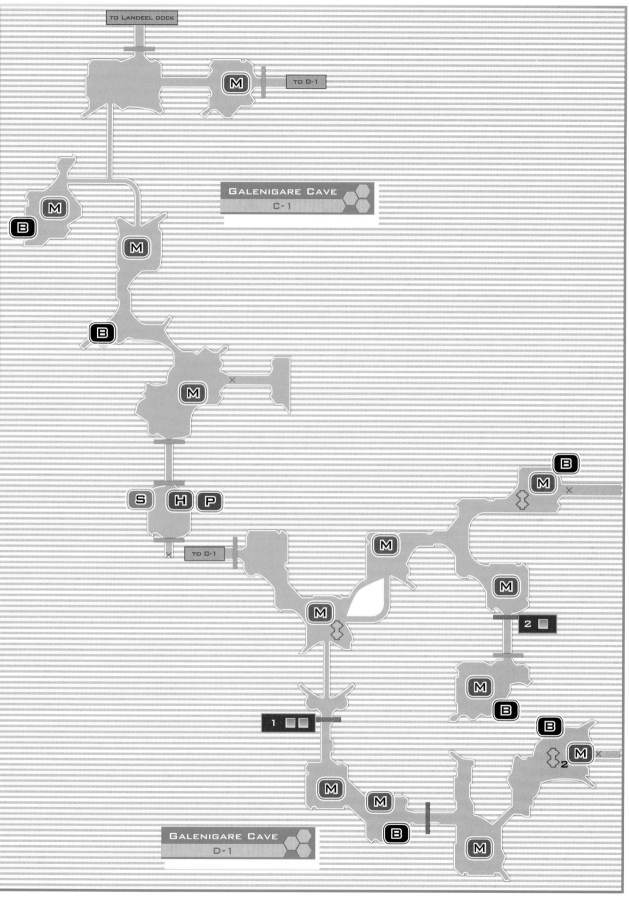

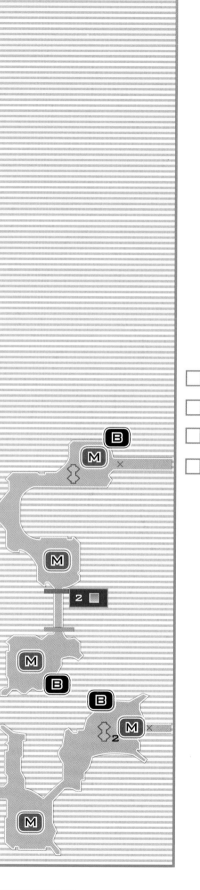

PHOTON SEALING

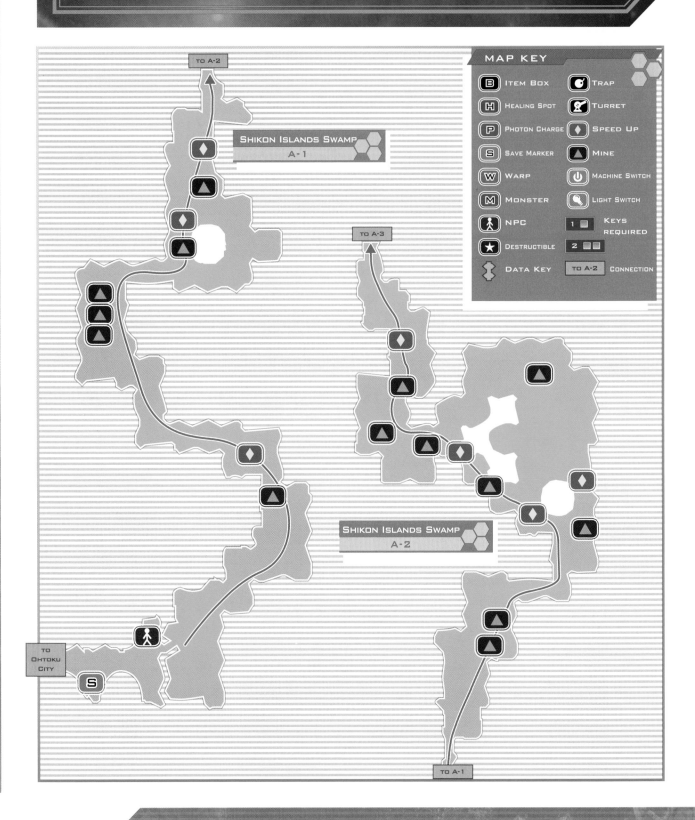

MAP KEY

B	ITEM BOX	🎯	TRAP
H	HEALING SPOT	🔫	TURRET
P	PHOTON CHARGE	◆	SPEED UP
S	SAVE MARKER	▲	MINE
W	WARP	⏻	MACHINE SWITCH
M	MONSTER	🔍	LIGHT SWITCH
🚶	NPC	1 ▯	KEYS REQUIRED
★	DESTRUCTIBLE	2 ▯▯	
🦴	DATA KEY	TO A-2	CONNECTION

TO A-2

SHIKON ISLANDS SWAMP
A-1

TO A-3

SHIKON ISLANDS SWAMP
A-2

TO OHTOKU CITY

TO A-1

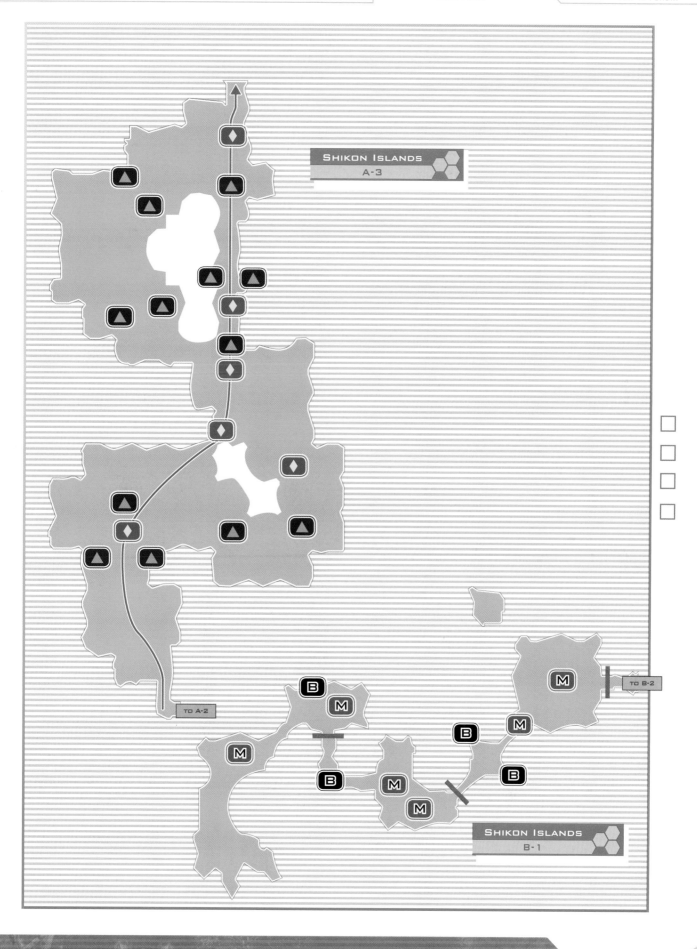

SHIKON ISLANDS
A-3

SHIKON ISLANDS
B-1

TO B-2

TO A-2

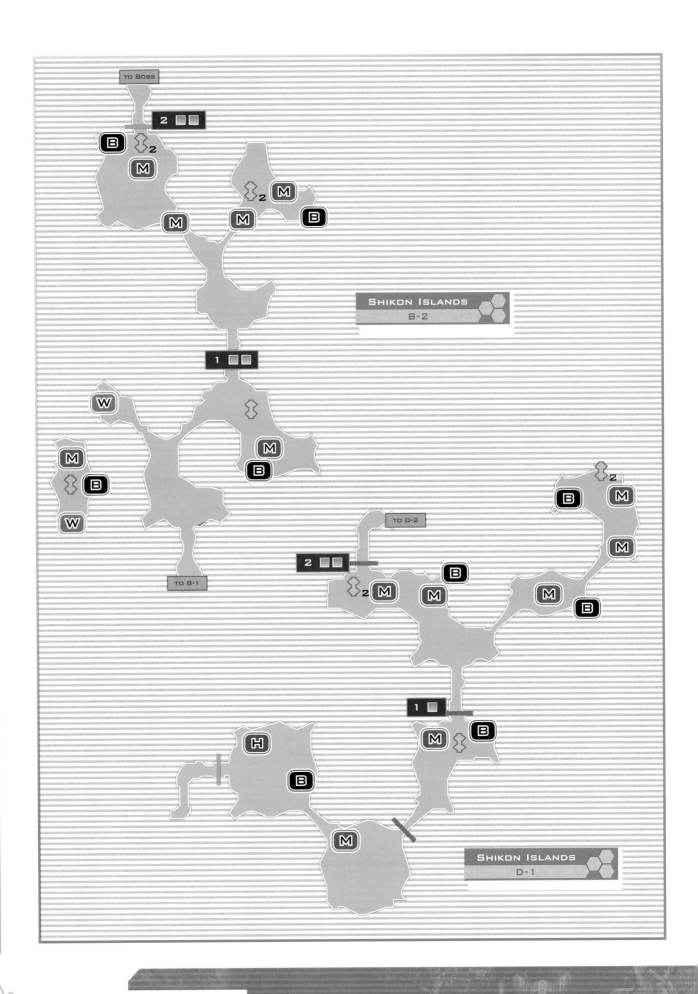

TO BOSS

SHIKON ISLANDS
8-2

TO 8-1

TO D-2

SHIKON ISLANDS
D-1

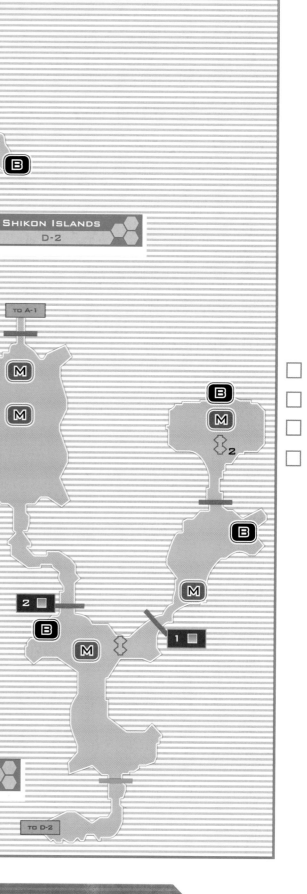

SHIKON ISLANDS
D-2

SHIKON ISLANDS
D-3

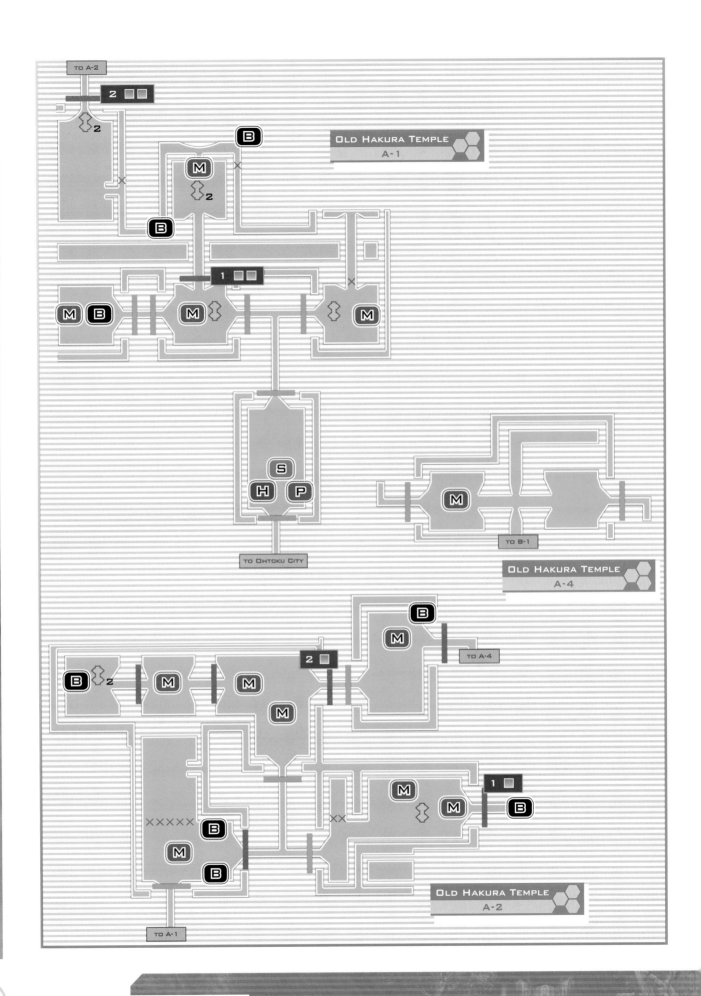

TO A-2

2

B

OLD HAKURA TEMPLE
A-1

M

B

1

M B

M

M

S
H P

M

TO B-1

OLD HAKURA TEMPLE
A-4

TO OHTOKU CITY

B

M

2

TO A-4

B

M

M

M

1

M

M B

XX

XXXXX B

M

B

OLD HAKURA TEMPLE
A-2

TO A-1

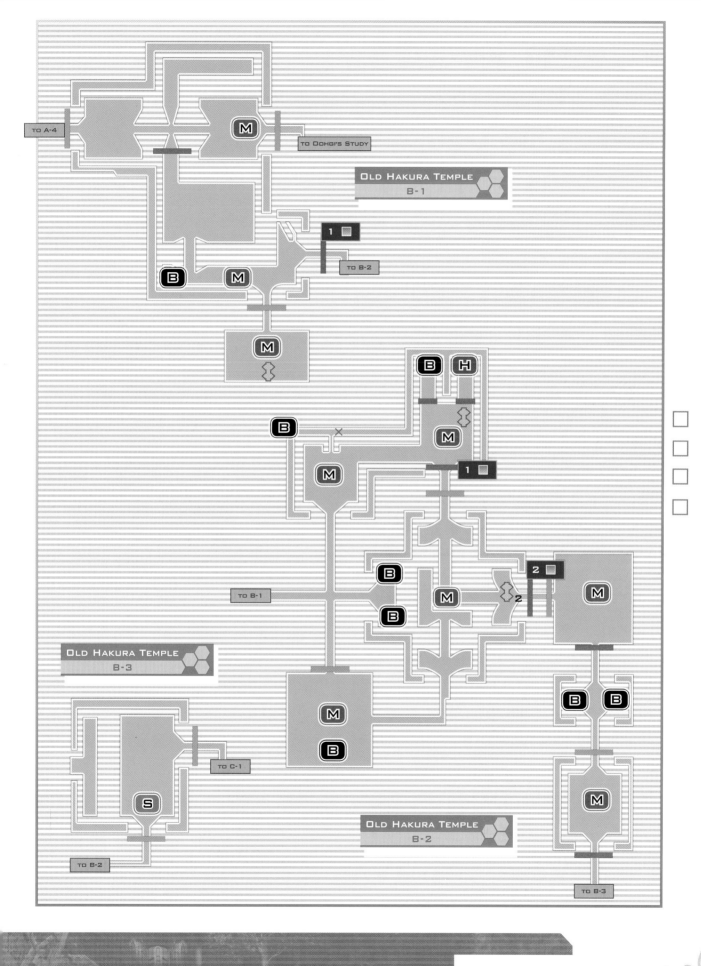

TO A-4

M

TO OOHGI'S STUDY

OLD HAKURA TEMPLE
B-1

1 □

TO B-2

B   M

M

B   H

B

M

M

1 □

2 □

B   M

M

TO B-1

B

B

OLD HAKURA TEMPLE
B-3

M

B

B   B

TO C-1

M

S

OLD HAKURA TEMPLE
B-2

TO B-2

TO B-3

GETTING STARTED

STORY MODE

FREE MISSIONS

NETWORK MODE

IN MELLVORE'S WAKE

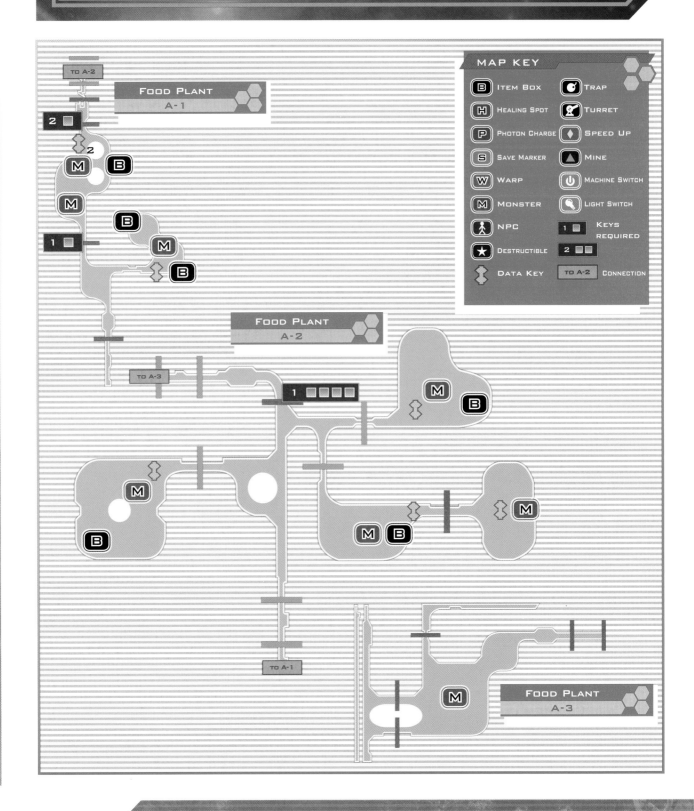

MAP KEY

B ITEM BOX
H HEALING SPOT
P PHOTON CHARGE
S SAVE MARKER
W WARP
M MONSTER
NPC
★ DESTRUCTIBLE
DATA KEY

TRAP
TURRET
SPEED UP
MINE
MACHINE SWITCH
LIGHT SWITCH
1 KEYS REQUIRED
2
TO A-2 CONNECTION

FOOD PLANT
A-1

TO A-2

FOOD PLANT
A-2

TO A-3

TO A-1

FOOD PLANT
A-3

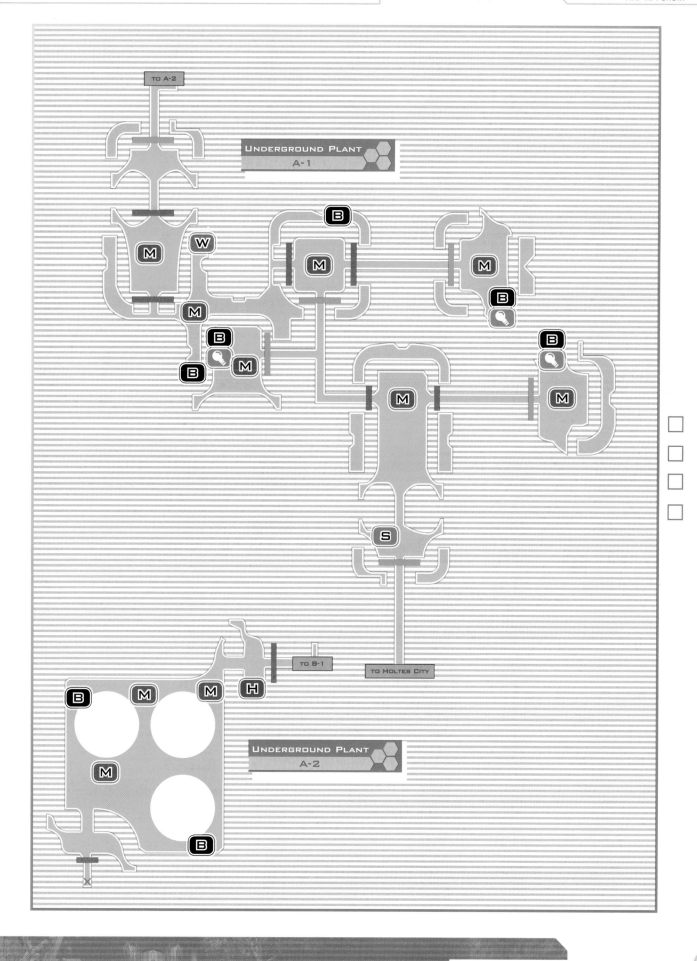

UNDERGROUND PLANT
A-1

TO A-2

UNDERGROUND PLANT
A-2

TO B-1

TO HOLTES CITY

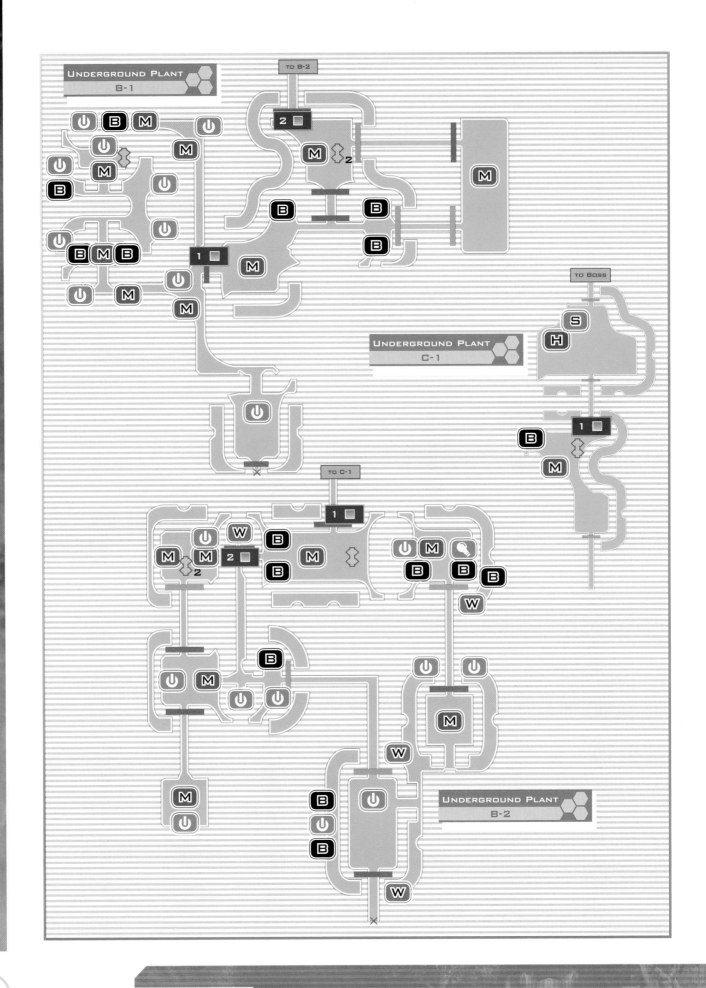

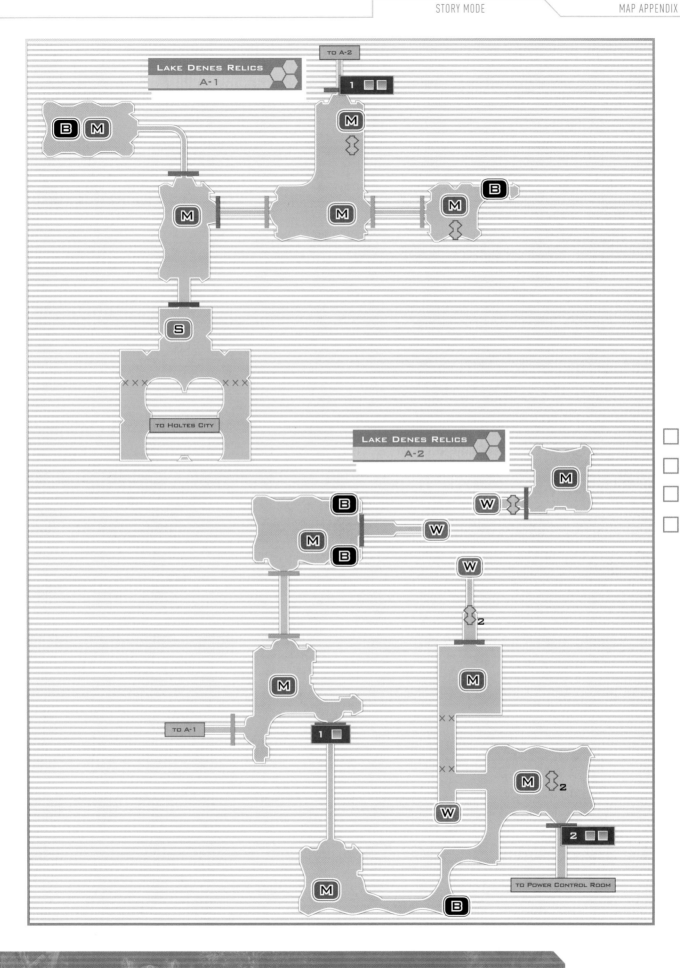

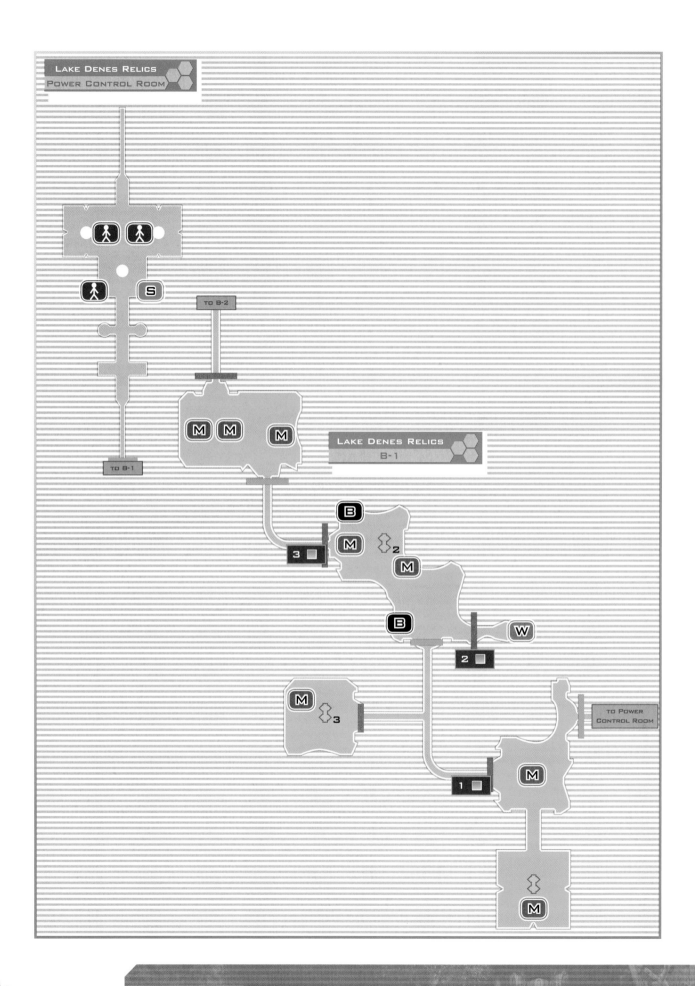

TO B-2

TO B-1

LAKE DENES RELICS
B-1

TO POWER
CONTROL ROOM

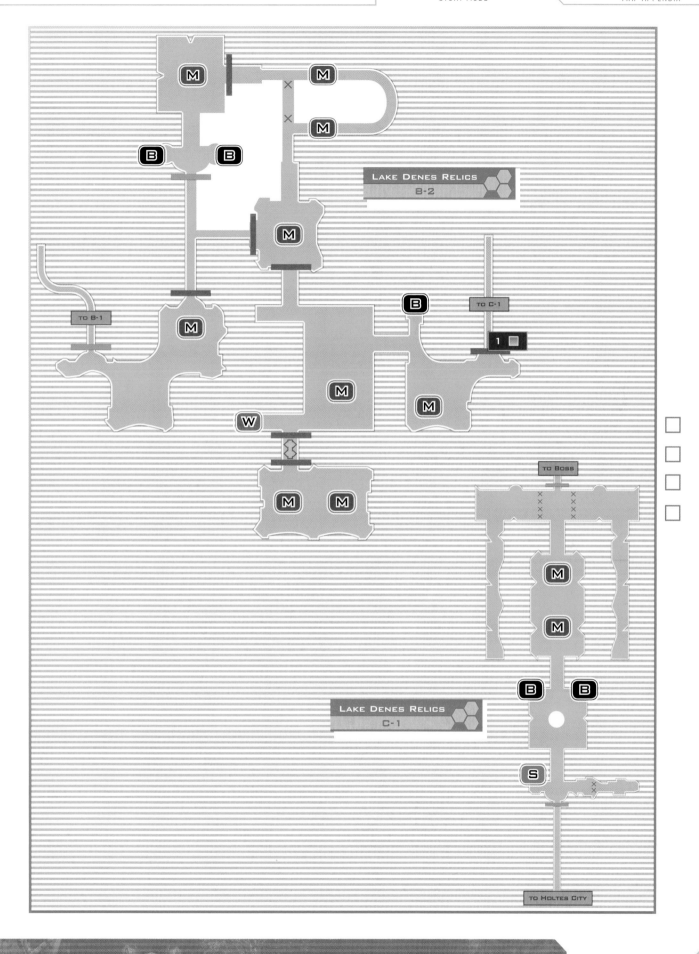

LAKE DENES RELICS
B-2

LAKE DENES RELICS
C-1

TO B-1

TO C-1

TO BOSS

TO HOLTES CITY

GETTING STARTED

STORY MODE

FREE MISSIONS

NETWORK MODE

HOT SOS

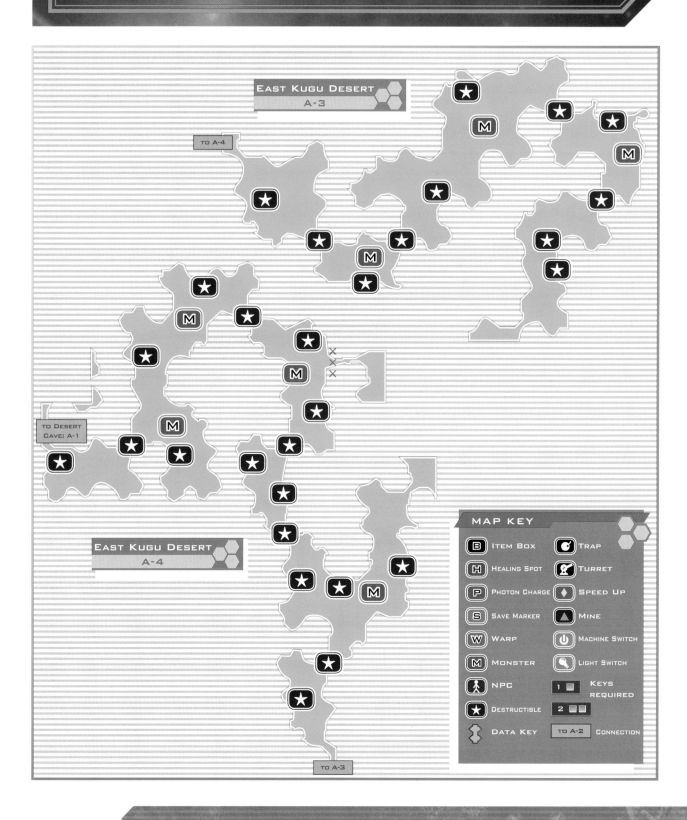

EAST KUGU DESERT
A-3

TO A-4

EAST KUGU DESERT
A-4

TO DESERT
CAVE: A-1

TO A-3

MAP KEY

B	ITEM BOX		TRAP
H	HEALING SPOT		TURRET
P	PHOTON CHARGE	◆	SPEED UP
S	SAVE MARKER	▲	MINE
W	WARP	⏻	MACHINE SWITCH
M	MONSTER		LIGHT SWITCH
NPC		1 ▢	KEYS REQUIRED
★	DESTRUCTIBLE	2 ▢▢	
DATA KEY		TO A-2	CONNECTION

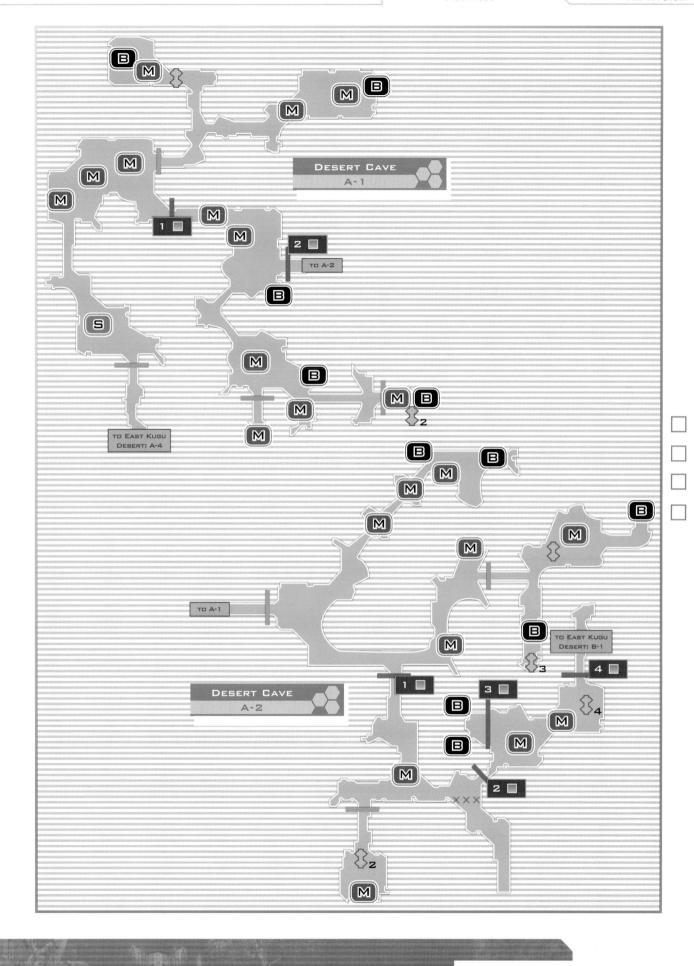

DESERT CAVE
A-1

TO A-2

TO EAST KUGU
DESERT: A-4

TO A-1

TO EAST KUGU
DESERT: B-1

DESERT CAVE
A-2

GETTING STARTED

STORY MODE

FREE MISSIONS

NETWORK MODE

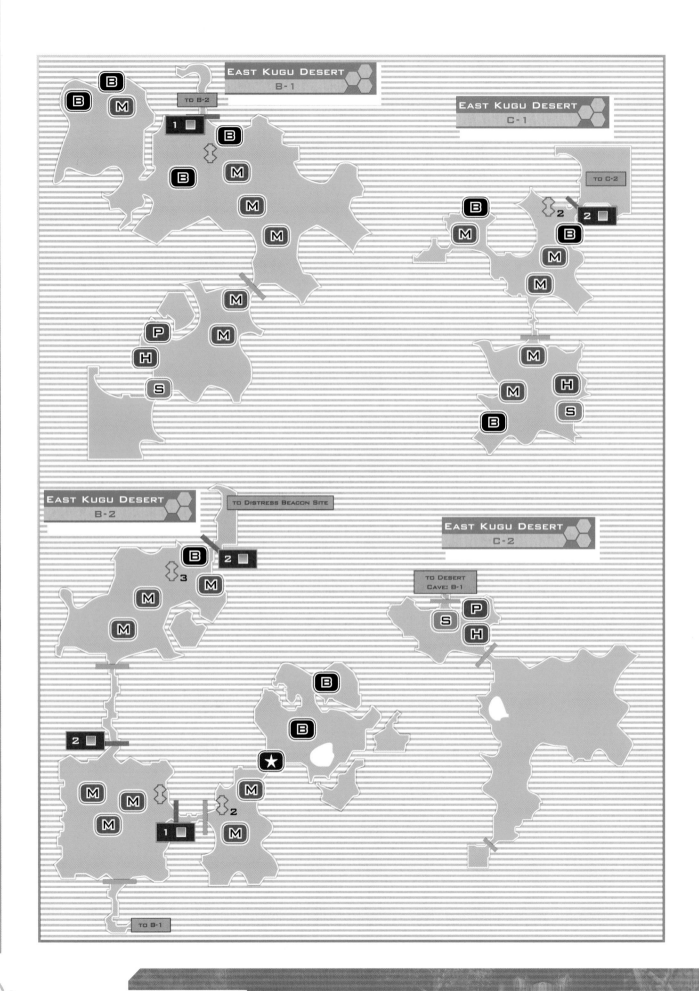

EAST KUGU DESERT
B-1

TO B-2

EAST KUGU DESERT
C-1

TO C-2

EAST KUGU DESERT
B-2

TO DISTRESS BEACON SITE

EAST KUGU DESERT
C-2

TO DESERT
CAVE: B-1

TO B-1

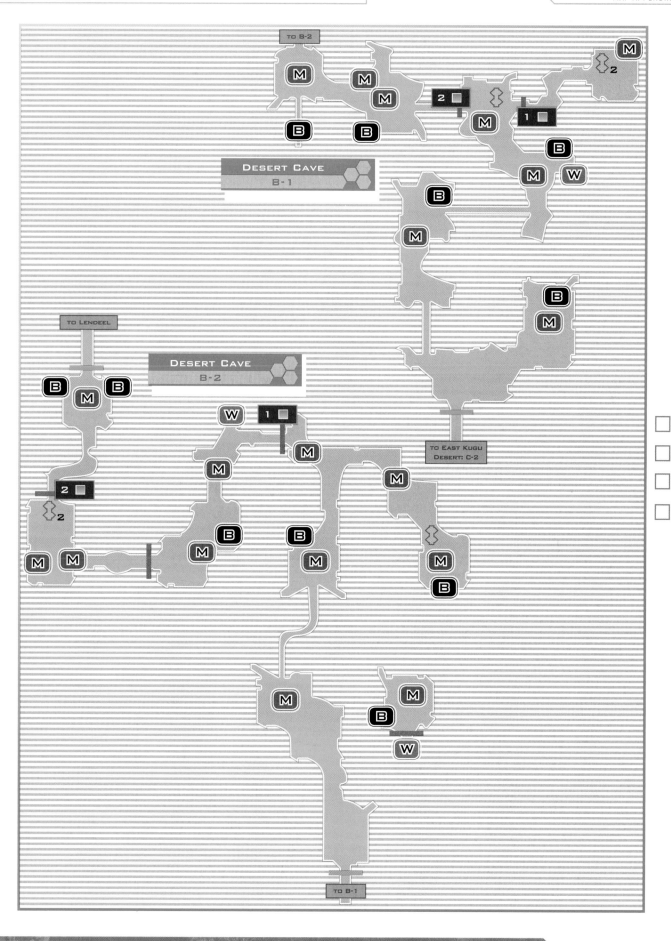

TO B-2

M

M

M

M

2 □

1 □

2

M

B

B

B

M

W

DESERT CAVE
B-1

B

M

B

M

TO LENDEEL

DESERT CAVE
B-2

B M B

W

1 □

M

M

2 □

2

B

M M

M

B

M

M

B

M

TO EAST KUGU
DESERT: C-2

M

B

M

B

B

M

M

B

W

TO B-1

GETTING STARTED
STORY MODE
FREE MISSIONS
NETWORK MODE

RITE OF DIVINATION

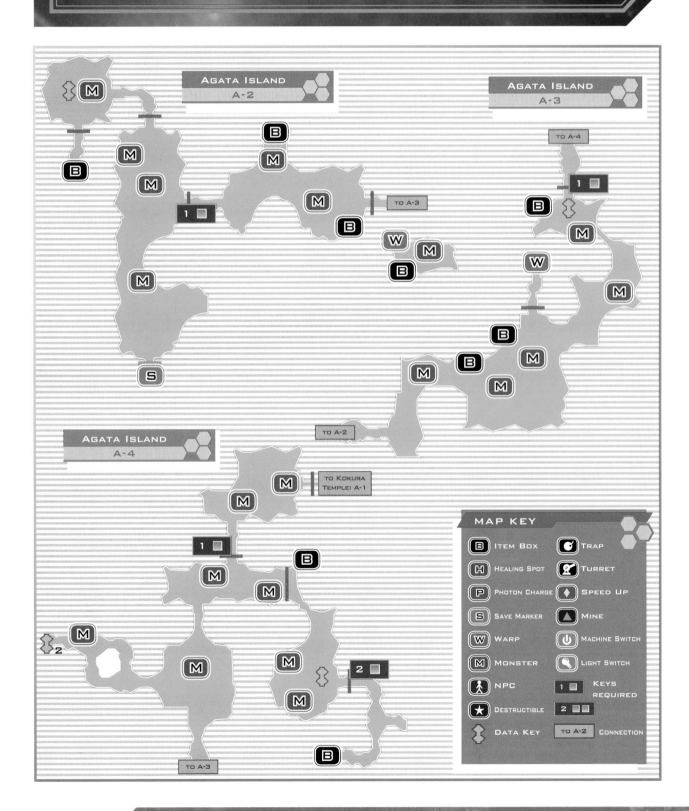

AGATA ISLAND
A-2

AGATA ISLAND
A-3

TO A-4

TO A-3

TO A-2

AGATA ISLAND
A-4

TO KOKURA
TEMPLE: A-1

MAP KEY

B	ITEM BOX		TRAP
H	HEALING SPOT		TURRET
P	PHOTON CHARGE		SPEED UP
S	SAVE MARKER		MINE
W	WARP		MACHINE SWITCH
M	MONSTER		LIGHT SWITCH
	NPC	1	KEYS REQUIRED
	DESTRUCTIBLE	2	
	DATA KEY	TO A-2	CONNECTION

TO A-3

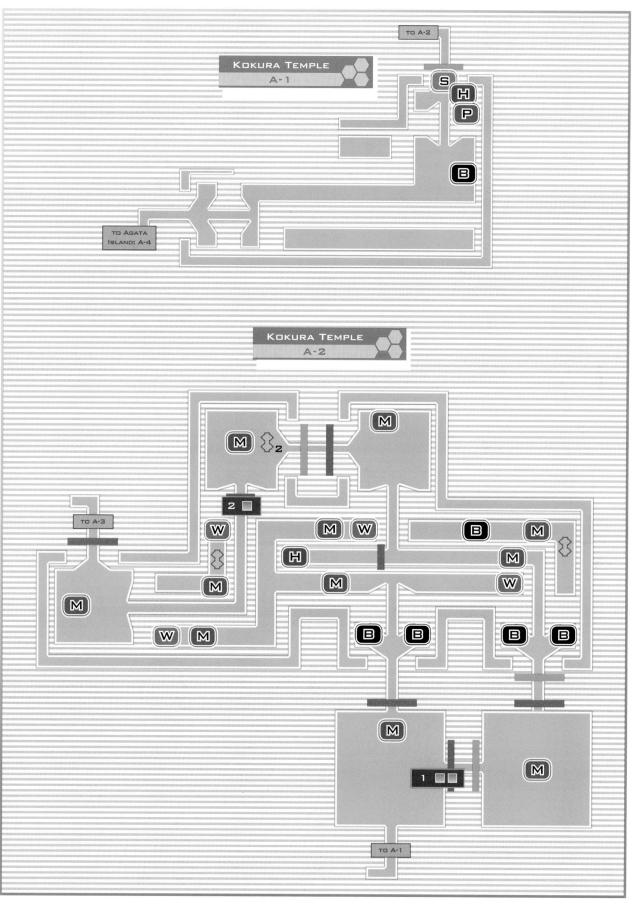

KOKURA TEMPLE
A-1

TO A-2

S
H
P

B

TO AGATA
ISLAND: A-4

KOKURA TEMPLE
A-2

TO A-3

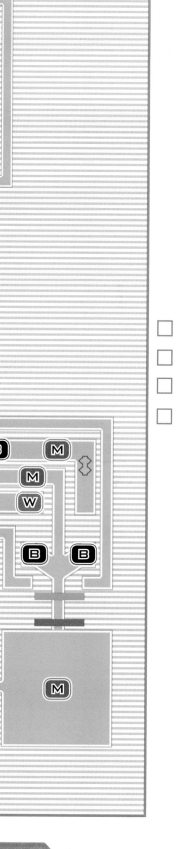

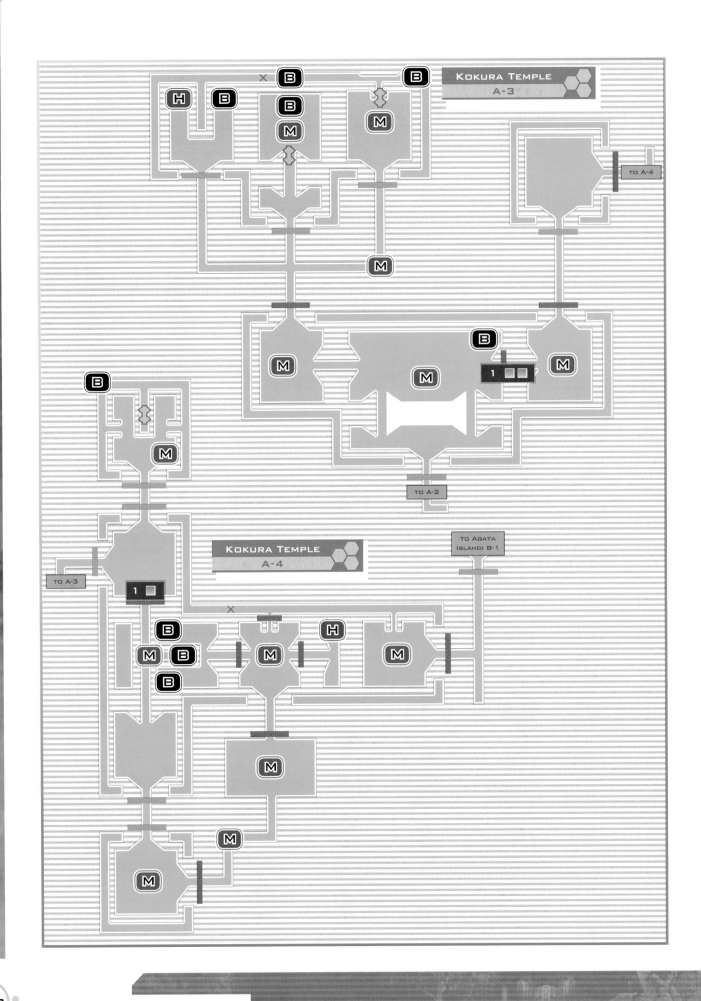

KOKURA TEMPLE
A-3

TO A-4

TO A-2

TO AGATA
ISLAND: B-1

KOKURA TEMPLE
A-4

TO A-3

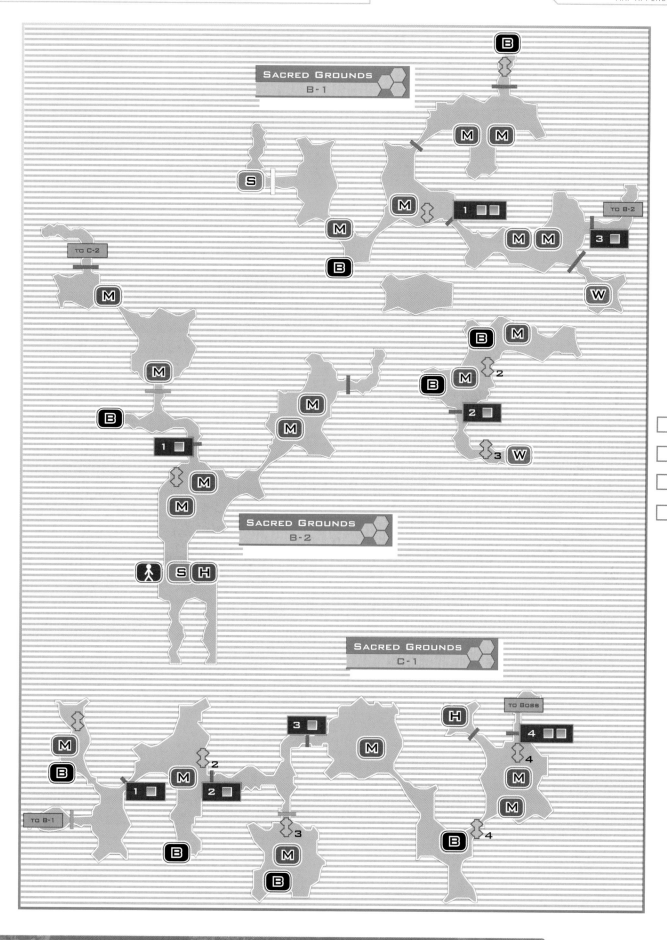

UNIFICATION POINT

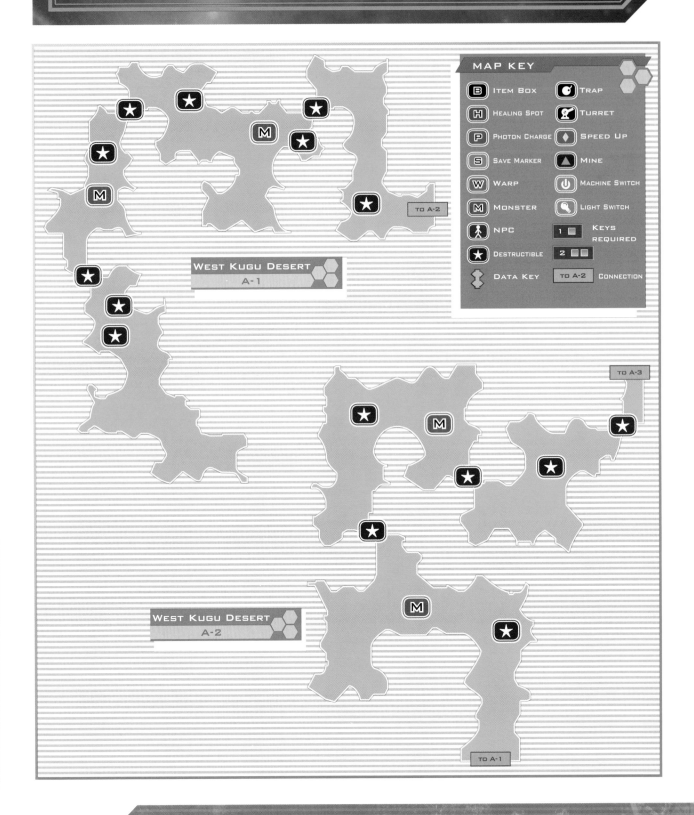

MAP KEY

B	ITEM BOX		TRAP
H	HEALING SPOT		TURRET
P	PHOTON CHARGE		SPEED UP
S	SAVE MARKER		MINE
W	WARP		MACHINE SWITCH
M	MONSTER		LIGHT SWITCH
	NPC	1	KEYS REQUIRED
★	DESTRUCTIBLE	2	
	DATA KEY	TO A-2	CONNECTION

WEST KUGU DESERT
A-1

TO A-2

TO A-3

WEST KUGU DESERT
A-2

TO A-1

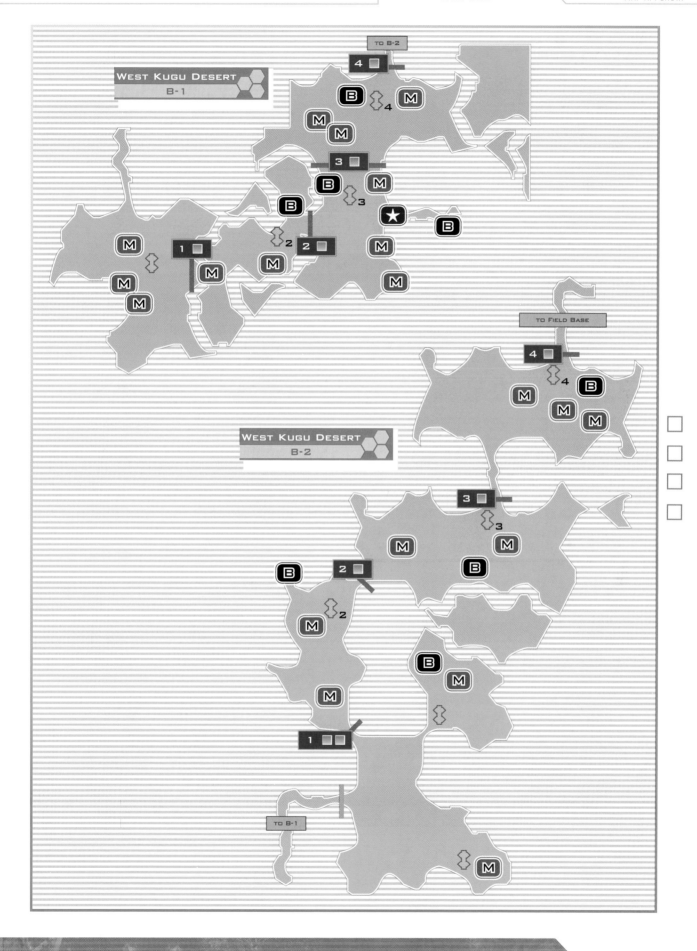

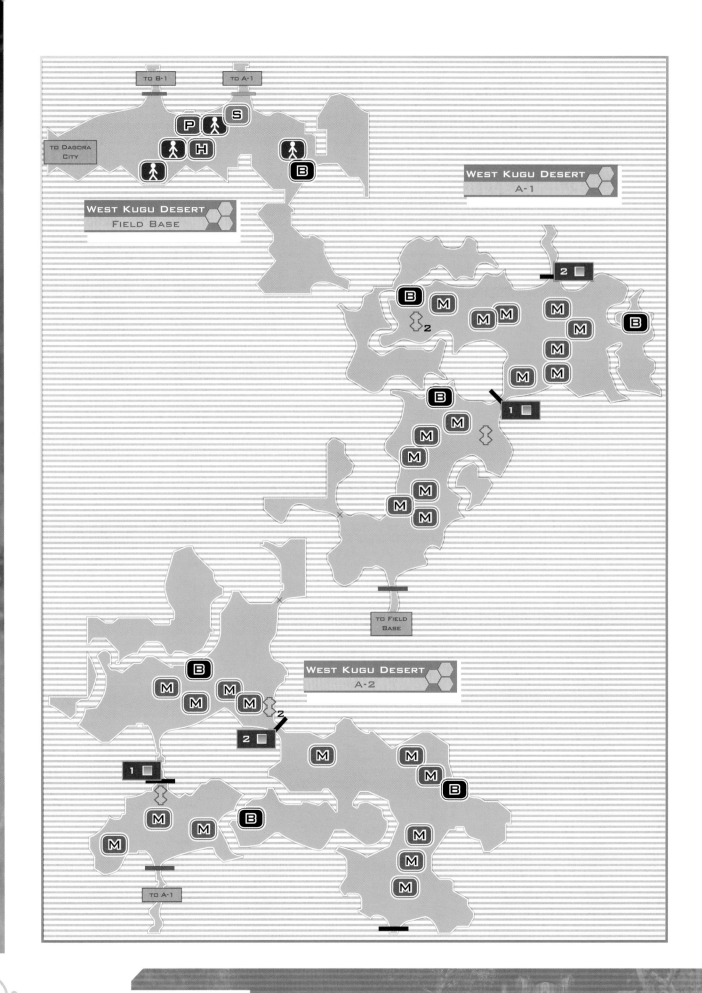

TO B-1   TO A-1

P 👤 S

TO DAGORA CITY

👤 H

👤

👤

B

WEST KUGU DESERT
A-1

WEST KUGU DESERT
FIELD BASE

2 ▢

B M

2

M M

M

M M

M

M M

B

M

B

M

1 ▢

M

M

M

M

M

TO FIELD BASE

B

M

M M

WEST KUGU DESERT
A-2

M

M

2

2 ▢

M

M

M

1 ▢

B

M

M

M

M

TO A-1

M

M

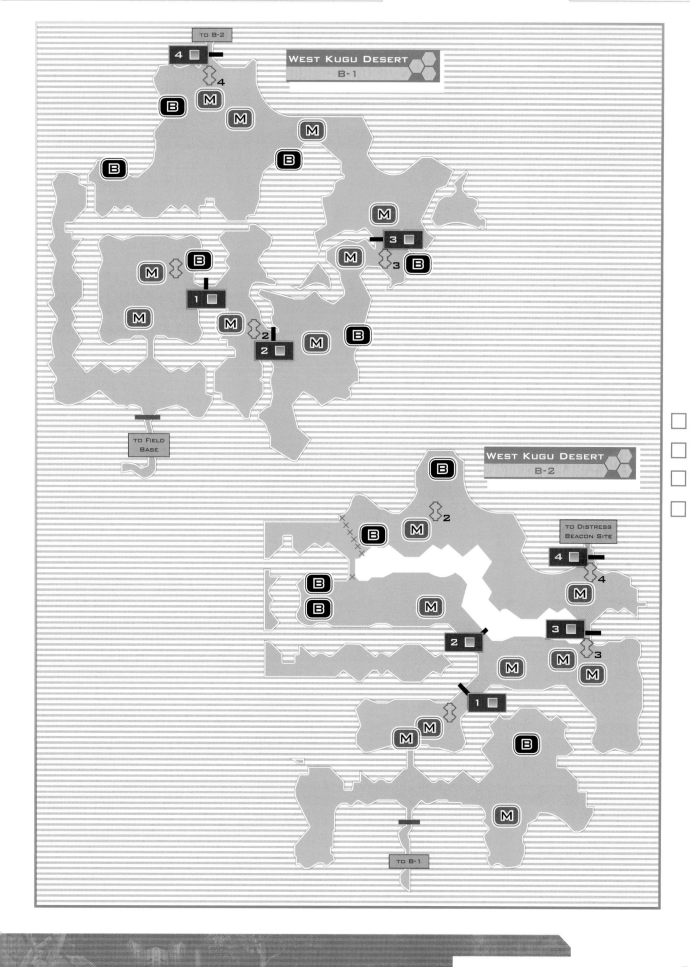

LIFE CHOICES

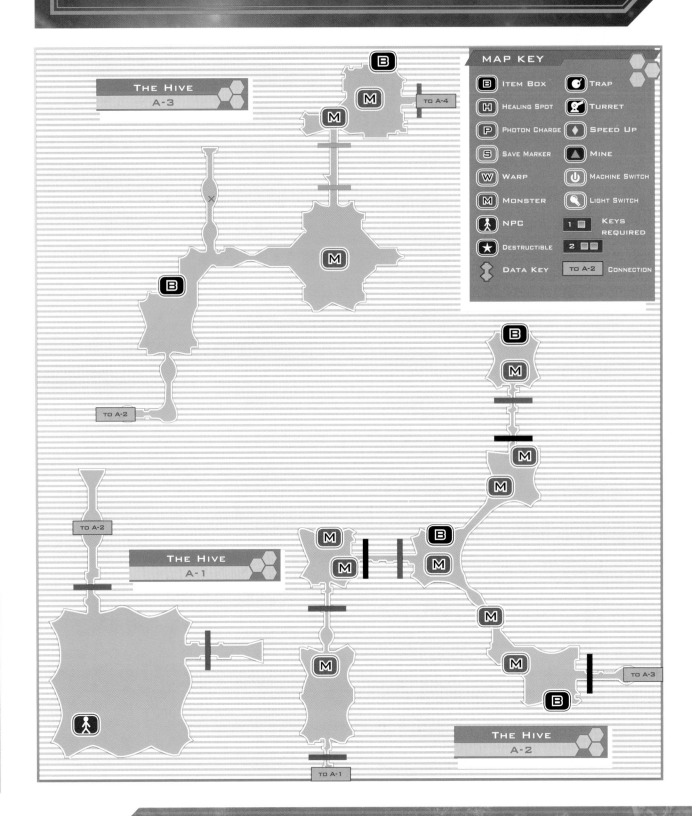

THE HIVE
A-3

TO A-4

TO A-2

TO A-2

THE HIVE
A-1

TO A-3

THE HIVE
A-2

TO A-1

MAP KEY

B	ITEM BOX		TRAP
H	HEALING SPOT		TURRET
P	PHOTON CHARGE		SPEED UP
S	SAVE MARKER		MINE
W	WARP		MACHINE SWITCH
M	MONSTER		LIGHT SWITCH
	NPC	1	KEYS REQUIRED
	DESTRUCTIBLE	2	
	DATA KEY	TO A-2	CONNECTION

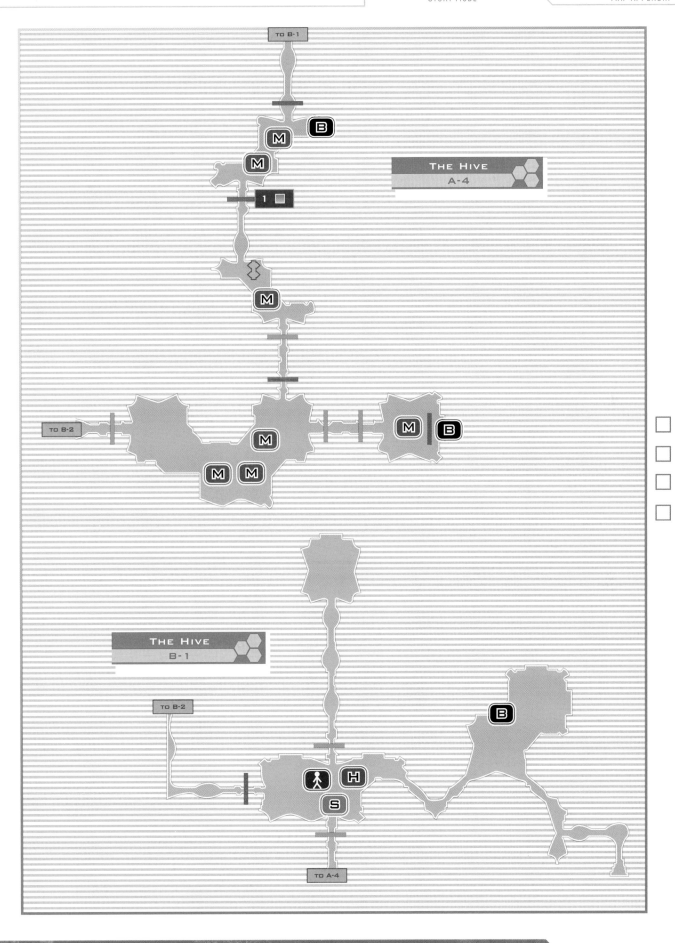

THE HIVE
A-4

THE HIVE
B-1

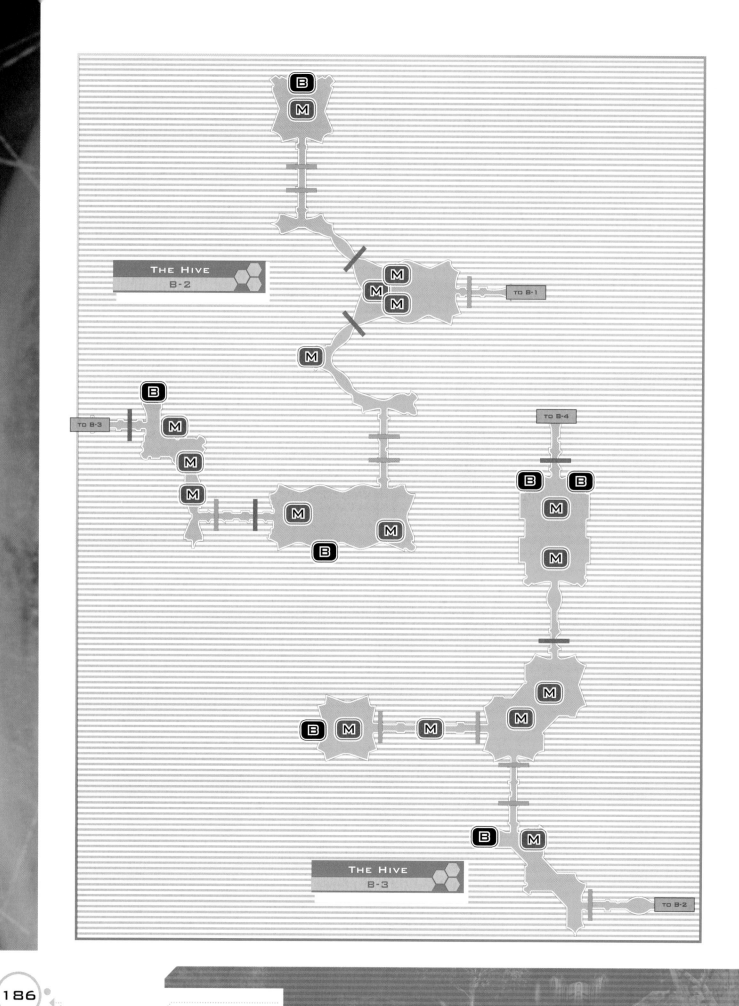

FREE MISSIONS

As you play Story Mode, you'll unlock Free Missions that you can play any time that you want a break from the main quest. The first one is unlocked during Chapter 3, and after that a new batch will be made available at the end of each chapter. The Free Missions you unlock will also be made available in Extra Mode. You can view lists of newly unlocked Free Missions by checking the Vision Phone in Ethan's room.

LEVEL-UP YOUR CLASSES

Free Missions provide a great opportunity to level Ethan up and each of his selectable classes. Each mission is a time trial, so if you can beat it quickly and slay all the enemies on the way, you'll earn Mission Points that will increase your class level. Diligent Free Mission players can easily max out all three of their classes by the end of the game. Free Missions also offer an opportunity to farm for Meseta, supplies, and synthesis materials. But if you're gunning for an S-Rank, there won't be any time for item-gathering.

WIN EXCLUSIVE PRIZES

Each mission offers a room decoration prize for S-Rank winners. Missions that end in a boss will usually reward you with a trophy of that boss's head, while other missions award replica ships or insect-themed prizes that are based on Sega's popular-in-Japan Mushi King games. In Extra Mode, certain missions also offer SUV Weapons Units (which can only be used by CASTS of level 20 or higher).

SUV WEAPON PRIZES

The following missions offer additional SUV Weapon Prizes to those who earn an S Rank in Extra Mode.

- Cargo Train Rescue (Holtes City Linear Train)
- Grove of Fanatics (Ohtoku City Flyer Base)
- Endrum Underground (Holtes City Linear Train)
- Tunnel Infestation (Dagora City Flyer Base)

CHOOSE THE RIGHT TEAM

One of the keys to success in Free Missions is choosing the right party. Maya Shidow is one of the best allies for Rangers and Forces, as she will cast stat-boosting Technics while you attack from a distance (other allies will typically just stand around). Free Missions also provide an opportunity to use a fully-evolved Pete in combat, and you won't be disappointed by the results.

When choosing your party, you'll also have to consider the Photon Arts they may give you if you earn an S-Rank. Except for Maya, who gives you purchasable spells, each party character has up to two Photon Arts that they may randomly bestow on Ethan when he earns an S-Rank. Unfortunately, not every character is always available—in Story Mode Karen, Hyuga and Maya will often be occupied by storyline events, so if you covet their Photon Arts, use them repeatedly in the few chapters in which they're available. In Extra Mode, the availability of party characters is based on your progress in Story Mode. If you've beaten the game, all seven characters will always be available.

SPECIAL S-RANK REWARDS

When you earn an S Rank at any trial, there is a small chance (around 1 in 10) that a party member will reward you with an exclusive Photon Art.

	Character	Prize 1	Prize 2
	HYUGA	GRAVITY STRIKE (1-HAND SWORD)	ASSAULT CRUSH (TWIN BLADES)
	KAREN	MOUBU SEIRAN-ZAN (TWIN DAGGERS)	–
	LEO	SPINNING BREAK (LONG SWORD)	DUS ROBADO (SPEAR)
	LUCAIM	BOBBA DONGA (KNUCKLES)	RENZAN SEIDAN-GA (TWIN CLAWS)
	MAYA	DIGAS (WAND/ROD)	RENTIS (ROD/WAND)
	TONNIO	BUTEN SHOUREN-ZAN (DAGGER)	SENTEN KANZAN-GA (CLAW)
	LOU	SPIRAL DANCE (DOUBLE BLADE)	–

[GUARDIANS COLONY]
LINEAR LINE PLATFORM

MISSION: EVACUATION

Due to a sudden SEED attack, there are people trapped in one section of the Linear Line. SEED-Forms are blocking their escape route.

		Required	-
LOC	Linear Line Corridor	Party	1-4

UNLOCKED AFTER COMPLETION OF CHAPTER 3

Bring a wide array of weapons into this trial so you can sweep groups with a Sword or home in on solitary targets with double dagger or 1-hand Saber Photon Art. The enemies won't put up much of a fight, but time is so tight that you have only a few seconds to devote to each of them.

When you enter Block 2, bear east at the fork and don't turn around until you've cleared out the wave of Pannon at the dead end. Then run to the west end of the map and blast the nearest item box to generate the wave of foes that holds the key. This is the one and only item box you should smash on the trial; everything else will just waste time.

MONSTERS

- **DELSABAN** LVL 10 TYPE: DARK
- **DELSABAN** LVL 11 TYPE: DARK
- **PANNON** LVL 10 TYPE: DARK
- **PANNON** LVL 11 TYPE: DARK
- **SENDILLAN** LVL 10 TYPE: DARK

TRIAL RANKING

CONDITIONS

1. CLEAR TIME 8:00 VALUE 700pts
   PENALTY -1 point per second late

2. ENEMIES 72 VALUE 300pts
   PENALTY -5 points per enemy missed

RANKING INFORMATION

SCORE	RANK	MESETA	MP	PRIZE
1000	S	1000	60	Linear Line
700 - 999	A	500	30	-
400 - 699	B	300	10	-
0 - 399	C	-	1	-

MISSION: ANNIHILATION

Many SEED-Forms appeared in the agricultural plant and damage is increasing. At this rate, the colony will face an inevitable food shortage.

Required	Must be at least level 30
LOC	Food Plant
Party	1-4

UNLOCKED AFTER COMPLETION OF CHAPTER 8

MONSTERS

SENDILLAN
LVL **35**
TYPE: DARK

DELSABAN
LVL **35**
TYPE: DARK

PANNON
LVL **35**
TYPE: DARK

SEED-VANCE
LVL **45**
TYPE: DARK

By the time you unlock this mission, you should be skilled enough at slaying Pannon and Delsaban to earn an easy S-Rank. Anti-dark Technics and Photon Arts (any bullet with "Rising" in its name) should be used liberally, as the chests here are full of Photon Charges you can use to restore your weapons' PP. The mission ends with the familiar SEED-Vance fight, but after you slay it two more will appear. If your health is at risk and you still have time on the clock, back up and use ranged tactics. But otherwise take the hits and go all-out with Rising Strike for quick kills.

TRIAL RANKING

CONDITIONS

1 CLEAR TIME 9:00 VALUE 1000pts
PENALTY -1 points per second late

RANKING INFORMATION

SCORE	RANK	MESETA	MP	PRIZE
1000	S	10000	80	Walking Pannon
700 - 999	A	4000	50	-
400 - 699	B	1500	30	-
0 - 399	C	-	20	-

MISSION: CREATURE DISCOMFORT

Native creatures in Raffon Meadow have gone savage because of SEED influence. Stop them from causing damage.

Required -

LOC Raffon Meadow

Party 1-4

UNLOCKED AT BEGINNING OF CHAPTER 3

MONSTERS

		TYPE:
DISTOVA	LVL 5	FIRE
SHAGREECE	LVL 6	FIRE
VAHRA	LVL 5	ELEC

To complete this mission in 1:50 you can't afford to waste a single second. Tear off to the east as soon as the mission begins and follow the wall to your right. Blast two Shagreece, then turn and move on before the bodies even hit the ground. Blast all the enemies as you run to the northwest, and switch to a Wand or Rod as you approach the end. You'll need to kill the four waves of Vahra with one area-effect Technic each, so link up Rabarta or Ramegid in advance.

TRIAL RANKING

CONDITIONS

1 CLEAR TIME 1:50 VALUE 600pts
PENALTY -1 point per second late

2 ENEMIES 25 VALUE 400pts
PENALTY -5 points per enemy missed

RANKING INFORMATION

SCORE	RANK	MESETA	MP	PRIZE
1000	S	300	20	PPT Shuttle
700 - 999	A	150	10	-
400 - 699	B	50	5	-
0 - 399	C	-	1	-

MISSION: BURNING PLAINS

The SEED have attacked a section of Raffon Meadow. The surrounding area is being severely damaged by fire-based SEED contamination.

Required	Must be at least level 5

LOC	Raffon Meadow	Party	1-4

UNLOCKED AFTER COMPLETION OF CHAPTER 3

MONSTERS

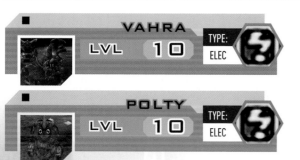

VAHRA — LVL 10 — TYPE: ELEC

POLTY — LVL 10 — TYPE: ELEC

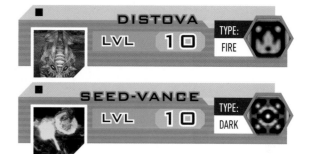

DISTOVA — LVL 10 — TYPE: FIRE

SEED-VANCE — LVL 10 — TYPE: DARK

00:05:45

The time required to locate and purify 20 blewmes makes this one of the toughest Free Missions on which to score an S-Rank. Do a trial run and focus on memorizing the blewme locations, especially the ones that are hidden behind tall grass and on the SEED-Vance-guarded hill. At least you don't have to worry about missing foes; all of the enemies are on the main path and you'll need to kill them all to make the keys to each door appear. You won't have much time for combat, so use Photon Arts and powerful Technics exclusively. While being high-level will make combat easier, you'll need to accept this mission by Chapter 5 if you want Karen and Hyuga's help with purifying the blewmes.

TRIAL RANKING

CONDITIONS

1. **CLEAR TIME 9:00 VALUE 300pts**
   PENALTY -1 point per second late

2. **ENEMIES 43 VALUE 300pts**
   PENALTY -5 points per enemy missed

3. **SEEDS PURIFIED 5 VALUE 400pts**
   PENALTY -200 points per SEED-Zoma missed

RANKING INFORMATION

SCORE	RANK	MESETA	MP	PRIZE
1000	S	1000	60	Beetle
700 - 999	A	500	30	-
400 - 699	B	300	10	-
0 - 399	C	-	1	-

MISSION: THE MAD BEASTS

The Distova altered by the SEED are attacking people. Also, an oversized variant of Koltova has appeared and is wreaking havoc.

| Required | Must be at least level 10 |

| LOC | Raffon Meadow | Party | 1-4 |

UNLOCKED AFTER COMPLETION OF CHAPTER 3

MONSTERS

VAHRA	LVL 16	TYPE: FIRE	
DISTOVA	LVL 15	TYPE: FIRE	
DISTOVA	LVL 16	TYPE: FIRE	
POLTY	LVL 15	TYPE: FIRE	
GOL DOLVA	LVL 25	TYPE: FIRE	

Eliminate the aggressive koltova!

Charge toward the cave to the left the instant this trial begins. Clear out the Distova there, then turn and run back to the main route, which will take you to Block 2. When you enter that block's cave, bear left again and keep killing until the key appears. The other cave path will take you to another pair of enemy-filled rooms and onto the final block; save some PP on your best Technic or combo Photon Art for the Gol Dolva at the end!

TRIAL RANKING

CONDITIONS

1 CLEAR TIME 8:00 VALUE 600pts
PENALTY -1 point per second late

2 ENEMIES 69 VALUE 400pts
PENALTY -5 points per enemy missed

RANKING INFORMATION

SCORE	RANK	MESETA	MP	PRIZE
1000	S	1000	60	Koltova Transport
700 - 999	A	500	30	-
400 - 699	B	300	10	-
0 - 399	C	-	1	-

MISSION: RULER OF THE PLAINS

The De Ragan has built its nest in Raffon Meadow and making nearby residents uneasy.

Required	Must be at least level 15

LOC	Raffon Meadow	Party	1-4

UNLOCKED AFTER COMPLETION OF CHAPTER 4

You've traveled through Raffon Meadow several times, and you should know the lay of the land. Remember to hang a left at the first cave to reach the dead-end meadow patrolled by two Shagreece; you'll need to kill them to earn your S-Rank. When you reach the De Ragan at the end, you should be strong enough to battle without worrying about dodging its attacks; go berserk with your best Photon Arts or Technics for a quick win.

MONSTERS

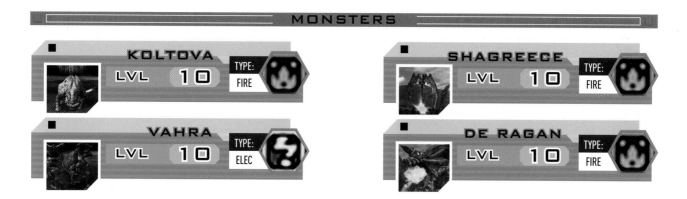

KOLTOVA LVL **10** TYPE: FIRE

VAHRA LVL **10** TYPE: ELEC

SHAGREECE LVL **10** TYPE: FIRE

DE RAGAN LVL **10** TYPE: FIRE

TRIAL RANKING

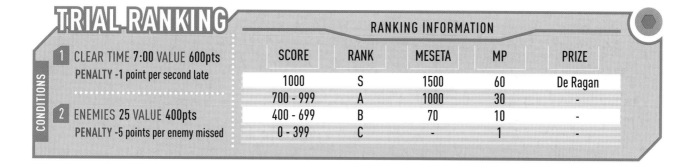

CONDITIONS

1. CLEAR TIME 7:00 VALUE 600pts
   PENALTY -1 point per second late

2. ENEMIES 25 VALUE 400pts
   PENALTY -5 points per enemy missed

RANKING INFORMATION

SCORE	RANK	MESETA	MP	PRIZE
1000	S	1500	60	De Ragan
700 - 999	A	1000	30	-
400 - 699	B	70	10	-
0 - 399	C	-	1	-

MISSION: WHAT IS IN THE RUINS

Teams investigating the Raffon RELICS site have been disappearing one after another.

Required	Must be at least level 10

LOC	Raffon RELICS	Party	1-4

UNLOCKED AFTER COMPLETION OF CHAPTER 4

MONSTERS

BADIRA LVL **16** TYPE: FIRE

GOLMORO LVL **16** TYPE: LIGHT

SVALTUS LVL **25** TYPE: LIGHT

POLAVOHRA LVL **19** TYPE: ELEC

Whatever class you play, make sure you have plenty of ranged weapons and Technics to use against the evasive Golmoro. The same attacks that are effective against them should be useful against the Svaltus at the end, but don't waste all your PP on the first Svaltus, since two more will appear when it dies! Technics are your best choice, since they can be used from out of the Svaltus' attack range and can penetrate their energy shields. If you have trouble with this mission, wait until Chapter 7 when you can buy the dark-element Megid-series Technics that are very strong against this area's light-type foes.

TRIAL RANKING

CONDITIONS

1. CLEAR TIME **10:00** VALUE **600pts**
   PENALTY **-1 point per second late**

2. ENEMIES **82** VALUE **400pts**
   PENALTY **-5 points per enemy missed**

RANKING INFORMATION

SCORE	RANK	MESETA	MP	PRIZE
1000	S	1500	60	Svaltus Edge, Bruce's Cargo Ship
700 - 999	A	1000	30	-
400 - 699	B	700	10	-
0 - 399	C	-	1	-

[PARUM]
LINEAR TRAIN PLATFORM

MISSION: CARGO TRAIN RESCUE

There is a request for assistance from a cargo train that is under attack by rogues.

Required	Must be at least level 15. Cannot return to the city.

LOC	Onboard the Cargo	Party	1-4

UNLOCKED AFTER COMPLETION OF CHAPTER 5

MONSTERS

DILLA GRIENA LVL **21** TYPE: FIRE

GOHMA DILLA LVL **21** TYPE: FIRE

ROGUE (JASSE) LVL **21** TYPE: --

ROGUE (OGG) LVL **21** TYPE: --

This Free Mission is a repeat of the trial in Chapter 4, and it uses all the same monster-hiding tricks it did back then. After leaving the Forward Car, return immediately and run back to the start of the level to spawn another Dilla Griena. You don't need to use the key it drops to open the Forward Car treasure room, but you will need to take key #2 at the end of the Middle Car and use it to unlock the Middle Car treasure room. Slay the three Rogues in there, then move on to clear out the Rear Car.

TRIAL RANKING

			RANKING INFORMATION			
		SCORE	RANK	MESETA	MP	PRIZE
1	CLEAR TIME 6:30 VALUE 700pts PENALTY -1 point per second late	1000	S	2500	70	Military PPT Shuttle
		700 - 999	A	1300	40	-
2	ENEMIES 32 VALUE 300pts PENALTY -5 points per enemy missed	400 - 699	B	1000	20	-
		0 - 399	C	-	10	-

CONDITIONS

197

MISSION: ENDRUM UNDERGROUND

Endrum Collective have occupied an underground plant. They are calling for the release of their former representative, Harness.

Required | Must be at least level 35

LOC | Underground Plant | **Party** | 1-4

UNLOCKED AFTER COMPLETION OF CHAPTER 9

MONSTERS

GSM-05 SEEKER — LVL **40** — TYPE: ELEC

GSM-05B BOMALTA — LVL **40** — TYPE: ELEC

SPECIAL OPS (SODA) — LVL **40** — TYPE: --

SPECIAL OPS (ASSAULT) — LVL **40** — TYPE: --

GRINNA BETE C — LVL **40** — TYPE: ELEC

GRINNA BETE S — LVL **50** — TYPE: ELEC

Finding all the enemies in this confusing installation is no easy task. In Block 1, run to the northwest, climbing to the top level of the plant before descending down to challenge some GSM units for the first key. Before you use it, run north of the gate until you trigger two waves of Special Ops. In Block 2, run up the pathway to the right to reach the room to the northeast. Kill a bunch of GSM, then continue north to a dark room full of soldiers. No time to waste looking for a light switch—use a Technic like Regrants to wipe out the unseen foes. Then backtrack and complete your tour of the installation. You'll find switches in the two rooms on the west side of the map, and while you don't need to flip them, you do need to get very close to trigger the enemy waves in each room.

You'll earn a key that way, but you won't need it; it only unlocks a teleporter, and all of the teleporters on this map are a waste of time. Run onward towards Block 3, where you'll fight two lower-level Grinna Bete C before challenging a familiar trio of Grinna Bete S. Run in half-circles to dodge their bullets and tear into them with Tornado Dance when you close the distance.

TRIAL RANKING

CONDITIONS

1 CLEAR TIME 12:00 VALUE 700pts
PENALTY -1 point per second late

2 ENEMIES 66 VALUE 300pts
PENALTY -5 points per enemy missed

RANKING INFORMATION

SCORE	RANK	MESETA	MP	PRIZE
1000	S	5000	90	Grinna Bete S
700 - 999	A	3500	60	-
400 - 699	B	2000	40	-
0 - 399	C	-	30	-

MISSION: TWO-HEADED SENTINEL

The De Ragnus that dwells in the Denes RELICS is obstructing the investigation of the site.

Required	Must be at least level 55

LOC	Denes RELICS	Party	1-4

UNLOCKED AFTER COMPLETION OF CHAPTER 10

MONSTERS

BADIRA	LVL 56	TYPE:	FIRE
GOLMORO	LVL 56	TYPE:	LIGHT
ZAMVAPAS	LVL 59	TYPE:	LIGHT
ORGDUS	LVL 59	TYPE:	LIGHT
VOLFU	LVL 56	TYPE:	ELEC
DE RAGNUS	LVL 60	TYPE:	--

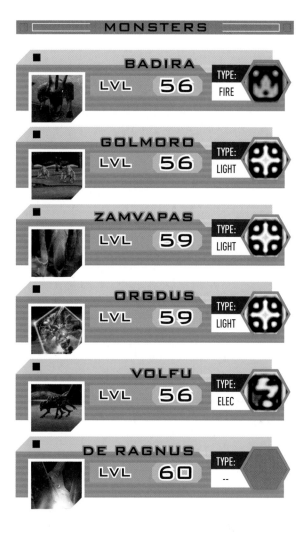

You'll face a constant onslaught of foes that ends in a De Ragnus battle, so you'll want to keep your Shifta Wand at the ready. There isn't anything too fancy here, and none of the enemies are off the main path. Use teleporters whenever you have a chance, and use your auto-map to spot the locked doors when you score a key. You'll usually spawn a new wave of enemies as you run to the doors, so watch for yellow dots on your map to make sure no Golmoro or Badira slip by as you rush on to the next area.

Shifta-enhanced Dus Daggas or Gravity Strike combos are the best way to quickly kill Zamvapus or Orgdus foes, but projectile attacks and Technics are more effective against the Golmoro. If you intend to use ranged attacks, run through the Golmoro pack and fire from the other side of the room to pull your allies into the battle. De Ragnus won't be tough if you have a number of powerful weapons to cycle through as you burn your PP on Photon Art combos.

TRIAL RANKING

CONDITIONS

1. CLEAR TIME 12:00 VALUE 700pts — PENALTY -1 point per second late
2. ENEMIES 66 VALUE 300pts — PENALTY -5 points per enemy missed

RANKING INFORMATION

SCORE	RANK	MESETA	MP	PRIZE
1000	S	5000	90	Glaring De Ragnus or Smiling De Ragnus
700 - 999	A	3500	60	-
400 - 699	B	2000	40	-
0 - 399	C	-	30	-

MISSION: MIZURAKI DEVASTATION

Altered Tengohgs are devastating the Mizuraki C.D.

Required	Must be at least level 15

LOC	Mizuraki C.D.	Party	1-4

UNLOCKED AFTER COMPLETION
OF CHAPTER 5

MONSTERS

AGEETA — LVL 20 — TYPE: ICE

TENGOHG — LVL 20 — TYPE: FIRE

OLLAKA — LVL 20 — TYPE: FIRE

GOSHIN — LVL 20 — TYPE: FIRE

There are a few tricks on this one, including one wave of Ageeta that only spawn when a rock is destroyed (early in Block 2) and another wave that guards the key to the treasure room in the northeast corner of the same map. To score a time under 9:30 you need the ability to kill a Goshin in a single hit—you don't have time to chase them around the battlefield. Play as a Force and load up your Wand or Rod with a fire Technic like Damfoie to clear the waves of Ageeta and an ice Technic like Rabarta to give you an edge in the triple-Tengohg battle at the end of the mission. Either Technic should be capable of killing a Goshin with a well-timed hit.

TRIAL RANKING

CONDITIONS

1. CLEAR TIME 9:30 VALUE 600pts
   PENALTY -1 point per second late

2. ENEMIES 81 VALUE 400pts
   PENALTY -5 points per enemy missed

RANKING INFORMATION

SCORE	RANK	MESETA	MP	PRIZE
1000	S	2500	70	Stag Beetle
700 - 999	A	1300	40	-
400 - 699	B	1000	20	-
0 - 399	C	-	10	-

MISSION: FROZEN WOODS

A section of the Mizuraki C.D. has come under SEED attack and is contaminated with ice-based SEED.

Required	Must be at least level 20

LOC	Mizuraki C.D.	Party	1-4

UNLOCKED AFTER COMPLETION OF CHAPTER 6

MONSTERS

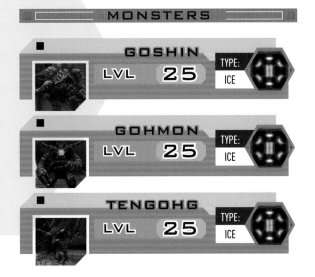

GOSHIN LVL **25** TYPE: ICE

GOHMON LVL **25** TYPE: ICE

TENGOHG LVL **25** TYPE: ICE

This was a tough one in Chapter 5, and now you have stronger foes and a fifth SEED-Zoma to worry about. Prep for the trial by making sure your Goggles and Photon Reflector are in your action palette, next to Wands filled with fire Technics and projectile weapons with fire Photon Arts (Damfoie is a particularly effective way to eliminate Tengohg quickly). Locating and purifying the SEED-Zoma won't be difficult in these straightforward blocks, but don't forget that after you purify the final one you need to run southwest to the teleporter to clear out more foes before you can run northeast to the exit.

TRIAL RANKING

CONDITIONS

1. CLEAR TIME 13:00 VALUE 300pts
   PENALTY -1 point per second late

2. ENEMIES 58 VALUE 200pts
   PENALTY -5 points per enemy missed

3. SEEDS PURIFIED 5 VALUE 500pts
   PENALTY -200 points per SEED-Zoma missed

RANKING INFORMATION

SCORE	RANK	MESETA	MP	PRIZE
1000	S	3500	70	Maiden's Ship
700 - 999	A	1800	40	-
400 - 699	B	1300	20	-
0 - 399	C	-	10	-

MISSION: THE DEMONS ABOVE

The Onmagoug has become more aggressive due to SEED influence.

Required	Must be at least level 30

LOC	Mizuraki C.D.	**Party**	1-4

UNLOCKED AFTER COMPLETION
OF CHAPTER 7

MONSTERS

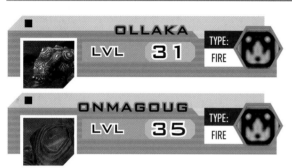

OLLAKA — LVL **31** — TYPE: FIRE

GOHMON — LVL **31** — TYPE: ICE

ONMAGOUG — LVL **35** — TYPE: FIRE

TENGOHG — LVL **31** — TYPE: FIRE

The two blocks before the boss give you plenty of opportunities to go astray, so plan your course before the timer starts ticking. After you take the first Warp in Block 1, clear out the foes to reveal one key, but don't use it until you've taken the second Warp (on the left) to reach an island with a second key. Use that to open the right of the two gates and clear out the foes there. (Then take the left gate to the exit.) At the halfway point of Block 2, you'll need to take a hard turn to the west to pick up a key. Continue past the key and smash the rocks in the caves to reveal two new waves of monsters on your way back. Save all your best melee Photon Arts for the Onmagoug, and if your level is high enough you may now be able to beat it the first time you shoot it out of the sky.

TRIAL RANKING

CONDITIONS

1 CLEAR TIME **11:00** VALUE **600pts**
PENALTY -1 point per second late

2 ENEMIES **57** VALUE **400pts**
PENALTY -5 points per enemy missed

RANKING INFORMATION

SCORE	RANK	MESETA	MP	PRIZE
1000	S	4000	80	Onmagoug
700 - 999	A	2500	50	-
400 - 699	B	1500	30	-
0 - 399	C	-	20	-

MISSION: DEFEND THE ISLANDS

There is a large outbreak of creatures throughout the Shikon Islands.

Required	Must be at least level 25
LOC	Shikon Islands
Party	1-4

UNLOCKED AFTER COMPLETION
OF CHAPTER 7

MONSTERS

Monster	LVL	Type
AGEETA	30	ICE
OLLAKA	31	FIRE
KAMATOZE	34	ICE
GOSHIN	31	FIRE
GOHMON	30	ICE

Beating the 12-minute clock won't be tough if you're willing to rush headlong into battle against some dangerous foes. You'll need to charge Kamatoze and Gohmon kings as soon as they appear and destroy them before they can cast Technics or use evasive moves that will drag out the battle. Photon Arts like the Double Saber's Tornado Dance and the Damfoie Technic are great ways to deal heavy damage quickly.

On each of the three blocks, take the path that leads away from the exit first. That means taking the right fork at the northern junctions in Block 1 and Block 3. You can skip the teleporter in Block 2, however, as it leads only to treasure, not foes.

TRIAL RANKING

CONDITIONS

1 CLEAR TIME 12:00 VALUE 700pts
PENALTY -1 point per second late

2 ENEMIES 79 VALUE 300pts
PENALTY -5 points per enemy missed

RANKING INFORMATION

SCORE	RANK	MESETA	MP	PRIZE
1000	S	4000	80	Tornado Throw
700 - 999	A	2500	50	-
400 - 699	B	1500	30	-
0 - 399	C	-	20	-

MISSION: WOODLAND FLAMES

The Sacred Grounds of the Agata Islands are under SEED attack and in danger of fire contamination.

Required Must be at least level 45

LOC Agata Islands **Party** 1-4

Unlocked after completion of Chapter 10

MONSTERS

AGEETA LVL **51** TYPE: FIRE

OLGOHMON LVL **52** TYPE: FIRE

SEED-VITACE LVL **55** TYPE: DARK

OLLAKA LVL **52** TYPE: FIRE

KAGAJIBARI LVL **54** TYPE: LIGHT

With a little help from your friends, you should be able to make it through this Free Mission in well under 15 minutes. Bring Lou, since she has a Photon Eraser, and Hyuga and Karen if they're available. If they're not, rely on Lou to help with the purification and fill up the rest of your party with melee fighters. That will allow you to run right past minor foes like Ageeta and Ollaka and hunt for blewmes while your party handles the combat. You don't need to worry that a foe will slip through the cracks, since every room must be cleared completely before you'll be allowed to proceed. Take on the deadlier Olgohmon, SEED-Vitace, and Kagajibari yourself, using melee combos like Gravity Strike and Tornado Dance to defeat them quickly.

TRIAL RANKING

CONDITIONS

1 CLEAR TIME 15:00 VALUE 700pts
PENALTY -1 point per second late

2 ENEMIES 57 VALUE 300pts
PENALTY -5 points per enemy missed

RANKING INFORMATION

SCORE	RANK	MESETA	MP	PRIZE
1000	S	6000	90	BR Burning Poster
700 - 999	A	4000	60	-
400 - 699	B	2500	40	-
0 - 399	C	-	30	-

MISSION: GROVE OF FANATICS

Some members of Dohgi's faction in the Communion of Gurhal are illegally occupying the old Hakura Temple.

Required | Must be at least level 35

LOC | Old Hakura Temple | **Party** | 1-4

UNLOCKED AFTER COMPLETION OF CHAPTER 8

The Bysha are very weak to magic, so make sure your Hunter has a Wand with a pair of Zonde-series Technics (a pure Force will have trouble with the Armed Servants and boss). The trickiest part of the mission comes right at the beginning of Block 1. Run east to get the key from some servants, then fight off another pair in the hallway to the south. When they fall, run past them to the west and search for a hidden key behind some item boxes—the ones that are hiding in plain sight are always the easiest to miss. If you've picked up the Tornado Dance Photon Art for the Double Saber, use it to hit Adahna Degahna from behind for a quick boss victory.

MONSTERS

BYSHA TYPE-KOH21 — LVL 36 — TYPE: GROUND

BYSHA TYPE-OTSU32 — LVL 36 — TYPE: GROUND

ARMED SERVANT (TAGUBA) — LVL 37 — TYPE: --

ARMED SERVANT (OZUNA) — LVL 37 — TYPE: --

ADAHNA DEGAHNA — LVL 40 — TYPE: GROUND

TRIAL RANKING

CONDITIONS

1 CLEAR TIME 12:00 VALUE 600pts
PENALTY -1 point per second late

2 ENEMIES 57 VALUE 400pts
PENALTY -5 points per enemy missed

RANKING INFORMATION

SCORE	RANK	MESETA	MP	PRIZE
1000	S	4500	80	COG Cargo Shuttle
700 - 999	A	3000	50	-
400 - 699	B	1800	30	-
0 - 399	C	-	20	-

MISSION: TEMPLE OF ICE

The Kokura Temple that protects the Sacred Grounds has been overrun by monsters.

Required | Must be at least level 40

LOC | Kokura Temple | **Party** | 1-4

UNLOCKED AFTER COMPLETION OF CHAPTER 10

AGEETA LVL **46** TYPE: ICE	OLGOHMON LVL **50** TYPE: ICE
OLLAKA LVL **48** TYPE: ICE	DILNAZEN LVL **48** TYPE: DARK

Clearing three blocks and killing a hundred foes in ten minutes is a difficult task. To earn an S Rank on this one you'll probably need to be at least level 60 and have access to high-level fire-element weapons.

In Block 1, head north from the entrance to a central hallway that has Warps at both of the dead ends to the left (the Warps will not appear until nearby foes are slain). Take them in either order, as both lead to #1 keys that open the door in the first room of the map. In Block 2's northwest wing, ignore the monster-free room to the left and search for keys in the center and right rooms only. The trick in Block 3 is to not miss the wave of item box-triggered enemies (the only ones in this dungeon). Run north from the entrance to find a key, then use that to open the door south of the entrance. The boxes are at a dead end that branches off the elevated hallway to the left.

TRIAL RANKING

CONDITIONS

1 CLEAR TIME 10:00 VALUE 700pts
PENALTY -1 point per second late

2 ENEMIES 100 VALUE 300pts
PENALTY -5 points per enemy missed

RANKING INFORMATION

SCORE	RANK	MESETA	MP	PRIZE
1000	S	6000	90	COG Limousine Shuttle
700 - 999	A	4000	60	-
400 - 699	B	2500	40	-
0 - 399	C	-	30	-

[MOATOOB]
DAGORA CITY FLYER BASE

MISSION: THE PANDEMONIUM

There has been an outbreak of altered creatures in the mountains of the Galenigare area. This is causing trouble for workers at a nearby coalmine.

Required	Must be at least level 20

LOC	Galenigare Canyon	Party	1-4

UNLOCKED AFTER COMPLETION
OF CHAPTER 6

TRIAL RANKING

CONDITIONS

1 CLEAR TIME 12:00 VALUE 700pts
PENALTY -1 point per second late

2 ENEMIES 84 VALUE 300pts
PENALTY -5 points per enemy missed

RANKING INFORMATION

SCORE	RANK	MESETA	MP	PRIZE
1000	S	3500	70	Lapucha Figure
700 - 999	A	1800	40	-
400 - 699	B	1300	20	-
0 - 399	C	-	10	-

VANDA	LVL 25	TYPE: FIRE
VANDA	LVL 25	TYPE: FIRE
LAPUCHA	LVL 26	TYPE: ICE
KOG NADD	LVL 28	TYPE: LIGHT
JISHAGARA	LVL 26	TYPE: ICE

The two blocks in this Free Mission consist of three loops that are rendered impassable by rock walls. You'll need to hit both sides of every wall to find all of the 84 monsters on the map. In Block 1, begin by running east from the entrance and slay the enemies you find in that direction before returning to the correct northern path. After three straight rooms of monsters that drop keys, head south to the opposite side of the same wall to slay another pack of foes. Repeat the process in Block 2, by first heading east to slay two waves of enemies. Ignore the treasure room key and return to the main path, where you'll eventually come across a Warp. Hop in, slay three enemies, then hop back out without exploring farther. In the northeast section of the map, search each of the three dead-end tunnels to reveal both monsters and the keys needed to open the final door.

MISSION: TUNNEL INFESTATION

An important tunnel in the East Kugu Desert is becoming a nest for a large number of native creatures.

	Required	Must be at least level 35
LOC	East Kugu Desert	Party	1-4

UNLOCKED AFTER COMPLETION OF CHAPTER 9

This Free Mission is a straightforward brawl until you reach the Warp towards the end of Block 2. To kill all of this mission's enemies, you must ignore the Warp, clear out a wave of enemies deeper into the cave, unlock the door, and clear out two waves of enemies in the room beyond it. Only when the key appears in that second room should you turn and run back to the Warp. The Warp will take you to an island with a few additional enemies, and after you clear the island a second Warp will take you straight to the exit. If you hadn't cleared those two rooms first, you'd be on the wrong side of a locked door and it would be impossible to earn an S-Rank.

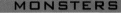

| JISHAGARA | LVL 43 | TYPE: ICE |
| NAVAL | LVL 43 | TYPE: GROUND |

| ZOONA | LVL 43 | TYPE: FIRE |
| VANDA | LVL 43 | TYPE: FIRE |

GETTING STARTED

STORY MODE

FREE MISSIONS

NETWORK MODE

TRIAL RANKING

CONDITIONS

1 CLEAR TIME 8:30 VALUE 700pts
PENALTY -1 point per second late

2 ENEMIES 76 VALUE 300pts
PENALTY -5 points per enemy missed

RANKING INFORMATION

SCORE	RANK	MESETA	MP	PRIZE
1000	S	5000	90	Zoona
700 - 999	A	3500	60	-
400 - 699	B	2000	40	-
0 - 399	C	-	30	-

MISSION: ABSOLUTE ZERO

A new SEED attack has been confirmed in the West Kugu Desert. A large number of creatures are ice-contaminated.

Required	Must be at least level 60

LOC	West Kugu Desert	Party	1-4

UNLOCKED AFTER COMPLETION OF CHAPTER 11

This is a monster-for-monster replay of the time trial in Chapter 11 where you had to slay an entire battalion of monsters. The same strategies will work this time, too: Use fire-element weapons and Technics, boost your power with Shifta every few minutes, and don't get distracted by the chests and item containers. In addition to the usual prize of a room decoration, victors will win the [B] Svaltus Sword Board, a recipe for a 10-star Sword that is the ultimate weapon of Story Mode.

MONSTERS

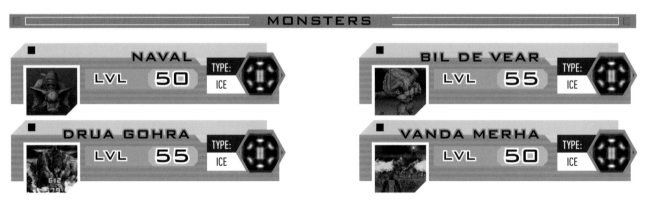

	NAVAL	LVL 50	TYPE: ICE

	BIL DE VEAR	LVL 55	TYPE: ICE

	DRUA GOHRA	LVL 55	TYPE: ICE

	VANDA MERHA	LVL 50	TYPE: ICE

TRIAL RANKING

CONDITIONS

1 CLEAR TIME 12:00 VALUE 1000pts
PENALTY -1 points per second late

RANKING INFORMATION

SCORE	RANK	MESETA	MP	PRIZE
1000	S	9000	100	[B] Svaltus Sword, Vanda
700 - 999	A	5000	70	-
400 - 699	B	3000	50	-
0 - 399	C	-	40	-

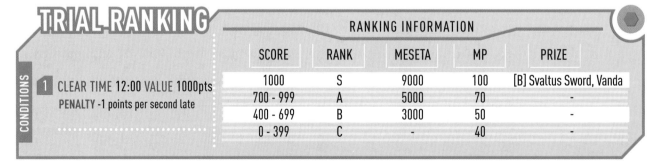

MISSION: TERROR IN THE DESERT

In the West Kugu Desert, the Dimmagolus has become even more ferocious due to SEED infection.

Required	Must be at least level 60

LOC	West Kugu Desert	Party	1-4

UNLOCKED AFTER COMPLETION OF CHAPTER 11

The two blocks of this trial are full of long side paths, and if you miss the right one, it could be fatal to your ranking. In Block 1 you'll find all of the enemies on the clear path from door to door, but in Block 2 finding all the enemies will take a bit of effort. Hang a right as soon as you enter the area to find an out-of-the-way Zoona nest, then head through the center of the base until you reach the exit door. Instead of unlocking it, run to the left to uncover another Zoona nest, and use the key they give you to open the remaining locked gate in the center. After slaying the pack of Naval who rush you near the gate, you can return to the exit to battle this mission's boss, the Dimmagolus.

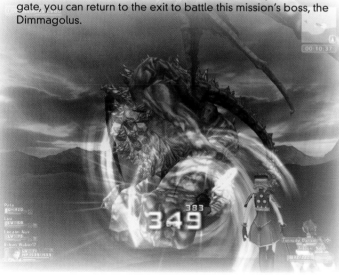

MONSTERS

JISHAGARA	LVL	61	TYPE: ICE

BUL BUNA	LVL	61	TYPE: GROUND

DRUA GOHRA	LVL	65	TYPE: FIRE

ZOONA	LVL	61	TYPE: FIRE

NAVAL	LVL	61	TYPE: GROUND

BIL DE VEAR	LVL	65	TYPE: GROUND

DIMMAGOLUS	LVL	65	TYPE: GROUND

TRIAL RANKING

CONDITIONS

1 CLEAR TIME 12:00 VALUE 600pts
PENALTY -1 point per second late

2 ENEMIES 75 VALUE 400pts
PENALTY -5 points per enemy missed

RANKING INFORMATION

SCORE	RANK	MESETA	MP	PRIZE
1000	S	2500	70	Landeel A or Landeel B
700 - 999	A	1300	40	-
400 - 699	B	1000	20	-
0 - 399	C	-	10	-

NETWORK MODE

[GUARDIANS COLONY]
UNSAFE PASSAGE

LOCATION:
LINEAR LINE ACCESS CORRIDORS

Parts of the Linear Line are shut down due to the SEED. Walking along the access corridors is the only way to get to some parts of the colony.

BEGINS:	Linear Line Line Platform	ENDS:	Transfer Terminal

∨∨ MONSTERS ENCOUNTERED ∨∨

MONSTER	TYPE	C. LVL	B. LVL	A. LVL
DELSABAN	DARK	1	20	30
PANNON	DARK	1	20	30
SENDILLAN	DARK	1	20	30

UNSAFE PASSAGE C

No prerequisites.

CREATURES: LV1+

RANK S REWARDS:
MESETA: 100
MP: 2

UNSAFE PASSAGE B

All party members must be LV5+

CREATURES: LV20+

RANK S REWARDS:
MESETA: 450
MP: 5

UNSAFE PASSAGE A

All party members must be LV20+

CREATURES: LV30+

RANK S REWARDS:
MESETA: 650
MP: 7

OVERVIEW

This is the first mission most players will embark upon, and it is certainly the easiest mission in Network Mode. While the A and B versions feature enemies with much higher stats, they have the same simple attack patterns and should not pose much of a threat to characters who meet even the minimum prerequisites to enter.

Among the mission's charms are its high percentage of weapon drops. Delsaban foes frequently drop 1-hand Swords (Saber, Buster, and Pallasch in versions C, B, and A respectively), and the Sendillan are a reliable source of Handguns (Handgun, Autogun, and Lockgun). There is also a very small chance you'll encounter super-rare Rappy enemies in place of the Pannon in this mission.

TACTICS

The geography of all three variations is very straightforward, and players who get turned around can follow the glowing green signs to their destinations. Treasure boxes are fairly common (although breaking some will trigger enemy attacks), especially at optional dead ends. Don't miss the trio of treasure boxes that can almost always be found at the end of the partially blocked-off loops in the corners of some rooms.

Delsaban monsters move slowly and are only a threat to targets in front of them. When battling them at close range, you can usually turn and flee when they lift their claws and successfully dodge the attack. But there isn't much of a reason to battle them head-on when they turn so slowly; Forces and Rangers should act as bait to lure them away, making it even easier for Hunters to get behind them for easy kills. If you use quick weapons like Knuckles to continuously hit Delsaban in the back, they have no chance of escape.

At rank C, this is a great mission for Forces to gather Meseta and experience. Their basic Foie fireball can kill almost any enemy in a single hit and the enemies move too slowly to pose a threat. The only exception is the Sendillan, who can charge at distant characters quite quickly. Forces who lack the support of Hunters should use their own melee weapons to strike the Sendillan in their sides. Forces and Rangers who don't want to risk it can always back out through a doorway and snipe from the other side; most foes cannot leave the area in which they're spawned.

[GUARDIANS COLONY]
FIGHT FOR FOOD

LOCATION:
FARMING PLANT

SEED have fallen on the farming plant, and damage is spreading. Secure the farms and protect the colony's food supply!

BEGINS: Transfer Terminal   **ENDS:** Aurorey Viewing Plaza

MONSTERS ENCOUNTERED

MONSTER	TYPE	C. LVL	B. LVL	A. LVL
DELSABAN	DARK	5	25	35
PANNON	DARK	5	25	35
SENDILLAN	DARK	5	25	35
SEED-VANCE	DARK	5	25	35

FIGHT FOR FOOD C

No prerequisites.

CREATURES: LV5+

RANK S REWARDS:

MESETA: 200
MP: 3

FIGHT FOR FOOD B

All party members must be LV10+

CREATURES: LV25+

RANK S REWARDS:

MESETA: 700
MP: 7

FIGHT FOR FOOD A

All party members must be LV25+

CREATURES: LV35+

RANK S REWARDS:

MESETA: 950
MP: 9

OVERVIEW

The Unsafe Passage mission ends at the Transfer Terminal area, where players can recharge, buy supplies, and continue on to the Aurorey Viewing Plaza. (No further missions are available at the Aurorey Viewing Plaza, at least not yet.) To reach the plaza you'll need to cross the Farming Plant as part of the Fight for Food mission, a slightly harder version of Unsafe Passage that ends with a SEED-Vance boss encounter.

The difference in enemy levels is not enough to reach a higher tier of item drops, so you'll find the same items here that were available in Unsafe Passage. The one exception is the 1-, 3-, and 4-star Twin Handguns (in mission versions C, B, and A respectively) that are dropped very rarely by the SEED-Vance boss.

TACTICS

The dungeon layouts get a bit more confusing here, and many variations have rooms with a lock that requires four separate keys. You'll need to search every possible dead end to find them all; large parties can split up to search individually or stick together for safety. The keys are often hidden in seemingly empty rooms where a surprise wave of enemies will appear when an item box is destroyed. Blast the box from afar with a Handgun so you won't be surrounded when the monsters spawn.

In the dungeon's final block you'll face a SEED-Vance enemy that is much tougher than the kind that appeared in Story Mode. Forces who choose to battle at long range should stay moving and use Handguns until after SEED-Vance fires a projectile or attacks with one of its tentacles. Only then will you have the time to cast Foie without being interrupted.

Melee fighters should be careful about dodging SEED-Vance's spin attack. If you use normal attacks from a quick weapon you'll be able to turn and run to dodge the attack, which it warns you about by lurching downward. After an attack misses, you can use Photon Arts combos like Rising Strike without fear of interruption. Of course, if you have plenty of hit points and don't mind using a few recovery items, you can simply rush the SEED-Vance and wail on it from all sides. If this is your tactic, do it immediately, before SEED-Vance can use the Shifta technique to boost its own attack power.

Players who are challenging the A version of the mission will discover a nasty surprise when they slay SEED-Vance— two more will pop up in its place! Focus your attacks on just one of them and circle your target as you attack it so the second one can't get an easy bead on you with its projectile attacks.

GETTING STARTED

STORY MODE

FREE MISSIONS

NETWORK MODE

[PARUM]
MAD CREATURES

LOCATION:
RAFFON MEADOW

The SEED influence has caused many of the creatures in Raffon Meadow to become vicious and they are causing damage in the local area.

BEGINS: Holtes City Flyer Base   **ENDS:** Raffon Field Base

∨∨ MONSTERS ∨∨
ENCOUNTERED

MONSTER	TYPE	C. LVL	B. LVL	A. LVL
DISTOVA	FIRE	10	20	30
KOLTOVA	FIRE	10	20	30
POLTY	ELECTRIC	10	20	30
VAHRA	ELECTRIC	10	20	30
SHAGREECE	FIRE	10	20	30

MAD CREATURES C

No prerequisites.

CREATURES: LV10+

RANK S REWARDS:
MESETA: 150
MP: 2

MAD CREATURES B

All party members must be LV10+

CREATURES: LV20+

RANK S REWARDS:
MESETA: 300
MP: 3

MAD CREATURES A

All party members must be LV25+

CREATURES: LV30+

RANK S REWARDS:
MESETA: 400
MP: 4

OVERVIEW

The Mad Creatures mission leaves from the Holtes City Flyer Base and takes you to the Raffon Meadow Field Base, from which you can accept the Plains Overlord and Sleeping Warriors missions. Mad Creatures C is a great mission for low-level characters, and the wide-open areas should make it easy for Rangers and Forces to get hits in without having to risk life and limb at melee range.

TACTICS

The Koltova/Distova, Polty, and Vahra foes here are cousins to the Sendillan, Pannon and Delsaban foes (respectively) that you battled in the Guardian Colony's Linear Line missions. Ice-element spells like Barta are very effective here, since they'll deal additional damage to Fire-type foes and can often hit three or more Vahra at once, since the Vahra typically maintain tight formations in battle.

Among the toughest foes you'll face are the Vahra kings, which can be distinguished from normal Vahra by the purple horns on their heads and the crown icon in their status box. Vahra kings can cast stat-boosting Technics on their tribes and recover their health with Resta. Fight very conservatively against such tribes, as they will all likely have a strength boost and deal extraordinary amounts of damage! Pick at the hordes with ranged weapons and back away; many of Raffon Meadow's large areas have invisible barriers that will teleport monsters back to their starting points if they cross it, and retreating behind one is an effective way of dividing enemy ranks.

Ranged weapons are your best option against airborne Shagreece foes, as melee attackers will have a hard time getting close and Technic-users will often find their target has flown away before their spells can connect. If Shagreece appear near a cave, back up into it; the Shagreece will have trouble following and you can usually pick them off safely by using first-person targeting.

[PARUM]
PLAINS OVERLORD

LOCATION:
RAFFON MEADOW

SEED contamination has driven a De Ragan from the mountains and it is nesting in Raffon Meadow, threatening nearby settlements.

BEGINS: Raffon Field Base

ENDS: Lakeshore Park Area

MONSTERS ENCOUNTERED

MONSTER	TYPE	C. LVL	B. LVL	A. LVL
DISTOVA	FIRE	15	25	35
KOLTOVA	FIRE	15	25	35
POLTY	ELECTRIC	15	25	35
VAHRA	ELECTRIC	15	25	35
SHAGREECE	FIRE	15	25	35
DE RAGAN	FIRE	20	30	40

PLAINS OVERLORD C
No prerequisites.

CREATURES: LV15+

RANK S REWARDS:
MESETA: 700
MP: 8

PLAINS OVERLORD B
All party members must be LV15+

CREATURES: LV25+

RANK S REWARDS:
MESETA: 1050
MP: 11

PLAINS OVERLORD A
All party members must be LV30+

CREATURES: LV35+

RANK S REWARDS:
MESETA: 1450
MP: 14

OVERVIEW

The Mad Creatures mission will take you to the Raffon Meadow Field Base, where those who want another crack at the rare weapon drops of the Raffon monsters can continue on to the Plains Overlord mission. Virtually all of the monsters in Raffon Meadow hold something of value; Koltova carry Knuckles, Distova carry Spears, Vahra hold Twin Blade weapons and Shagreece drop Rifles quite frequently. All are 1-star rarity in version C, 3-stars in version B, and 4-stars in version A. The exception is the Boards dropped by the Polty, which can allow you to make higher-level Daggers if you have the right materials.

TACTICS

This is a great mission to lead new players on, since the experience rewards are high and there is no shortage of safe places from which to use ranged weapons. Snipers can try to catch foes behind the corners of cliffs and blast them from there or stay near the entrances of the vast fields and back up to where the monsters cannot follow. Feel free to burn all your PP on the road to the boss, since there will be a PP Charger before the boss Warp.

Gather your troops before entering the boss Warp and make sure everyone is standing within range before you select "yes," because no one will be allowed to enter the battlefield late. Use a Moon Atomizer on anyone who dies—if your party is wiped out, all progress against De Ragan will be lost.

Hunters should aim for the neck and, if possible, use Photon Arts that lift them into the air (like Rising Strike or Rising Crush) so that they can connect with De Ragan's head for additional damage. Forces should use ice-type Technics, although when Gizonde is added to Network Mode they should switch to that instead. Rangers who have a steady hand and ice bullets can dish out heavy damage if they switch to first-person view and strive for headshots. But don't try it alone—this tactic requires a Hunter or two to keep De Ragan distracted with melee attacks.

[PARUM]
SLEEPING WARRIORS

LOCATION:
RAFFON RELICS

Teams investigating the Raffon Relics site are being held back by Stateria, the reactivated ancient weapons. Clear the way for the research teams!

BEGINS: Raffon Field Base   **ENDS:** Raffon Field Base

V V MONSTERS ENCOUNTERED V V

MONSTER	TYPE	C. LVL	B. LVL	A. LVL
GOLMORO	LIGHT	16	31	41
BADIRA	FIRE	16	31	41
POLAVHORA	ELECTRIC	16	31	41
SVALTUS	LIGHT	16	31	41

SLEEPING WARRIORS C
No prerequisites.

CREATURES: LV15+

RANK S REWARDS:
MESETA: 600
MP: 6

SLEEPING WARRIORS B
All party members must be LV20+

CREATURES: LV30+

RANK S REWARDS:
MESETA: 1050
MP: 10

SLEEPING WARRIORS A
All party members must be LV35+

CREATURES: LV40+

RANK S REWARDS:
MESETA: 1350
MP: 13

OVERVIEW

Sleeping Warriors is the most challenging of the Parum missions, and despite the lack of prerequisites, version C should not be attempted by low-level characters. Hunters will struggle here, but the combination of power and range will make Forces invaluable. If you don't have one in your party, consider a class change.

Of all the Parum missions, this one has the most to offer high-level characters. Weapon drops are fairly common and the level-41 foes in the A version drop five-star weapons that cannot be bought anywhere, including Twin Daggers (from the Golmoro) and Wands (from the Polavhora). The Svaltus boss occasionally drops special Long Swords that have a 20% fire photon at any rarity level, making them valuable prizes for Hunters.

TACTICS

There are many light-type foes in the Relics, and since Megid Technics are not yet available in Network Mode, Forces should stick to Barta in most situations. It will deal extra damage to the Badira, hit multiple targets in Golmoro packs and conform to the many ramps and stairs in the terrain. Hunters should keep a handgun handy for the evasive Golmoro, or fall back and let the Rangers wipe them out.

Hunters can return the favor when going up against the Polavhora, which have so many hit points that they can drain a fully-charged rifle and still not die. Hit them from the sides with melee weapons and prepare to run as soon as they rear up on their hind legs. Rangers and Forces should use fire-type attacks—the burn effect will deal damage based on a percentage of the Polavhora's Max HP, which will amount to hundreds of points of additional damage. Use Photon Arts liberally throughout the Relics, because you can always find a Photon Charger in the second and/or third block.

The Svaltus boss will be a chore for Hunters but a snap for Forces and Rangers. Use the ample room on the battlefield to strafe the Svaltus, side-stepping its attacks and returning fire with bullet volleys and Foie fireballs. Only attack while the Svaltus moving—when it stops you need to focus on dodging. Hunters should reverse their usual role and play the opportunist while Rangers and Forces do the bulk of the work. Keep a respectful distance out of Sword range, and move in for quick back-attacks when Svaltus uses an energy shield or attacks a distant ally with a projectile.

[NEUDAIZ]
MIZURAKI DEFENSE

LOCATION:
MIZURAKI C.D.

Violent creatures are wreaking havoc at the Mizuraki C.D. The fragile Mizuraki ecosystem is taking irreparable damage. Stop the creatures and save the trees!

BEGINS: Ohtoku City Flyer Base **ENDS:** Kego Clearing

MONSTERS ENCOUNTERED

MONSTER	TYPE	C. LVL	B. LVL	A. LVL
AGEETA	ICE	15	25	35
GOSHIN	FIRE	15	25	35
GOHMON	ICE	15	25	35
OLLAKA	FIRE	15	25	35

MIZURAKI DEFENSE C
No prerequisites.

CREATURES: LV15+

RANK S REWARDS:
MESETA: 450
MP: 5

MIZURAKI DEFENSE B
All party members must be LV15+

CREATURES: LV25+

RANK S REWARDS:
MESETA: 700
MP: 7

MIZURAKI DEFENSE A
All party members must be LV30+

CREATURES: LV35+

RANK S REWARDS:
MESETA: 900
MP: 9

OVERVIEW

The Ohtoku City Flyer Base hosts two missions: Mizuraki Defense and Forested Islands. Mizuraki Defense ultimately leads to an area known as the Kego Clearing, where you can sign up for the Demons Above mission. Both missions are dream assignments for Rangers, who will have an edge against the native fauna and are the most effective type for battling the boss at the end of Demons Above.

Players can find a wide variety of new materials in this mission, as well as several random room decorations. Good enemy item drops are fairly rare, although the Goshin have been know to carry wands and the Ageeta commonly drop Boards from which you can synthesize Yohmei Corp Line Shields.

TACTICS

You'll encounter a wide variety of new monsters here. Ageeta can be slain quite easily as they rush at you, but become a threat if you let them stand still and charge up their ice blasts.

Goshin are trickier. They burrow underground and attempt to pop up at your feet, hitting their targets with a strength-lowering condition when they do. Fortunately, they don't disappear from the auto-map when they're burrowing, so it's easy to track their movements. Guns and Technics are the best way to defeat them; let them rise up as you back away and blast them from just out of attack range. Hunters who lack ranged attacks should step back as they rise, then pound them with Photon Arts.

Gohmon are slow-moving bipeds that use the Barta Technic to attack distant targets. Once again, guns are a safe solution, provided you move laterally after each shot to shake off the incoming Barta waves. Fire-type bullets will do extra damage, but ground-type bullets can shut down their Technic-casting capability, and are the better choice when you have Hunter and Force friends battling at close range. Note that Rifles have a longer range than the Barta Technic, so Rangers need not ever expose themselves to harm.

Note: If you ever get stuck and can't find the key to proceed, search for the mossy, crystal-embedded rocks that can be destroyed with any weapon. Sometimes you'll need to destroy one to generate the wave of foes that holds the key.

GETTING STARTED

STORY MODE

FREE MISSIONS

NETWORK MODE

[NEUDAIZ]
DEMONS ABOVE

LOCATION:
MIZURAHI C.D.

The Onmagoug, long feared for its ferocity, has become even more aggressive due to SEED influence. Stop it before there are casualties!

BEGINS: Kego Clearing

ENDS: Kugo Hot Springs

MONSTERS ENCOUNTERED

MONSTER	TYPE	C. LVL	B. LVL	A. LVL
AGEETA	ICE	15	30	40
GOSHIN	FIRE	15	30	40
GOHMON	ICE	15	30	40
OLLAKA	FIRE	15	30	40
TENGOHG	FIRE	15	30	40
ONMAGOUG	FIRE	20	35	45

DEMONS ABOVE C

No prerequisites.

CREATURES: LV15+

RANK S REWARDS:
MESETA: 400
MP: 8

DEMONS ABOVE B

All party members must be LV20+

CREATURES: LV30+

RANK S REWARDS:
MESETA: 1200
MP: 12

DEMONS ABOVE A

All party members must be LV35+

CREATURES: LV40+

RANK S REWARDS:
MESETA: 1550
MP: 15

OVERVIEW

Demons Above is a repeat of the Mizuraki Defense mission, featuring the same enemies and several blocks with identical geography. The only real differences are the enemies—in some variations you'll encounter rare winged Tengohg in place of other foes, and every variation ends with the challenging Onmagoug boss. In the A & B versions, you'll face foes that are five levels higher than their Mizuraki Defense equivalents, and since the foes in the A variation have hit the 40 mark, they'll provide superior item when slain.

This mission ends at the Kugo Hot Springs, which is one of the coolest lobby areas in the game. There are no new missions to accept there, but it's a great place to relax after a grueling boss fight.

TACTICS

All the exciting stuff is on Block 3 of this mission. There you'll find new Tengohg enemies (possibly), and a series of Warps that may lead to a rare item from an item container. You'll also find a PP Charger and a Warp gate that leads to an extremely difficult boss encounter.

If you've played Story Mode, you know the trick to defeating the Onmagoug is shooting out its wings while it flies, and then attacking it with the Photon Arts of powerful weapons when it crashes to the ground. That trick still works, but it is no longer required; the Onmagoug will voluntarily land at regular intervals, so Hunter-heavy parties can skip the shooting and simply concentrate on dodging its attacks while it's in the air. You'll take a few hits if you stand between its legs and attack while its wings are intact, but you'll have plenty of time to tend to your wounds after the Onmagoug flies away.

Rifle-wielding Rangers and Bow-equipped Forces can use first-person targeting to blast out the Onmagoug's wings as it flies. But the Onmagoug is much stronger than it was in Story Mode, and you'll need to put more effort into dodging its damaging boulders, fireballs and lightning bolts. Only enter the first-person targeting mode after it attacks, or you'll be a sitting duck.

[NEUDAIZ]
FORESTED ISLANDS

LOCATION:
SHIKON ISLANDS

A large outbreak of violent creatures is putting the pilgrims of the Shikon Islands in danger. Clear the forest of the creatures.

BEGINS:	Ohtoku City Flyer Base	ENDS:	Tanze Pilgrimage Route

MONSTERS ENCOUNTERED

MONSTER	TYPE	C. LVL	B. LVL	A. LVL
AGEETA	ICE	15	30	40
GOHMON	ICE	15	30	40
KAMATOZE	ICE	15	30	40
OLLAKA	FIRE	15	30	40
GOSHIN	FIRE	15	30	40

FORESTED ISLANDS C
No prerequisites.

CREATURES: LV15+

RANK S REWARDS:
MESETA: 250
MP: 3

FORESTED ISLANDS B
All party members must be LV20+

CREATURES: LV30+

RANK S REWARDS:
MESETA: 450
MP: 5

FORESTED ISLANDS A
All party members must be LV30+

CREATURES: LV40+

RANK S REWARDS:
MESETA: 600
MP: 6

OVERVIEW

You'll have to pass through the Forested Islands mission to reach the Tanze Pilgrimage Route, your base for both the Rainbow Beast and Grove of Fanatics missions. The rewards are disappointing in terms of Meseta and Mission Points, but you can earn some rare synthesis Boards from enemy item drops. While Boards aren't as immediately useful as new weapons and armor, the ability to customize them with specific photons can make them far more valuable in the long run. Fire-type weapons are particularly useful in this mission, for example, but you don't necessarily need to synthesize them. Hunters who have 8600 Meseta to burn (and a high enough ATP score) can buy Ryo-Sagazashi twin daggers with a 30% fire photon at the Yohmei shop.

TACTICS

Foie fireballs are the Technic of choice for Forces, as they'll allow casters to destroy Ageeta with ease and deal heavy damage to the Kamatoze. They can even be used against the Goshin effectively, allowing Forces to target them from farther away than Rabarta will allow (although Rabarta is a better choice at mid-range). But Forces will want to swap their Rods for a 1-hand Sword or Dagger and rush into melee range when large packs of Gohmon appear—Technics take so long to cast that they'll leave Forces unable to dodge the Gohmons' Barta

The king of the islands is the powerful Kamatoze. While Forces and Rangers can burn its life away from a distance, Hunters will need to tread very carefully, attacking its sides with wide weapons like the Spear or Long Sword and refraining from long combos that would leave them unable to turn and run when the first of the spreading ice crystals appear. It's amazing how quickly a Hunter can go from full health to death when he or she is encased in ice and unable to dodge further attacks—Forces should keep an eye on the Hunters' life bars and be ready to rush in with a Resta Technic.

GETTING STARTED
STORY MODE
FREE MISSIONS
NETWORK MODE

[NEUDAIZ]
RAINBOW BEAST

LOCATION:
AGATA ISLANDS

Mission ends when 1 member arrives at lobby.

The COG has requested help dealing with the Kagajibari near their Sacred Grounds, due to its resistance to Technics.

BEGINS: Tanze Pilgrimage Route   **ENDS:** Agata Islands Sacred Grounds

MONSTERS ENCOUNTERED

MONSTER	TYPE	C. LVL	B. LVL	A. LVL
AGEETA	ICE	15	35	45
GOHMON	ICE	15	35	45
KAMATOZE	ICE	15	35	45
OLLAKA	FIRE	15	35	45
GOSHIN	FIRE	15	35	45
KAGAJIBARI	LIGHT	15	35	45

RAINBOW BEAST C
No prerequisites.

CREATURES: LV15+

RANK S REWARDS:
MESETA: 500
MP: 5

RAINBOW BEAST B
All party members must be LV20+

CREATURES: LV35+

RANK S REWARDS:
MESETA: 1000
MP: 10

RAINBOW BEAST A
All party members must be LV35+

CREATURES: LV45+

RANK S REWARDS:
MESETA: 1300
MP: 13

OVERVIEW

What a difference five levels can make! Rainbow Beast is one of the hardest missions in the game, offering four straight blocks of combat with no Heal Spots or Photon Chargers (in most variations) to provide succor to weary fighters. Don't be afraid to use the crystals to Warp back to the clearing and recharge your weapons, because you'll want to be able to make heavy use of Photon Arts against the Kagajibari boss.

At least your success will be well rewarded. Instead of the usual item boxes that appear when the boss is slain, you'll discover a large quantity of the striped containers that hold rare recovery items like Sol Atomizers and Scape Dolls!

TACTICS

Kamatoze monsters appear with alarming frequency here, and pose a grave threat to Hunters. Rangers and Forces should try to burn them with fire effects, while Hunters should fight conservatively to avoid their spreading ice crystals. This is a wonderful mission for Beast and CAST Hunters, who can put their SUV Weapons and Nanoblasts to excellent use against the Kamatoze. Hunters who have access to these techniques should arrange for the party's Forces to support them with Resta Technics, and then fight recklessly to charge up their special attacks.

The Kagajibari boss appears as the final wave in a long series of enemies at the end of Block 4. Unlike the Story Mode version that was content to trade projectiles with Forces and Rangers, this one will leap at characters who uses ranged tactics and attempt to battle them at close range. While this leap can be dodged by immediately running to the side, it's actually more effective to battle the Kagajibari at close range anyway. Slip behind it after it uses a shield or its spin attack, and unload your melee weapons' Photon Arts. Weapons with long combos can be used repeatedly to lock up the Kagajibari and leave it unable to attack or even turn around—the Twin Blades' Rising Crush Photon Art is especially effective.

[NEUDAIZ]
GROVE OF FANATICS

LOCATION:
ABANDONED TEMPLE

A radical faction of the Communion of Gurhal has occupied Old Hakura Temple, with the stolen Adahna Degahna as their main weapon. Stop them!

BEGINS: Tanze Pilgrimage Route   **ENDS:** Tanze Pilgrimage Route

MONSTERS ENCOUNTERED

MONSTER	TYPE	C. LVL	B. LVL	A. LVL
BYSHA TYPE-KOH21	GROUND	16	36	46
BYSHA TYPE-OTSU32	GROUND	16	36	46
ARMED SERVANT (TAGUBA)	--	16	36	46
ARMED SERVANT (OZUNA)	--	16	36	46
ADAHNA DEGAHNA	LIGHT	21	41	51

GROVE OF FANATICS C
No prerequisites.

CREATURES: LV15+

RANK S REWARDS:
MESETA: 700
MP: 8

GROVE OF FANATICS B
All party members must be LV20+

CREATURES: LV35+

RANK S REWARDS:
MESETA: 1450
MP: 14

GROVE OF FANATICS A
All party members must be LV35+

CREATURES: LV45+

RANK S REWARDS:
MESETA: 1850
MP: 17

OVERVIEW

You will need a well-rounded party to succeed at this difficult mission. Neither Rangers nor Hunters can do much damage against the temple's heavily armored Bysha, so parties without a good Force or two shouldn't even bother to sign up. But while Forces are fantastic against the Bysha, they won't be able to defeat the boss without a lot of help from melee fighters.

Players can find a wide variety of new materials in this mission, as well as several random room decorations. Item synthesis specialists will find a ton of interesting Boards here, mixed into item boxes and dropped by enemies.

TACTICS

Before this mission, fire and ice were the only truly relevant elemental types. But the common Bysha enemies in this mission are Ground-types and have Defense scores that are far higher than their Mental Strength stats. This makes a Force with Zonde-series Technics (Razonde in particular) the best possible character for this mission—at least until the boss.

There is a clear division of party labor here: Rangers and Hunters should immediately hunt down and slay the Armed Servants before they can cast their Technics, while Forces should fry the Bysha with Razonde. When the servants are cleared, Rangers can join the Bysha war by switching to plasma bullets, while Hunters should focus on knocking them back with skills like Rising Strike, which will protect the party and set the Bysha up for follow-up Technics.

Low-level Forces who have enjoyed being the party MVP throughout the mission will be in for a rude awakening when they meet the boss. The Adahna Degahna can slay low-Defense characters in a single hit, and Forces have so little to contribute in the battle that they might as well just wait by the boss Warp and ask their party to go on without them. Hunters and Rangers should do quite well by themselves—as in Story Mode, players need only charge at the Adahna Degahna as soon as the battle begins, slip behind it and between its treads, and dish out all the damage they can with heavy weapons like long Swords and Spears. If it warps away, chase after it to repeat the process.

SEGA Goes Mobile!!!

OFFICIAL STRATEGY GUIDE

BradyGAMES® Publishing
An Imprint of DK Publishing
800 E. 96th Street
3rd Floor
Indianapolis, Indiana 46240

Please be advised that the ESRB rating icons, "EC", "K-A", "E", "T", "M", "AO" and "RP" are copyrighted
works and certification marks owned by the Entertainment Software Association and the Entertainment
Software Rating Board and may only be used with their permission and authority. Under no circumstances
may the rating icons be self-applied or used in connection with any product that has not been rated by the
ESRB. For information regarding whether a product has been rated by the ESRB, please call the ESRB at
1-800-771-3772 or visit www.esrb.org. For information regarding licensing issues, please call the ESA at
(212) 223-8936. Please note that ESRB ratings only apply to the content of the game itself and does NOT
apply to the content of this book.

ISBN: 0-7440-0869-7
Printing Code: The rightmost double-digit number is the year of the book's printing; the rightmost single-
digit number is the number of the book's printing. For example, 06-1 shows that the first printing of the
book occurred in 2006.

09 08 07 06   4 3 2 1

Manufactured in the United States of America.

BradyGAMES Staff

Publisher David Waybright	**Director of Marketing** Steve Escalante	**Creative Director** Robin Lasek	**Designers** Craig Keller Reka Janosi
Editor-in-Chief H. Leigh Davis	**Licensing Manager** Mike Degler	**Project Manager** Christian Sumner	